THE LAKE POETS AND PROFESSIONAL IDENTITY

The idea that the inspired poet stands apart from the marketplace is considered central to British Romanticism. However, Romantic authors were deeply concerned with how their occupation might be considered a kind of labor comparable to that of the traditional professions. In the process of defining their work as authors, Wordsworth, Southey, and Coleridge – the "Lake school" – aligned themselves with emerging constructions of the "professional gentleman" that challenged the vocational practices of late eighteenth-century British culture. They modeled their idea of authorship on the learned professions of medicine, church, and law, which allowed them to imagine a productive relationship with the marketplace and to adopt the ways eighteenth-century poets had related their poetry to other kinds of intellectual work. Brian Goldberg explores the ideas of professional risk, evaluation, and competition that the writers developed as a response to a variety of eighteenth-century depictions of the literary career.

BRIAN GOLDBERG is Associate Professor of English at the University of Minnesota.

CAMBRIDGE STUDIES IN ROMANTICISM

This series aims to foster the best new work in one of the most challenging fields within English literary studies. From the early 1780s to the early 1830s a formidable array of talented men and women took to literary composition, not just in poetry, which some of them famously transformed, but in many modes of writing. The expansion of publishing created new opportunities for writers, and the political stakes of what they wrote were raised again by what Wordsworth called those "great national events" that were "almost daily taking place": the French Revolution, the Napoleonic and American wars, urbanization, industrialization, religious revival, an expanded empire abroad, and the reform movement at home. This was an enormous ambition, even when it pretended otherwise. The relations between science, philosophy, religion, and literature were reworked in texts such as *Frankenstein* and *Biographia Literaria*; gender relations in *A Vindication of the Rights of Woman* and *Don Juan*; journalism by Cobbett and Hazlitt; poetic form, content, and style by the Lake School and the Cockney School. Outside Shakespeare studies, probably no body of writing has produced such a wealth of response or done so much to shape the responses of modern criticism. This indeed is the period that saw the emergence of those notions of "literature" and of literary history, especially national literary history, on which modern scholarship in English has been founded. The categories produced by Romanticism have also been challenged by recent historicist arguments. The task of the series is to engage both with a challenging corpus of Romantic writings and with the changing field of criticism they have helped to shape. As with other literary series published by Cambridge, this one will represent the work of both younger and more established scholars, on either side of the Atlantic and elsewhere.

For a complete list of titles published see end of book.

THE LAKE POETS
AND PROFESSIONAL
IDENTITY

BRIAN GOLDBERG

CAMBRIDGE
UNIVERSITY PRESS

CAMBRIDGE UNIVERSITY PRESS
Cambridge, New York, Melbourne, Madrid, Cape Town, Singapore, São Paulo

Cambridge University Press
The Edinburgh Building, Cambridge CB2 8RU, UK

Published in the United States of America by Cambridge University Press, New York

www.cambridge.org
Information on this title: www.cambridge.org/9780521866385

First published 2007

Printed in the United Kingdom at the University Press, Cambridge

A catalogue record for this publication is available from the British Library

ISBN 978-0-521-86638-5 hardback

Contents

Acknowledgments

It gives me great pleasure to thank the many people who contributed to the writing of this book. The teaching and scholarly energy of Charlotte Zoe Walker and Patricia Gourlay, two professors at SUNY-Oneonta, have been an ongoing source of inspiration since I was first introduced to literary study in their classrooms. At Northeastern University, Stuart Peterfreund provided an enduring, admirable model of Romantic scholarship. For subsequent acts of kindness and intellectual generosity, I am also indebted to William H. Buchholz and Bruce Herzberg at Bentley College; Charles Rzepka; and Herbert Tucker. Colleagues at the University of Washington were invariably helpful during my time there, and I am especially grateful for the conversation of Jane Brown, Henry Staten, and Raimonda Modiano. At the University of Minnesota, thanks are due to Shirley Nelson Garner, Michael Hancher, and Gordon Hirsch. John Watkins has been an especially supportive and stimulating presence.

Two anonymous readers at Cambridge University Press gave more good advice than I have been able to follow, and I am deeply grateful for the generosity of the editors of the series, Marilyn Butler and James Chandler, and for the help and patience of Linda Bree and Maartje Scheltens. Also at Cambridge University Press, this project has benefited greatly from the help and attention of Rosina Di Marzo and Sara Barnes. Versions of this manuscript were read by Stephen Behrendt, Stuart Curran, William Galperin, Marilyn Gaull, Nancy Moore Goslee, Jon Klancher, and Peter Manning – in some cases, opposition has proved to be true friendship; in all cases, I am thankful for the valuable insights of these scholars.

A version of Chapter Six has appeared as "Romantic Professionalism in 1800: Robert Southey, Herbert Croft, and the

Letters and Legacy of Thomas Chatterton," in *ELH* 63:3 (1996), 681–706. © The Johns Hopkins University Press. Material from this essay is reprinted with permission of the Johns Hopkins University Press. Parts of Chapter Seven have appeared in *Studies in Romanticism* (36:3, Fall 1997). I thank the editors and anonymous reviewers of these journals.

This project began as a Ph D dissertation at Indiana University, and special acknowledgment is due to the committee that guided my work there: Kenneth R. Johnston, Mary Favret, Patrick Brantlinger, and M. Jeanne Peterson. The intellectual debt I owe to the individual members of this committee is profound. Thanks also to Andrew Miller, Nicholas Williams, and Julia Williams. Marshall Brown, at Washington, and Andrew Elfenbein, at Minnesota, have been generous, personally and intellectually, in many more ways than can be documented here.

In Boston, Pam and David Benson and Jon Diamond, and in Wisconsin, Teresa, Mike, and Taylor Kemp, have been valuable friends. In Chicago, Susie Phillips has shared many magical trials. Abundant thanks are due to the gentlemen in the condo. Duncan has contributed indispensable energy, mischief, and good cheer. Finally, my parents, Michael Goldberg and Janet Stamm, Rachel Singer, and Robert Stamm, my in-laws, William and Mary Krug and Heather Martin, my sister, Jessica Goldberg, and actor/ screenwriter/NYPD detective (ret.) Michael Kaycheck have all contributed to this book extensively and immeasurably. I am grateful for their love and kindness. My last and deepest thanks goes to Becky Krug, whose brilliance and insight have been vital at every step. Without her, this project, and its author, would be nowhere.

Introduction: Professionalism and the Lake School of Poetry

When William Wordsworth, Robert Southey, and Samuel Taylor Coleridge – the Lake school – formulated their earliest descriptions of the role of the poet, two models of vocational identity exerted special pressure on their thinking. One was the idea of the professional gentleman. In their association of literary composition with socially useful action, their conviction that the judgment of the poet should control the literary marketplace, and their efforts to correlate personal status with the poet's special training, the Lake writers modified a progressive version of intellectual labor that was linked, if sometimes problematically, to developments in the established professions of medicine, church, and law. In short, they attempted to write poetry as though writing poetry could duplicate the functions of the professions. The other model, and it is related to the first, is literary. Like the Lake poets, earlier eighteenth-century authors had been stimulated, if occasionally frustrated, by the puzzle of how to write poetry in the face of changing conceptions of intellectual work. While ideals of medical, legal, and theological effectiveness that measured "technique" were competing with those that emphasized "character," literary production was moving (more slowly and less completely than is sometimes thought) from a patronage- to a market-based model.[1] Eighteenth-century writers developed a body of figural resources such as the poetic wanderer that responded to new constructions of experience, merit, and evaluation, and the Lake writers seized on these resources in order to describe their own professional situation.

To invoke the concept of the "professional" in this context is to allude to a number of separate issues. Kant's declaration that "beautiful art ... must not be a matter of remuneration" participates in a centuries-long insistence that virtue is dependent on leisure, whereas authors motivated by an "abject devotion to their private interests," as Isaac Disraeli puts it, "like Atalanta, for the sake of the apples of gold, lose the glory of the race."[2] Critics interested in the historical fortunes of this idea have found that the eighteenth century, with its growing consumer economy and expanding book trade, is a crucial developmental period.[3] By the end of the century, as Roger Chartier describes the situation, there has emerged a "somewhat paradoxical connection" between a "desired professionalization," meaning the possibility of earning a living through writing, and "an ideology of literature founded on the radical autonomy of the work of art and the disinterestedness of the creative act."[4] Romantic theories that replace didactic or effect-oriented "instrumentalism" with art for its own sake may be understood as a reaction to market conditions, which is to say, as Martha Woodmansee does, that there is an "interest" in "disinterestedness": "As literature became subject to a market economy, the instrumentalist theory ... was found to justify the wrong works," while theories of an autonomous aesthetic sphere justified imaginative writing that was rejected by the marketplace.[5]

The possibility I investigate here, however, is that Romantic authors had a more productive relationship to the idea of audience than rejection followed by reaction, and that the professional model offered a fruitful alternative to the hack and the brilliant recluse. To understate the case, it is not difficult to find Romantic writers explicitly distinguishing their own aims and motivations from commercial ones, but, it should be added, such accounts often come in close proximity to other kinds of concerns. When, in one of his 1802 letters to the gentleman-poet William Sotheby, Coleridge declares that his "*true Call* to the Ministry of *Song*" gives him confidence in the face of criticism, his sense of vocation and the intellectual independence his ministry entails are forcefully expressed. Nobody ministers in isolation, however, and Coleridge follows up by joking about the money his publisher has lost on his recent translation of *Wallenstein*: "I am sure, that Longman never thinks of me ... but the ghosts of his departed Guineas dance an ugly Waltz round my idea."[6] The ministry of song is logically separable from the dance of the ghostly guineas, but professionalism, which allows disinterest to coexist with the world of business, brings Coleridge's rhetorical performances into a single line.

Chartier's "somewhat paradoxical connection" between being free and working for pay is not necessarily a paradox, any more than it is only an associative accident for Coleridge to mention his prophetic call at the same time that he dwells upon his latest adventure in publication. The poet sings, but money dances, and sometimes it dances away.

Although getting paid is only part of what the term "professional" means in this context, it is worth remembering that the Lake poets, especially when they were first orienting themselves towards their work, were either willing or felt compelled to associate authorship with remuneration. "[Southey] knew that I published [*Lyrical Ballads*] for money and money alone," Wordsworth would complain in 1799, irked by Southey's unenthusiastic review of the volume. "I care little for the praises of any other professional critic, but as it may help me to pudding."[7] Southey had responded similarly, a few years earlier, to a qualified review of his own writing. "Have you seen Bob Banyard's review of Joan of Arc? 'a professional man must not step too much out of his way' granted – ergo I abjure public poetry: but a professional man must have a house and furniture – ergo I must write a book first."[8] The "book" Southey is laboring over is his Welsh epic *Madoc*, and as he mulls over his situation the poem's hero is pressed into un-princely service: "Poor Madoc! If he will buy me chairs tables linens etc. etc. it will be worth more than an eternity of posthumous credit."[9] A year later, Coleridge would propose that "things necessary for the body" should be purchased "by the labour of the body, and things necessary for the mind by the labour of the mind," but he also laments that, "Alas! this beautiful order of things, if not rendered impossible by the present state of society, is in most instances incompatible with our present state of education."[10] "The beautiful order of things" imagined by Coleridge will require reform at the public and the personal level. Meanwhile, he has been employed as a freelance journalist, as a lecturer, and as a newspaper poet, and he has been preparing to take up a living as a preacher, a fate from which he has only been rescued by a timely annuity settled on him as a form of patronage.

It would be a mistake to imagine that, at such moments, the poets are merely displaying an opportunistic careerism, or in Coleridge's case a fatalism, that negates their other claims on behalf of "the ministry of song." It is important, for example, to distinguish between "publishing" and "writing." Wordsworth may state that he publishes only for money, but he allows the composition of poetry to stem from a diviner impulse. A similar point may be made about Southey's plan to renounce "public poetry" once his identity as a professional man is established. It would remain acceptable, even desirable, to write privately, for a close circle of friends and relations. Of the three, Coleridge is most visibly torn between aesthetic idealism and the fallen world of work. Some writing is meant to be sold, for example the Wallenstein translation, but other works, the productions of "Genius," express a kind of freedom which must be supported differently. "Never pursue literature as a trade!" Coleridge eventually advises, and he, like Southey, is imagining that a gentleman might establish a stable professional life that would enable leisurely, not trade-driven, composition.

Yet if it is difficult to understand these varied careers as expressions of a single-minded entrepreneurialism, it is equally hard to believe that the genteel retirement that an author such as Gray pursued, or the legal career he spent his life avoiding, would really have provided adequate or desirable shelter for the Lake poets' efforts. These writers measured themselves against their audiences, and against other professionals, from beginning to end. Further, although Wordsworth is the only member of the Lake school whose best achievements may unambiguously be located in his poetry, writing poetry was always, for all of them, the most valued exercise of the author's calling. Their collective effort may thus be considered an attempt to redeem the idea of professional work for the practice of poetry, an attempt that was sometimes frustrated but other times energised by what eighteenth-century intellectual work was actually turning into. Although the Lake poets court vocational failure and sometimes disaster, their writing has an optimistic and pragmatic core, which may be why, in addition to their irreducible formal gifts, they become such important models for the poets who follow them. Chatterton was believed to have poisoned himself, after all, and Gray's Bard leaps "headlong" into the "roaring tide" of the Conway River. In the work of Wordsworth, Coleridge, and Southey, on the other hand, the poet almost always gets out alive.

I YOUNG POETS, OLD PROFESSIONS

"Professionalism," then, is one name for the poets' relationship to their culture, and it frames their relationship to their immediate predecessors. Yet the central importance of the learned professions for these poets has remained under-examined. There have been valuable treatments of poets and individual professions, for example of Coleridge and medicine or, especially, Wordsworth and the law.[11] There have also been studies that use the category "professionalism" to describe an aspect of modernity in which Romantic writing is directly implicated. However, in order to understand the way these poets conceived of their actual work, it is also necessary to generalize about the other kinds of work they might have expected to do. While the category of "authorship" has undergone intensive scrutiny in the past thirty years, structuralist and discursive approaches have treated it as a complexly isolated reflection of other kinds of social relations. Recent discussions of copyright, for example, have advanced our sense of the legal contours of authorship, but, by design, they leave the non-specific aspects of authorship unanalyzed.[12] In contrast, I argue that what Alan Liu calls the "vocational imagination," which is an author's "need to *place* [the work of writing] in the field of contemporary industry," is shaped by the "ecology" or the "system" of professional labor.[13] The ancient, learned professions that provided the basic template for professional identity, as well as other vocational groups that aspired to professional status, compete internally and externally for jurisdiction over tasks and problems of recognized importance, and they compete over the definitions of what successful solutions should look like.[14] For the Lake writers, poets are or should be a central part of this system, based on their training and their variously defined social mission. At a moment when differing versions of social order fill the air, some familiar metaphors – poet as prophet, poet as healer, poet as law-giver – turn out to have unpredictably literal referents.

Although the life-stories of the Lake poets have different textures, their early careers are defined by a common body of "life-chances," a specific combination of material necessity and educational resources.[15] As young men, each was in need of a dependable source of income, and, pursuing a standard trajectory, each followed up on a grammar-school education with attendance at Oxford or Cambridge. The differences among Wordsworth's rural Hawkshead, Southey's venerable Westminster, and Coleridge's charity school, Christ's Hospital, are thus partially ameliorated by the schools' preparatory function, which is exercised largely informally – as the career of Southey, ejected from Westminster but welcome at Balliol College, demonstrates. The writers were all intended by their families to enter the Church, a fact that bears directly on the ways they would describe the poetic profession, but other options were live at various times. In addition to their clerical prospects, Wordsworth also contemplated the law, and Coleridge and Southey both considered medicine. Further, the extra-professional jobs they imagined for themselves were based, by and large, on the education that suited them for the professions, and those options included work that was or would eventually become "professional" by many definitions: school teaching, tutoring, and journalism are central, and Coleridge's brief experience of military service, his pseudonymous enlistment in the Light Dragoons as "Silas Tomkyn Comberbache," is anomalous from the point of view of history not because he became a soldier but because he did not enter the army as an officer.

Potential entry into the professions contributes greatly to the writers' sense of identity, but it also generates an ongoing act of resistance toward the old regime. Any profession could be expensive or time-consuming to prepare for – "all professions have their inconveniencies," as Wordsworth would say.[16] More important, the perceived stability of the professions and their participation in the distributive dynamics of the establishment made them emblematic of old-style, oligarchic corruption. Coleridge's 1795 attack on Southey, shortly after the dissolution of Pantisocracy, is illustrative. Coleridge claims to be upset, not for his own sake, but on behalf of their partner George Burnett, who will be left without support now that the utopian community the men had been planning has been abandoned. As a radical intellectual with a short supply of cash, Burnett is financially as well as morally barred from the professions, Coleridge argues, even though professional work is the alternative for which his education has best suited him: "He cannot go into the Church – for you did 'give him principles'! .... Nor can he go into the Law – for the same principles declare against it ... for Law or Physic he could not take his degrees in or be called to," Coleridge adds, "without a sinking of many hundred pounds."[17] While Coleridge is implicitly separating himself from Burnett's haplessness, their situation is in many ways shared, and he is as precise in distinguishing among the professions as he is at ease combining them. One set of objections bears on the church, a related but extended set to the law ("a wicked profession," he calls it later in the same letter); and law and physic demand a substantial outlay of capital, whether one is "called to" the bar or "takes his degrees in" medicine.[18] Southey, Coleridge implies, is unfairly advantaged in being able to consider these courses of action. Coleridge might have added what he also knew, which is that Southey had had the option of a Church living available to him, held by his uncle, Herbert Hill, while he and Burnett lacked Southey's helpful connections.

A critique of established networks is equally implicit in Wordsworth's earlier declaration, generically representative of his radicalism, that "[h]ereditary distinctions and privileged orders of every species ... must necessarily counteract the progress of human improvement."[19] Wordsworth's sense of "human improvement" owes as much to Smith as to Godwin, since the existence of "privileged orders" is not only an impediment to efficient land use and the enforcement of law but to the proper distribution of places and positions. Significantly, Wordsworth's temporary intention is to fight these "institutions" as an entrepreneurial journalist, a quasi-profession that would struggle toward legitimacy over the course of the nineteenth century.[20] Yet such an appeal to the open market, which offers itself as an answer to inherited privilege, demands some framing. As Wordsworth had earlier written to Mathews:

You certainly are furnished with talents and acquirements which if properly made use of will enable you to get your bread unshackled by the necessity of professing a particular system of opinions. You have still the hope that we may be connected in some method of obtaining an Independence .... Nothing but the resolution is necessary. The field of Letters is very extensive, and it is astonishing if we cannot find some little corner, which with a little tillage will produce for us the necessities, nay even the comforts of life.[21]

While they tout the magic of the late-century literary marketplace, these lines reveal the problematic that would also define

Wordsworth's ongoing thinking about the relationship of poetic to professional work. The potentially shabby world of full-time journalism is transformed into an agricultural "field" that lies waiting for the desultory, non-competitive, and non-waged tillage of Wordsworth and Mathews, whose actions will require the classical, martial virtue of "resolution," who are figured optimistically as a pair of gentleman farmers, and whose goal is not a steady salary but "independence." Writing may be a trade, but it is not "trade," and it isn't the shop or the factory. It is the proper sphere for educated men of "talents and acquirements," and the independence it offers is multivalent. Wordsworth would be free of the establishment's "system of opinions," and he also wants to be free of its system of handing out money and jobs.

The proximity of professional to authorial careers is not surprising, since in each case so much could depend on a certain kind of educational background, and the Lake writers share this proximity with a wide body of precedent poets. Thomas Akenside is announced as "M.D." on the title page of *Pleasures of Imagination*; William Collins narrowly avoided becoming a clergyman; Thomas Gray spent much of his life preparing for a legal career he would never enter; Edward Young, as I will discuss, took orders, and other chapters of this book detail James Beattie's academic career and William Cowper's disastrous experience with the law. Further, while the professional or near-professional gentleman-author is one central figure for the Lake poets, just as relevant are poets such as Richard Savage and Thomas Chatterton, at either end of the century, who were excluded by circumstances from that profile yet were highly sensitive to the currents of professional authority that swirled around them. For writers of the Lake poets' generation, the stories of these marginal careers are also formative, insofar as Savage and Chatterton enact both the resistance and the imaginative accommodation that defines the Lake poets' response to professional work.

The history of the British professions unfolds within a number of overlapping chronological frameworks. While the institutional structure of the eighteenth-century professions, which includes the Universities, the Royal College of Physicians, and the Inns of Court, is medieval, the professions begin to take their modern form after 1688, when the anti-professional backlash of the civil wars and the subsequent court-centered regimes of Charles II and

James II give way to a revitalization of professional privilege.[22] Patterns of education also change after the wars, and professional preparation becomes more clearly separated from the generic education of the gentleman.[23] All of these shifts have precedents before 1642, and all provide connections between earlier and later professional forms. As Rosemary O'Day suggests, the development of a specifically professional ethic entails the dismantling of the early modern responsibilities of the aristocratic leader, but it also involves a recombination of those "humanist" tendencies on behalf of the professional project.[24] Romantic writers are able to draw on the oppositional heritage of various Whig and Country versions of patriotic "virtue" (versions that are not always mutually compatible) largely because professional self-justification makes formerly aristocratic values available in the context of authorized and sometimes regulated intellectual labor.

Over the course of the eighteenth century, the professions move toward the acknowledgment of new sources of status and of purportedly more rational measurements of effectiveness, but the process is not especially linear or evolutionary. As Roy Porter describes eighteenth-century medicine, for example, action on the part of apothecaries, lay practitioners, and (for Porter, most important) a growing population of clients makes "medicine a more lucrative profession, and doctors ... more prestigious," not because medical science becomes more technically proficient, but because a greater number of people are in a position to demand, and potentially to supply, "health."[25] More generally, during the early-century period that sees Queen Anne's bounty improve the status of the lower clergy by augmenting poorer church livings, the Act of 1729 combine attorneys and lawyers in the hope of regularizing their effectiveness, and, between 1720 and 1750, the founding of most of London's great teaching hospitals, demographic pressure is encouraging consolidation and specialization, increasing the chances of individual and collective mobility while contributing to the "intellectual" significance of intellectual work. Geoffrey Holmes, who has demonstrated that the Augustan professions "expanded and diversified [and] became increasingly valuable as instruments of social fusion," also describes the "rise in academic standards" that the professions experience during this early period.[26] Yet as an important counter-example, a post-1688 regularization of the church "career-structure" is immediately followed by increasing pluralism, elite defense of privilege, and a "chaotic" reward-structure.[27]

The process of rationalization would accelerate in the nine-teenth century, when, as Magali Sarfatti Larson has phrased it, the "move by merit against birth" that defines certain kinds of pro-fessionalism is energized by industrial take-off and political reform.[28] The years of the Lake poets' early careers are marked, however, by a confluence of factors that are crucial for later developments. New possibilities for political radicalism stimulated by events in France come together with the population's ever-increasing desire for professional service and its hostility towards the establishment's attempts to control intellectual work, all of which opens up new ways of imagining and pursuing a poetic or a professional career. In the intensified circumstances of the 1790s, when it has become more desirable than ever to look beyond the borders of the established professions and when the demand for "careers open to talents" would emerge as an inter-national imperative, the Lake poets set out to find ways of exploiting both their status as potential professional gentlemen and new and emerging ways of thinking about work. These cir-cumstances go some way toward substantiating Clifford Siskin's signal observation that the actual language of modern pro-fessionalism gets "written up" between the landmark phases of early eighteenth-century and mid- and late-Victorian professional growth.[29] I would add, though, that changes and inconsistencies within this period and within the professions themselves are cen-tral to associated developments in literary representation. Unlike the Foucauldian "disciplines" they may superficially resemble, that is, the professions are a real object of knowledge that binds the Lake poets to their precursors.[30] Their history thus offers one concrete and specific way of talking about a "long eighteenth century" that is marked by difference as well as continuity.

II ROMANTIC PROFESSIONALISM, THEN AND NOW

To move from a disparate and long-term phenomenon such as "the rise of the professions" to the specifics of three connected poetic careers is to raise a biographical and historical question, but it is not only that. It is to begin to re-examine the matter of whether or how any Romantic text or career can "represent" its historical moment, as James Chandler puts it, without being reduced to a misleadingly schematic diagram.[31] As Chandler's account, which poses Romantic theories of a featureless "chronological time" against the equal and opposite force of a unifying "spirit of the age," indicates, Romantic criticism has followed Romantic literature in its preoccupation with the relationship of the general to the particular, or as it is sometimes expressed, of the total to the local. As a category of thinking that comes to justify the ascendance of certain social groups, "profession" is a site where ideology is constructed and it demands to be considered abstractly, in terms of normative structures. At the same time, professional activities are involved in the rawest kinds of acquisition, of money and of status, and are best explained at the level of empirically available detail. This double-sidedness brings professionalism directly into contact with recent developments in Romantic studies.[32] Since the history of the professions joins subjective development and training, "*bildung*," to a particular institutional environment, "professionalism" offers a way in for readers who investigate one topic of continuing interest, the enabling conditions of high Romantic solitude and autonomy.[33] To discuss Romantic poetics in terms of the professions is also, necessarily, to consider poetry in light of topics that have been vital to what has been called "sociable romanticism," including generally professional ones such as patronage and education and specifically literary ones like the book trade, the practices of journalism, and the relations of authors with other authors.[34]

While the importance of professionalism to criticism reflects the importance of professionalism to the poets themselves, critics have grown appropriately wary of this kind of identification.[35] Yet the coincidence is revealing, not so much for what it tells us about the Romantic origins of our own categories as for how it retrospectively illuminates the situations and insights of the authors. Theorists of isolation are skeptical of individual agency, perceiving the deep, motivated self as an invention, and not necessarily a fortunate one. Such writers locate, as one critic puts it, "historical entombments – of Otherness, of revolution, of sublimity" in acts of "imagination" that claim to join a fully realized subject to its social world.[36] On the other hand, sociable critics tend to grant agency to biographical subjects, even while advancing with an impressive

generalizing force.[37] A key feature of this sociable work is a sense
of situated, individual authorship.[38] When the Lake poets confront the question of their own vocation, they are similarly
managing the difference between what they feel free to do and the
perceived constraints on their activities, and they develop what
Regina Hewitt calls a "sociological point of view" regarding the
relationships of subjects and structures.[39] The poets' continuous
and purposeful actions are informed by the kinds of knowledge
about agents and institutions, people and the social world, that it
has also been the business of contemporary Romantic criticism to
articulate, and their understanding is expressed not only in their
explicit social theorizing, but in any number of informed rhetorical gestures.[40]

In granting the Lake poets a degree of reflexive knowledge and
action that is the functional equivalent of later critical perspectives
on their historical moment, even when these later perspectives
seem to clash, I may appear to be offering up a theoretically
belated version of the man of letters as hero. Paradoxically,
though, this heroism, such as it is, is accomplished at the expense
of failures and mistakes that most writing on poets and professionalism has not been positioned to acknowledge. On the
contrary, as I will discuss in detail below, critics who have addressed this subject have generally been quick to agree that Romantic
writing converges with the intents and purposes of England's
professional middle classes, and by extension comes to form the
template for categories such as "modernity," "literature," "the
imagination," and "the self." In fact, I argue, at the moment of
composition and afterwards, the poets are trying but failing to
harness professional ideas that would remain stubbornly resistant
to poetic uses. Despite the Lakers' lifelong familiarity with the
professions, the individual poet could go seriously wrong with
regard to them, either by misunderstanding their characteristics
or by overestimating his own ability to change the way they worked.
(The life stories of even the most successful authors display lapses
in social tact.) As I have already suggested, the professions themselves contained tendencies or potentials which were not compatible, so that poets who succeeded in addressing one version of
professional self-establishment might fail in regard to a co-existing
set of terms. Or, to put this in a way that reflects the writers'
experience, a given poet might fail and succeed at the same time.

While the Lake poets attempt a series of acts of identification with an imaginary figure, the professional gentleman, these acts never in themselves add up to a symbolically coherent identity, and they occasionally threaten to become what Erving Goffman calls in a different kind of context a "spoiled identity," constantly defined in relation to a norm that it cannot live up to and that it sometimes rejects.[41]

Here, the role of the eighteenth-century author in forming the community of the noble living and the noble dead is essential. Obviously, it will not do to imagine the extraordinarily productive and innovative figures who make up the Lake school as deluded, defeated, or self-defeating, any more than it would make sense to dismiss the institutions of Romantic criticism just because contradictory positions may be sustained within them. In contrast to Goffman's "discreditable persons" or Erikson's "morbid" and "contradicted" subjects, figures whose attempts at identification are permanently thwarted or abandoned, the Lake poets always credibly insist on the virtue of their own positions, and they are able to do so in part because of the continuing relevance and prestige of their literary precedents. To be professional meant many different things, but there was some assurance to be had in the idea that a "poet" was inherently an integrated, extraordinary character. When the Lake poets confront the legacies of figures such as Savage, James Beattie, Chatterton, Herbert Croft, William Cowper, or John Henderson, it is part of a constant search for other kinds of models, other potentially productive acts of identification, that might stabilize their conception of themselves as a new, viable kind of intellectual worker.

This emphasis on identification and reconstruction distinguishes my approach particularly from two other ways of thinking about Romanticism and the professions, one which treats professionalism as a counter-term to poetic freedom, one which absorbs the Lake poets' project into a broader movement toward "the rise of professional society." Because of the presumed separation of poets from economic activity, the historical category of the professional man of letters, vaguely defined as any male writer who makes a living at writing, once sorted poorly with the idea of the Romantic poet. Two books on "the profession of letters," published decades apart, illustrate the point: A. S. Collins' *The Profession of Letters, 1780–1832* (1928) concentrates on novelists and reviewers, not poets, and J. W. Saunders' *The Profession of English Letters* (1964) very briefly defines "the Romantic dilemma" as the problem of reaching unperceptive audiences with writing that is "professional" only insofar as it is "honestly imaginative."[42] Either a Romantic poet cannot really be "professional," these books suggest, or their professionalism must be very narrowly construed as a special refusal of the marketplace.

However, to be professional, historically speaking, is not only to get paid or to not get paid. It is to possess certain attributes and a certain, albeit variable, standing in the culture-at-large.[43] Therefore, critics have re-emphasized that the utopian attitude Herbert Marcuse famously called "the affirmative character of culture" is functional, not critical, in the development and maintenance of the bourgeois state, and this line of inquiry has recently been pursued in persuasive detail.[44] Siskin argues that during and after the "long eighteenth century," professional "behavior was no longer simply the behavior of gentlemen ... because the task at hand, in an increasingly complex culture, was no longer to embody ... but to represent: to write up new kinds of power by writing them down."[45] Professional work comes to stand in for the work of the middle class, which is now defined not in terms of doing, or of getting and spending, but in terms of potentially literary "representing." From the topic of professionalism, Siskin's case moves to its claims about the broader significance of Romantic discourse. New forms of professional behavior may be attributed to the textual productions now called "Romantic," and Romanticism may in turn be held accountable for historically specific forms of subjectivity. Ultimately, Romantic tales of self-fashioning provided the middle class with the organic account of a deep, "revisable" self that is "valorizing and valorized by an 'open' society and a 'free' economy."[46] In a related way, enriched by a series of close, ingenious readings, Thomas Pfau's study of "Wordsworth's Profession" argues that various kinds of "cultural work," mobilized by shrewdly intuitive cultural producers, generate the contingent, imaginary relationships that finally constitute middle-class self-consciousness.[47] Both critics begin by assuming a fragmented social world, and both find in "professionalism" a productive discourse that succeeds by healing the psychic injuries inflicted upon the middle class by social change. Rather than presenting a Romantic textuality that escapes from or effaces history, this kind of argument gives us a Romanticism that is socially engaged (just not at the banal level of policy making) and is also, while potentially dangerous, very powerful.

The dissolution of "Romanticism" into a complex but coherent "professionalism" comes at the price of a certain distortion, however, and it remains helpful to insist on the real historical vagaries of the term "professional," which was used to mediate among individual practitioners, separate vocational practices, and larger narratives of authority or efficacy. The Lake poets respond directly to these vagaries. Because of the wide-ranging, intuitive nature of the poets' approach to their own work, their particular gift for writing conflict, the temporal structure of Romantic professionalism enacts the mechanism of identification in which "a single covering figure" condenses situations and desires shared by or pertaining to a number of different characters.[48] In the sociological imagination of Romantic professionalism, the separate and more familiar mechanism of "identification" with an admired person is also subjected to the processes of dream logic. Members of other professions as well as potentially professional writers who succeed or fail in the literary sphere are collapsed, critiqued, and reified, and ideas about work from a dozen different directions are anticipated or appropriated in a flurry of reflexive mental and rhetorical superordination.[49] At its most assertive, Romantic professionalism takes on the character of a constitutive social demand – what Wordsworth, Coleridge, and Southey are up to is the business of building a better "ideal type," where "ideal" is intended to carry its normative as well as its Weberian meaning. Insofar as the Romantic professional is only an ideal, though, attachment to it is an attachment to something that isn't there. Prophecy always has its melancholy as well as its projective or aggressive components.

III WHAT IS THE "LAKE SCHOOL"?

Given the categorical instability of the professions and of the poets' relationships to them, it is fitting that "Lake school" is itself a designation that functions contingently, organizing itself through a chain of circumstances to which the poets respond individually and initially called into existence by reviewers who wanted to categorize and contain poetic authority. It is possible to treat the term as a heuristic device along the lines of "Romanticism" itself. David Chandler, a critic who has defended Southey's distinctiveness and value in relation to the other writers, allows that "there were enough personal connections between Wordsworth, Southey, and Coleridge, and just about enough common purpose in their work, to merit the title of a 'School,' even if they never thought of themselves as such."[50] William St. Clair identifies the Lake writers as among the most highly regarded poets of the first half of the nineteenth century, and while it is evident that his list, which is based on an examination of contemporary commentary, is in some ways incomplete, it is in its own terms revealing. Its members, Byron, Campbell, Coleridge, Moore, Rogers, Scott, Southey, and Wordsworth all knew each other and acted out various streams of rivalry and influence, but the poets who would come to be known as the Lake school are aesthetically and chronologically prior – Scott, a practicing lawyer the same age as Southey, did not write his great original poetry until 1805, and he did so under the direct influence of Coleridge as well as of Percy's *Reliques*.[51]

It has also been possible to treat the category of the Lake school as a mistake, born of the exigencies of journalism and perpetuated by writers who didn't know or care about the many personal and aesthetic differences among the poets.[52] Francis Jeffrey's 1802 review of Robert Southey's *Thalaba*, for example, is often credited with making the Lake school into a unified object of scrutiny, but it is not always clear what he thinks holds this school or "sect" of poets together.[53] Yet the case of Jeffrey, both his critique of the Lake school and his own biography, also helps us see how professional rivalries are generated within the ranks of the educated and how the collective identity of the Lake school is formed out of this dynamic. That is, Jeffrey illustrates and anticipates Marilyn Butler's insight that "the search for Romanticism is not so much the quest for a certain literary product, as for a type of producer."[54] At the onset of Jeffrey's working life, he had had the makings of a literary dilettante or, at best, a bad poet. His approach to the study and practice of law was desultory, and he idly considered other options, including medicine, while waiting for his prospects to gel. However, while Jeffrey's career began hesitantly and offered to go in a number of directions, it is in retrospect coherent, and both its hesitations and its final shape illustrate an important characteristic of professional life that would also inform the efforts of the Lakers. He enacts the belief that a gentleman's habits of mind are transitive, so that the lawyer who can read quickly and widely enough is suited for the role of man of letters while, conversely, the University man who has a flexible outlook is fit for any of the professions.

Before the advent of the *Edinburgh*, Jeffrey's most strenuous thinking and writing was done privately, its aim and audience uncertain, and the establishment of the *Edinburgh Review* was itself a kind of accident, a result of the underemployment of various Whig intellects who were suffering through the chilliness of a party-conscious Tory regime.[55] Yet as editor of the *Edinburgh*, Jeffrey the law student became a great, and a well-paid, critic, and once the Tory hold on Scottish law was broken, he was also potent at the bar and in politics, finally leaving the journal for the sake of these activities in 1829.[56] In the move from writer-in-waiting to prominent public man, Jeffrey lived out an alternative to the very different kinds of trajectories that Wordsworth, Southey, and Coleridge would experience, but it was one that had always been possible for their careers, as well; at the moment of the *Thalaba* review, Jeffrey and the Lake poets were engaged in a rivalry based as much on similarity as on difference. The review makes this explicit. As he puts it, the Lake poets "vulgar" language is especially inexcusable coming from writers such as Southey who had "had the occasion to indite odes to his college-bell, and inscribe hymns to the Penates."[57] Because they share his prospects, Jeffrey suggests, the Lakers should also share his outlook.[58] He would himself leave *The Edinburgh Review* because he believed the position was incompatible with the high status he had attained as lord advocate, but his public reputation, as recalled for example in Carlyle's *Reminiscence*, accommodated both roles easily enough. Meanwhile, the Lake writers would elevate the poet largely in terms that made him "a member of the *best* profession," in Siskin's words, although the claim required some conceptual wrangling.[59]

Further, as Mark Schoenfield argues, Jeffrey's "attack against Wordsworth and the other Lake Poets ... is professionally defensive" particularly because Jeffrey, like Wordsworth, had attempted the labor of "curing the illness of despair which the recent history of England and France had inflicted on early enthusiasts of the French Revolution."[60] Schoenfield's interpretation of events indicates both a break and a return. It is a break, because the Lake poets' careers are shaped by the competition over a specific historical task that might fall to the professions, to the poets, or to the newly risen Quarterly reviews; it is a return, because authors and the professions had been called on to respond to a different historical crisis at the end of the seventeenth century and would continue to present an organized cure for conflict and despair, the prospect of individualized work and social cohesiveness, into the twentieth. Harold Perkin has influentially argued that Victorian professionals make up "a forgotten middle class … because they forgot themselves" in promulgating an ideology of testable merit that sought to transcend class struggle.[61] In the 1790s, we see the pre-conditions of this self-forgetting not in a mild, class-bound convergence, but in intraprofessional conflict.

IV SOUTHEY, WORDSWORTH, QUARLES: ONE EXAMPLE

It remains to indicate how such conflicts could play themselves out at the level of the text, and I conclude this chapter with a representative example. Letter XVI of Southey's *Letters from Spain and Portugal* (1797) ends with the inclusion in full of Frances Quarles' "Hieroglyph VIII," a "beautiful poem on monastic life" that laments the waste of human talent in the "darkness" of ascetic seclusion.[62] Southey's re-contextualization of Quarles demonstrates not only his openness to a range of poetic sources, but also his inclination to respond to vocational difficulties by way of literary citation. Nominally a reflection on religious cloistering, Letter XVI is at least partially a disquisition on Southey's own situation, and its relevance is made transparent by the circumstances of its composition. Southey had been brought to Spain and Portugal by his Uncle Hill, who continued to offer him the Church living Southey had determined to reject and who represented the expectation that Southey, educated at his family's expense, would enter one of the professions instead of pursuing literature, radical politics, and an unsuitable marriage. In fact, although the trip was an attempt to remain in Hill's good graces, Southey had quietly married Edith Fricker just before leaving for Lisbon.[63] Additionally, while Southey would consider other professional options, his refusal of the Church, once made, never wavered. These events were riddled with predictable psychological ambivalence, and Southey's encoding of this biographical material is not especially subtle. As Letter XVI observes:

Our professions are usually chosen for us, and our educations regulated accordingly, at an age when it is not possible that we can decide wisely for ourselves: when that arrives, if our principles militate against the choice, what course must we pursue? It is dangerous when we set out on the voyage of life in an ill-provisioned vessel, to reject the aid of the pilot, and seize the helm ourselves.[64]

Southey at first grants his elders the status of "pilots," but as the letter proceeds, his most striking examples of familial decision-making are the religious seclusion of children and the making of castratos for the opera, reflections which might have made the similarly beleaguered Wordsworth and Coleridge smile, or grunt, in sympathy.[65] The deployment of Quarles's anti-monastic verse at the climax of this letter thus performs two tasks. It condenses Southey's anxieties about familial obligation into the conflict between free British Protestantism and the despotism of the Catholic South, and it further condenses these into the struggle for evaluative control that Jeffrey's *Thalaba* review would later take up. As Francis Jeffrey would recognize, Quarles is a readily available resource for Southey, but as if in anticipation, Southey "make[s] no apology for enriching [his] volume" by including the other-than-prestigious Quarles.[66]

The appearance of "Hierogliph VIII" in the *Letters* gains further interest from the fact that Wordsworth would find a more enduring use for the vocational language that had first caught Southey's attention.[67] Critics have long speculated about the source for the ringing opening of the 1799 version of *The Prelude*, and especially for its very first phrase:

> Was it for this
> That one, the fairest of all rivers, loved
> To blend his murmurs with my nurse's song,
> And from his alder shades and Rocky falls,
> And from his fords and shallows, sent a voice
> That flowed along my dreams?

As Robert J. Griffin has recently discussed, the phrase in question appears in *The Rape of the Lock* ("Was it for this you took such constant care[?]") and has been traced back to similar language in

Book IV of the *Aeneid*, which Pope may be parodying ("Was all that pomp of woe for this prepared[?]").[68] There is no reason not to accept that the phrase accumulates resonances as it passes from context to context. Nonetheless, finding the source of this language in Pope is of a piece with finding it in Milton or Virgil. All of these gestures reproduce the investment in canonicity defended by Jeffrey. In fact, Wordsworth is most immediately following Southey's example (and perhaps his text) and quoting the beginning of "Hierogliph VIII":

> Was it for this, the breath of Heav'n was blowne
>   Into the nostrils of this Heaven'ly Creature?
> Was it for this, that sacred Three in One
>   Conspir'd to make this Quintessence of Nature?
>   Did heav'nly Providence intend
>   So rare a fabric for so poor an end?

Not only its suggestive and repeated opening, but this entire stanza, is relevant to Wordsworth's lines. Quarles's poem laments the squandering of human talent or "light" that results from monastic practice. Wordsworth is struggling with a moment at which his own poetic talent, granted to him by "voice" of the river, appears likewise to be going to waste. The inspiration of heaven has been replaced by the blended sounds of the Derwent River, and the forestalled task is now the still-hard-to-define ministry of the poet, but the passages, each centered on vocation, are parallel, and Quarles's urging that "a thousand Tapours may gaine light from thee" is a plea to which Wordsworth's lines may be said to respond. Jeffrey has underappreciated, but he has understood, Wordsworth's special sensitivity to a kind of epigrammatic writing that balances the sublimely scriptural with the more humbly instructive. It is a measure of the difference between Wordsworth and Southey that Wordsworth is able to transform these lines so completely even while remaining so close to them, largely by re-casting them in the first person. On the other hand, Southey's shrewd and interpretively active inclusion of them in their original form indicates his particular gifts as an anthologizer, a compiler, and a bricoleur.

Chapter 1, "Cursing Doctor Young, and after," continues this introductory section and examines some of the definitions of the term "profession" that are operative for the Lake poets. In particular, it argues, new forms of professionalism are partially based on the proper management of risk, a subject that, in its literary version, habitually calls up the question of the afterlife. The chapter's first example is Coleridge's response to John Henderson, a celebrated Bristol intellectual who died in 1788 and who in his lifetime resisted accepting a traditional, non-innovative professional identity. Especially because of Henderson's interest in the occult, the conversation surrounding his death generates competing ideas about how the afterlife might be depicted in conjunction with competing, risky and risk-averse, versions of professional identity, and Coleridge takes the opportunity to embrace a progressive ethic of sublime vocational danger. The chapter's second example addresses one of Wordsworth's principle accounts of risk, death and the professions. "Tintern Abbey" has long been understood as a text that "secularizes" the providential vision of eighteenth-century poets. As I argue, however, what is at stake in the poem is also the professionalism of the poet, which may be more vital than the waning public influence of the cleric. Edward Young's *Night Thoughts* depicts a priest who aspires to lay speech; the Wordsworth of "Tintern Abbey," an unconnected layman, aspires to present a rigorous and rational account of human "training" that founders, in the turn to Dorothy, on the gendered terrain of late-eighteenth-century education. Young thus appears in "Tintern Abbey," and again in *The Prelude*, as a poet whose career risk is creditable in its own terms but requires modification in light of new professional practices.

The second section of the book broadens out to address the eighteenth-century context from which Romantic professionalism emerges. Chapter 2, "Merit and reward in 1729," takes a long view of the author's professional situation and investigates changing conceptions of merit and virtue, patronage and independence, and origins and experience. It begins with the life and writings of the famous Grub Street poet, Richard Savage. Criticism has tended to read Savage's career as belatedly embracing an aristocratic patronage system that would be rendered moot by the burgeoning marketplace. On the contrary, I argue that Savage is visionary insofar as he borrows classical, aristocratic language in order to insist on an autonomous, professional identity for poets, a topic also taken up, or lived out, by David Hume, Samuel Johnson, and James Beattie. Describing autonomy in terms of magical afterlives, formative experiences, and literal poetic flight, Savage is, perhaps despite himself, an early proponent of a later professional mode.

Chapter 3, "James Beattie and *The Minstrel*," moves to the work of James Beattie, which is both an advance on and an intensification of the professional ideal enacted by Savage. Like Savage, Beattie attempts to describe a poetic profession that is defined by its independence from patrons and other audiences. Unlike Savage, he establishes this independence not in reference to a welter of public debates about origins and merit, but in reference to a special example of the theme, Hume's skepticism, which Beattie construes as an assault on public order. Because its corrosive effect on religion brings comfort to libertines while discomforting the poor and the isolated, skepticism severs the link between the "fashionable" and the marginalized. Embracing the Scottish Common Sense philosophy that was partially intended to reestablish this link, Beattie designs his wanderer figure, the minstrel, to be absolutely free from mere intellectual trends. However, such independence has the ironic consequence of negating the universality of the minstrel's experiences. Professional autonomy, then, is constituted for Beattie as both a connection to and a division from the audience to which he would minister.

The third section of the book returns to the work of the Lake poets. In Chapter 4, "Authority and the itinerant cleric," several strands of the argument are brought to bear on the earliest writing of the Lake school. Savage and Beattie help establish the wandering figure as a representative of poetic professionalism, and, along with Young, they help establish the significance of church order as both a model for crucial intellectual work and a barometer of established professionalism's waning prestige. In the 1790s, the Lake poets take up the wandering figure in order to address yet another model of professional autonomy, this one connected to their prospects as potential curates or priests. In a series of itinerant poems, bad training, failed landscapes, and suicide ministries provide the negative image from which positive versions of the poetic calling will eventually be developed. Chapter 5, "William Cowper and the itinerant Lake poet," argues that these negative examples are partially recovered through the Lake poets' reading of Cowper. Cowper is a prominent stylistic resource, but he also stands for a principled reluctance to speak in place of an authorized ecclesiastical establishment. Poems such as "John Gilpin" and *The Task* dramatize Cowper's authorial displacement. The Lake poets respond in *Peter Bell, Rime of the Ancient Mariner,* and *Madoc* by describing acts of persuasion that are self-sufficient and that offer to ground new, if ultimately indefinable, poetic institutions.

While Part III deals with a series of conflicts that are textually contained, Part IV describes two public interventions on behalf of the Lake poets' professional claims. Chapter 6, "Robert Southey and the claims of literature," describes Southey's attempts to establish a professional position in his debate with Herbert Croft regarding a group of letters by Thomas Chatterton. In this debate, Southey defends a new version of professional identity by emphasizing affiliations that are based on work, not on birth. He thus joins an argument about authorship and status that is also present in David Williams' *Claims of Literature* and is anticipated by Croft's novel *Love and Madness. Love and Madness* takes pains to distinguish the murdering priest James Hackman, who is the gentleman hero of the story, from the suicidal poet Chatterton, who serves as Croft's negative example. Throughout, the novel emphasizes the importance of gentility over vocation – just the relationship Southey wants to reverse.

As Chapter 7 demonstrates, Wordsworth's Preface to *Lyrical Ballads* argues specifically and publicly for a Romantic version of professionalism. As it does so, it reiterates a series of important distinctions that are present in the work of Savage and Beattie. Wordsworth insists, first of all, that the poet is distinguished from his client audience on the basis of his specialized and rigorous training – Nature's "ministry more palpable," as *The Prelude* would call it. In addition to the distinction between the poet and his client audience, the Preface also insists on the difference between the poet and other kinds of professionals. Yet the text's impulse is ultimately synthetic, and it draws on strategies and arguments from a range of sources in order to make its major, deceptively simple claim: the work of the poet, no less than the labors of the professional or the virtues of the aristocrat, can and should be perceived as both autonomous and honorable, no matter how contradictory contemporary definitions of autonomy and honor turn out to be.

PART I

Romanticism, risk, and professionalism

CHAPTER 1

Cursing Doctor Young, and after

I ROMANTIC PROFESSIONALISM

Wordsworth, Southey, and Coleridge belonged to a fraction of the English population that provided many of the nation's "professional gentlemen," and they hoped that their personal status, which existed at the beginning of their careers in the form of a culturally determined potential, might be lent to the pursuit of letters. Further, they hoped that the transference would generate an improving reciprocity between the individual poet and an emerging vocational identity. This formulation, which posits an already held kind of standing that is subsequently loaned out before it is earned, may appear circular, but it is an accurate depiction of the work of the sociological imagination as these poets exercised it. However, as we have seen, the professions as they actually existed were multiplicitous and, at least from the point of view of the Lake poets, they could be unacceptably associated with the shortcomings of the old regime. This chapter examines some of the relevant definitions of professional identity that the Lake poets would try to manage, and it traces some of the ways the poets would make the idea of "risk" into a principle that distinguished a traditional professional identity from a more progressive and acceptable one. As they did so, debates about the afterlife provided the poets with one metaphorical basis for measuring properly risky against moribund forms of professional practice.

The Lake poets' collective act of professional imagination, which depended upon a multidirectional act of identification with other professional figures, seemed often to contradict itself or to go awry. Coleridge notices the problem early on, and writing to Thomas Poole in March of 1797, he describes his first encounter with a "professional man" in a way that reveals how difficult it was to think about poetry as a new kind of profession while also mounting a criticism of the professions as they actually existed. His autobiographical account, organized around the subject of vocation, begins by describing his father's failed literary occupations and, briefly, his mother's home economies. Next, it details the fates of his older brothers, whose activities make up a substantial catalogue of the vocational choices available to men in their circumstances. These siblings include an officer in the East India company, a school-teacher, a soldier, a parson, a chaplain/school-teacher, a "medical man," and a midshipman-turned-soldier. Finally, after announcing his own birth and christening, Coleridge goes on to tell the following tale:

In [1774] I was carelessly left by my Nurse – ran to the Fire, and pulled out a live coal – burnt myself dreadfully – while my hand was being drest by a Mr Young, I spoke for the first time (so my mother informs me) & said – 'Nasty Doctor Young!' – The snatching at fire, & the circumstance of my first words expressing hatred to professional men, are they at all ominous?[1]

This is a highly wrought, highly condensed allegory regarding the mismatch between Coleridge's expectations and his achievements. As a visionary, self-destructive child, he snatches coal from the fire; Dr. Young, an adult with authority and expertise, attempts to mitigate some of the damage; but bawling baby Coleridge, entering language for the first time, cries out against "nasty Dr. Young!", and Coleridge's inaugural "hatred of professional men" appears to produce the doctor as an absolute term of difference. The rejection of the doctor is not the entire story, however. Coleridge is suggesting to Poole that he has been at war with the professionals into whose ranks his older brothers, following his father, had moved with such apparent ease, but while the medical gentleman is fundamentally distinct from the poet, he also focuses a quirky but deeply felt act of self-recognition. Evident in the story of Dr. Young is Coleridge's persistent, wishful idea that if a person of his talents were to earn his way in some as-yet undefined fashion, he might be able to take up at least the accoutrements of more conventional professional figures. He is lamenting both his failure to enter an established profession and his inability to make his literary pursuits resemble the financially secure, gentlemanly activity that he believes he should reasonably expect to take part in.

It would be easy to follow Coleridge's lead and blame his unstable personality for his vocational difficulties. However, the apparent effortlessness of his epistolary shorthand suggests that his anxieties about money and his daydreams about what literary success might finally look like are implicated in a broader, unresolved argument regarding the definition of professional identity, one that is as audible to the dissenting industrialist Poole as it is to Coleridge. While the learned professions of church, medicine, and law were readily understood as "professions" and their members honored, at least nominally, for their service to society, the adjective "professional" also referred to those who were solely and inappropriately motivated by money.[2] Further, within the learned professions themselves the term was applied, with a tactical lack of rigor, across a highly stratified situation. Apothecaries, surgeons, and physicians could equally be called professionals, but a series of legal struggles over licensing and remuneration underscored the essential point that some medical men were more equal than others, and this tripartite structure obtained in church and law as well.[3] Competing implications of the term "professional" also shifted and blended. A "professional journalist" might be a "party hack" at one historical moment and yet become respectable at a later date.[4] Various members of the working population sought after the adjective "professional" as a status marker, but status could be established neither independently of language nor entirely within it, and the term's volatility reveals the extent to which sources of cultural eminence were unstable, not only over time, but also at any given time. In the case of the medical profession, for example, Corfield reports that "an index of the rising prestige of the medical practitioners was their capture of the scholarly title," "doctor," from lawyers, divines, and musicians; but the term "doctor" remained without a legal definition, so that provincial practitioners could, in a phrase Corfield cites from Smollett, " 'graduate themselves.' "[5] In Coleridge's letter, the down-class-sounding "Mr. Young" becomes the respectable "Dr. Young" before finally subliming into the "professional man" who represents the best and the most general aspects of the case.

Although the rise of the professions has often been presented as a simple indicator of the rise of modernity, a problem of equal or greater urgency for these writers was how the established standing of intellectual workers could be maintained as an aging Whig order faced collapse.[6] Because Coleridge felt justified in using Dr. Young as a synecdoche for all "professional men," it may be speculated that the doctor, whatever his actual family circumstances, had apprenticed with a reputable practitioner and been validated by a respectable country clientele (including Coleridge's father, the vicar). However, we cannot infer the details of his qualifications with much precision. For the country practitioner of Coleridge's Devonshire boyhood, "professional" was not a logically delimiting category, and what would have made Dr. Young a "professional" in Coleridge's sense is simply that he was recognizable as such, largely, probably, on the basis of a network of personal relationships.[7] On the other hand, the primary emphasis of an emergent professionalism is on the supposed certainties of acquired and documented expertise, what Andrew Abbott calls a combination of "abstract knowledge" and "technique" and Philip Elliot has usefully characterized as the marker of "occupational" professionalism.[8] A qualified practitioner in an occupational profession is one who has been found through examination to have aptitude and has subsequently been trained by an accredited institution according to rigorous principles.[9] Confidence in this kind of professional is based on the successful completion of a specialized course of study, and his or her ability is guaranteed by state certification, or by some other documented and institutional evidence regarding preparation, and not by a mix of personal connections and informal testimony.

This formulation should not be allowed to obscure the complexities of the situation. Critics have regularly noted that studies of the professions are vexed by the tension between sociological theories, which often presume a progressive narrative culminating in an ideal twentieth-century type, and a disobliging mass of historical detail. Magali Sarfatti Larson, for example, has offered one interpretation of the professions that sharply distinguishes a preindustrial condition from an industrial one, arguing that modern professions act collectively to control their own markets in ways that were not possible before the consolidation of industrial capital over the course of the nineteenth century.[10] She has since concluded, however, that the history of the professions is too discontinuous to support her binary and "monopolist" view, and she has subsequently concentrated on a more generally conceived "production of knowledge" that creates dissymmetries between experts and lay actors in a range of institutional contexts.[11] Abbott, similarly resistant to "monopolist" and "functionalist" definitions that identify professions ideally, also accepts "expertise" as a key term, although he is more interested in the conditions under which professions are constituted in competition with each other and in how expertise is actually to put to work.[12] For both writers, the fundamental unit is not the individual practitioner but the corporate entity, yet each writer tells us something about the negotiations the free operator must undertake within the parameters of professional history. Expertise, abstract knowledge, and competition are crucial for the Lake poets, but, for them, making these elements central is only one way of solving the problem of professional authority. In order for the poets to establish their identity with and apart from the professional practitioner, knowledge and experience have to be associated so that experience is neither casually genteel – the kind of polish an indifferent student might pick up at an Inn of Court, or the kind of indolent reading (and scribbling) Wordsworth would dismiss in 1815 – nor rigidly preordained.

Coleridge's tale dramatizes a moment of uncertainty insofar as it does not choose but moves among these rival ideas. To the extent that the story of Dr. Young lumps together all "professional men" and comically disposes of them, underlining the contrast between the recklessness of the fire-snatcher and the routines of the doctor, it demonstrates Coleridge's envy but also his antipathy toward the dull rounds of traditional professionalism as he understood it. Yet in his fire-snatching impulse Coleridge discovers the freely inquiring, empiricist daring that would underlie the professional heroism of the progressive practitioner. The gently ironic tone of the story holds in suspense Coleridge's desire to differentiate two characters, the established gentleman and the fearless researcher, while ultimately appropriating the privileges of one for the benefit of the other. The two vocational dilemmas are separate but related. Dr. Young's financial security is a representation of what Coleridge longs for but cannot achieve, and Dr. Young's respectability represents the charismatic, anti-credentialing function that modern professionalism, itself pursued at times by perfectly authorized, perfectly well-born gentlemen, wants to reject yet also wants to reconstruct for its own purposes.

Coleridge's fire-snatching, and the ethic of professional daring
that this reckless act signifies, remind us that "risk" in one form or
another is always attached to the establishment of professional
privilege, particularly when the grounds of that privilege are in
transition. As a normalizing mechanism, as a source of anxiety, or
as an occasion for argument or riot, risk is one of the principles
that determine the shifting balance of individual and collective
prerogatives. Risk may be understood in several senses here. In
late eighteenth-century England, a generalized professional ethic
that drew increasingly on medicine's scientific model called for
new and progressive kinds of research that were metaphorically,
and sometimes really, dangerous. In Bristol, Coleridge was surrounded by medical adventurers such as Humphry Davy and
Thomas Beddoes, both highly trained chemists, both political
radicals, and both dedicated to the exploration of medical
knowledge even when, as in their famous course of experiment at
the Pneumatic Institution, the exploration involved a degree of
physical peril.[13] Dangerous research must have been at least partly
inspired by an inherited ethic of professional intervention, since
the three learned professions had always had the job of standing
between the general population and the triple threat of death,
damnation, and injustice. Conversely, a moribund institution was
one that had abjured its relationship to risk. Part of Evangelical
Christianity's great power over the course of the eighteenth century came from its vivid insistence that getting religion wrong
could be far more dangerous to the individual than sectarianism
was dangerous to the state.

More broadly, modernity itself has been said to produce a "risk
society."[14] Various perils are experienced collectively, but they are
managed on behalf of all by a collection of "expert systems" that
has become infinitely wider and more finely divided up in the post-
industrial age.[15] Such perils, which include the possible large-scale
failure of various support networks, can only be understood
abstractly and must usually be forgotten about in order for normal
life to go on, but moments in which lay skepticism and resistance
confront the tyranny of experts are symptomatic of a "reflexive"
or "high" modernity that is more democratic, if more nervous,
than its precedents.[16] Not that professional authority has ever
been elemental or unchallenged. Whose lot it is to endure risk
and whose job it is to control it are points on which clients and

practitioners may eternally fail to agree. Like professionalism itself, risk is both intensely individualizing, insofar as it is a main premise of client choice and of lay/professional conflict, and definitive of national experience, insofar as state institutions respond or fail to respond to it. The millennial rhetoric of a revolutionary age automatically generates an account of expertise on behalf of the radical intellectual, and the Lake poets' various interventions in politics mark an attempt to establish a position, relative to government and to rivals in the literary sphere, on this basis. When the prospectus of *The Watchman* announces Coleridge's aim to "preserve Freedom and her Friends from the attacks of Robbers and Assassins!" his heroics are, he explains, a response to the dangerously compromised journalism of his provincial rivals.[17] In this case, the author both fights against an old system and represents the possibility of a new one.

Another kind of risk, which occurs at the level of the practitioner, is also part of the professionalizing engine. It is socially risky, but sometimes necessary, for poets or other would-be professionals to move from an established order to one that remains ill defined and notional. (The possibility of "going wrong," or of going right by going wrong, is neglected in writing that mistakes class for a static category.) Nor is this kind of risk separate from the theories of "risk society" outlined above. The demand for innovation must carry with it the threat of failure, or else "originality" would be a dead category, unable to figure in the recursive procedure whereby individual accomplishment and institutional change are mutually defining. Although the end-point of risk society has been described as the end of class affiliation, the proper management of risk is for Wordsworth, Coleridge, and Southey one of the ways professional gentility is established and defended.[18] To a readership largely informed by Johnson's *Lives*, Pope's entrepreneurial energies are more respectable as well as braver than the sheltering curacies of figures like Gray and Collins. (Pope is also, not incidentally, the better earner.) Coleridge's brief biographical paragraph thus proves to be cleverly constructed and widely referential. Reaching in to grasp the "coal" with which "Coleridge," punningly, begins, the writer's pre-reflective quest for his own fiery origins announces an inexpressible independence. At the same time, the in-its-own-terms indefensible rejection of the country surgeon prophesies the later ideal of an identifiable and systematically trained "clerisy."

The rest of this chapter works outward from two poems, one obscure, the other a recognized exemplar of High Romantic lyricism, in order to highlight the historically linked themes of poetic specialization and professional risk. In the first, "To the Author of Poems Published in Bristol," Coleridge revises Joseph Cottle's theories of vocation by replacing Cottle's language of elegiac consolation with a language of professional daring. Doing so means that Coleridge has to reckon not only with Cottle but especially with John Henderson, a local symbol of resistance to the professions, and with Milton's "Lycidas," which proves to be a central intertext for Cottle and Coleridge both. In "Tintern Abbey," I argue, Wordsworth also produces an oppositional account of professional identity, but his response is to a prominent forbear, Edward Young. Young's *Night Thoughts* evoke a dramatic world controlled in every particular by homiletics, but Young sacrifices the cleric's special role in the course of his extended argument and begins to piece together a stylistic argument for lay authority. Although "Tintern Abbey" ironically and unexpectedly responds to *Night Thoughts* by attempting to re-invoke professional privilege, the attempt founders on the gendered politics on which eighteenth-century specialization depends.

II COLERIDGE, COTTLE, AND JOHN HENDERSON

Coleridge's generic promiscuity has made his career famously difficult to define, but his lifework can provisionally be described as a quest for a framework within which religious, philosophical, and literary research might be pursued, as he puts it, "ad libitum."[19] In 1796, that quest was in danger of being stalled. He had become a well-known poet, journalist, and lecturer in Bristol and had also launched his own periodical, *The Watchman*, but he was finding that after his strong start, literary success was increasingly difficult to maintain. At this moment of uncertainty, Coleridge was brought into contact with the figure of the Bristol/Oxford celebrity John Henderson, who would play a part in Coleridge's ongoing search for models or counterparts. Cottle's first collection of verse had appeared in July of 1795, and despite the casual disdain with which Wordsworth, Coleridge, and Southey always treated Cottle's writing, his ability to compose and his financial resources made him an arbiter in the literary sphere.[20] Particularly because Cottle is Coleridge's patron and because, in early 1796, Coleridge is late in supplying him with copy, Cottle's fluency and his prerogatives as a bookseller are beginning to throw the literary calculus of his relationship with Coleridge out of whack. One response to the dilemma comes in verse. Some time in February 1796, while still at work on the preface to *Poems on Various Subjects* and the final version of "Religious Musings," Coleridge also finished "To the Author of Poems published anonymously in Bristol." Coleridge particularly praises Cottle's "Monody on the Death of John Henderson," and while there are other reasons for him to single out this text, the figure of Henderson is significant because it reminds Coleridge how to develop an oppositional version of authorship based on various forms of the risky acquisition and exercise of knowledge.

Henderson is a character with whom Coleridge can identify, where identification means not only shared opportunities but shared pathologies. The son of a Bristol school-teacher, Henderson was a famous local intellect who advanced to Oxford with the aid of a patron he met and impressed, as the story was often told, during an accidental meeting on a coach. He knew John Wesley, Samuel Johnson and Hannah More and may have had more than one personal connection to Coleridge's circle; he was also known, via the Oxford/Bristol connection, to Southey and probably to Beddoes.[21] As Kathleen Coburn remarks, Cottle seemed to have associated Henderson with Coleridge from the start, and among Coleridge's projected works is Henderson's biography.[22] The reasons Henderson would have reminded Cottle of Coleridge, and would have been of interest to Coleridge himself, are clear enough. Henderson's serendipitous ascent to Oxford is a dream version of Coleridge's unassisted struggle into (and out of) Cambridge, and the two men also shared widely praised linguistic and philosophical attainments. Coburn also observes that the men resembled each other physically.[23] Coleridge might further have taken note of some of the disabling symptoms of Henderson's character. Most pressing, there is the question of professional achievement. Henderson was plagued by the charge that "with as great talents as most men in England he had ... done just nothing," and in 1796 Coleridge has already begun to hear the same kinds of critiques.[24] Henderson is both a drinker and an opium user, and on this point, too, Coleridge is becoming increasingly vulnerable. As Coleridge had cursed the professionally adequate Doctor Young, so he appears to share a different curse with Henderson, the doom of squandered talents and squandered chances. While Cottle would attempt to rehabilitate his friend in a monody that comes to an almost surreally orthodox conclusion, Coleridge would suggest a more positive reading of Henderson's career. Failure is relative and can be honorable, and there is no regret and no withdrawal in Coleridge's "To the Author" and its once-removed approval of Cottle's troubled tutor. Here, disappointment and stigma are not the source of a shared embarrassment but of a shared, lived critique.

Henderson graduated from Pembroke but remained an impoverished fellow there, and his resistance or hostility to the institutions of professionalism is a significant aspect of his career. One of the few texts he ever published excoriates the law, and, in a manner reminiscent of the young Wordsworth, Coleridge, and Southey, he forever resisted the attempts of his friends to place him at the bar or in the Church. The DNB reports one potentially professional act on his part, but it takes place in suitably spontaneous, indeterminate circumstances:

[H]is benevolence led him, after he had acquired a knowledge of medicine, and an epidemic of fever was raging in Oxford, to practise gratuitously among its poor. At this crisis all his spare money was spent in drugs, and he sold his polyglot bible to purchase more.[25]

Henderson is a kind of medical man, as it turns out, but he is not the retiring, Youngian kind. Having "studied the healing art" at Pembroke, where Beddoes began his career in chemistry and where Coleridge's professional brothers also went to school, he would have found advances in medical science relatively accessible.[26] As important as the progressiveness of his training are the perils he undergoes in order to implement his knowledge. Exposing himself to the fevers of the poor, even at the expense of selling that testament to progressive theology, his "polyglot bible," he pursues a course of professional risk and scientific service. Yet he does so without submitting his talents or his knowledge to any institutional test, formal or informal, and in this way, he pursues the genteel, freelance healing of the eighteenth-century cleric.[27] He is at once the best prepared practitioner and the most complete amateur.

Cottle's memoir delves into the sensitive question of what, given his tremendous talents, Henderson actually accomplished during his life, and this leads him to the topic of Henderson's death. Cottle reports a conversation that would appear to excuse the fact that Henderson, who talked much, wrote very little:

Upon my expressing to him some concern at his not having benefited mankind by the result of his deep and varied investigations – he replied, "More men become writers from ignorance than from knowledge. – Many claims to originality must be pronounced null, unless the Authors can convict their forefathers of plagiarism. – Let us think slowly and write late." Thus the vastness and variety of his acquirements, and the diffidence of his own mental maturity alike prevented him from illuminating mankind, till DEATH called him to graduate in a sphere more favorable to the range of his soaring and comprehensive mind.[28]

The comments are reminiscent of Coleridge's own endlessly deferrable ten-year plan, but they also mark an important difference between the two careers. Henderson dies young, and according to the memoir, it's a good thing. Death is a vocational interruption insofar as it "prevent[s Henderson] from illuminating mankind," but it is also a "graduat[ion] in a sphere more favorable," a release from an impossible present to an eternal future of infinite intellectual activity. Cottle's memoir may be understood as a complaint about the workings of this world or as a statement of faith in the beneficence of the next one, but taken together the two readings reinforce the urgency of a question that will also guide Coleridge. Will poetic professionalism be allowed to emerge as a real possibility, or does Cottle's language of posthumous consolation foreclose the possibility of vocational improvement?

Discussions of Henderson's life after death are particularly motivated by a pressing fact of his intellectual biography. Henderson himself was well-known for his belief in spirits and in the possibility of communication with the dead, a proclivity that was the occasion for some satire in his lifetime. As Richard G. Swartz has recently suggested in a discussion of John Clare's autobiography, such thinking was, by the end of the eighteenth century, a potential sign of vulgarity.[29] Ghosts had no standing in formal Anglican doctrine, and to credit their existence was to embrace a suspect traditionalism and to run counter to the skepticism of the culture's educated ranks.[30] Yet the abiding interest in various emanations, angels, and specters would not go away. Drawing on Swedenborg for its intellectual impetus but on the work of Isaac Watts and the Wesleys for much of its affective power, an anthropocentric version of heaven, in which relationships there were continuous with those on earth and in which personal inclinations and talents remained intact, was struggling to earn respectability.[31] Belief in this kind of continuing existence for the departed is the bright flip-side of late-eighteenth-century occultism.

Henderson's interest in ghosts and the occult is not as distant from a progressive interest in medicine as it first appears. For the young Coleridge, for example, an anthropocentric afterlife defined by the materiality of human nature was of a piece with another tempting monism, Brunonian medicine. As Neil Vickers has explained, Brunonianism, an advanced form of vitalism which posited "excitability" as the fundamental force of life, was of interest to Coleridge through the 1790s and as late as 1823, largely because as a system of thought it promised to reconcile body and soul.[32] Brunonianism also offered to reform the profession of medicine itself by calling into question "the convoluted and often incoherent doctrines of the established profession."[33] Coleridge's poetic interest in the spirit world similarly has "its intellectual origin in his profound understanding of the value and also the limitation of the eighteenth-century skeptical philosophers," as Anya Taylor puts it.[34] Although unable finally to believe in the "descending, & incarcerated soul" on which popular accounts of spirits generally depend, and which is also the basis for certain consoling visions of reunion, such a faculty was to him at least "intelligible poetry."[35] In Coleridge's encounters with the invisible and with the patently corporal, his experience is exemplary – the progressive, the empirical, and the systematic suddenly find their counterpart in a mix of abstruse post-Renaissance metaphysics and a deeply felt folk life.

How this cluster of interests is imbricated in a tenuous but recurring re-thinking of professional authority is also shown in William Agutter's Anglican sermon on Henderson's death, which demonstrates some of the ways Henderson's occultism could be at least tentatively accommodated to more orthodox institutions and structures of beliefs. Agutter begins his sermon by positing that "Death is only the continuation of life," praises Henderson for refusing to join the "indolent cry of Ignorance and Affectation to brand with odium the occult sciences, before he had examined them for himself," and then offers, a little defensively, that "it appears highly probable, both from scripture and reason, that the angels of Heaven were once human beings; and that the friends of our purest affections may become our guardian angels."[36] Of particular interest is Agutter's yoking of scripture and reason as well as his desire to cast Henderson's occultism as a matter of having an empirically oriented, open mind. Tradition and research will join to confirm intimations of immortality that have always been common property, and, as in Agutter's discovery of the "guardian angel," rational speculation may even go beyond those intimations. The systematic inquirer proves to be a highly informed sub-type of the population to whom he ultimately ministers.

Henderson's pursuit of the occult also shows how closely related spiritualism could be to more explicitly professional impulses. Although an intense student of Lavater and Swedenborg, his public statements on his own necromancy are briskly Johnsonian. Of successful communications with the dead, Henderson informs Joseph Priestley that "1. I have no reason to think them absurd or impossible; 2. They are commonly asserted in all ages; 3. and generally believed. 4. I find myself more at ease in believing them; my notions are suitable."[37] With an affected urbanity, Henderson continues to speak the language of experiment familiar to educated gentlemen while suggesting that such language will not quite do. Having refused to assert that he has himself raised spirits, Henderson informs the famous Christian materialist, "You see you need not be in any apprehensions for your philosophy on account of any experiential knowledge of mine."[38] However, Henderson's treatment of the afterlife solicits even as it rejects the certainties of methodological rigor. In taking up the matter of eternal punishment, he likens his deductive argument to Bacon's experiments in chemistry, and not to Bacon's credit: "Nor let it displease the reader if [Henderson's argument about divine punishment] be brought in as some of Bacon's experiments, in his Natural Philosophy, 'solitary.' Though in truth they are more nearly relative than his experiments to the first topic."[39] Henderson is responsive to those moments in Bacon's thought where materialism shades into alchemy and spiritualism, but he emphasizes that in certain situations, Bacon's

announced methods may not serve open inquiry.[40] The axio-
matic method of Henderson's "Dissertation" implicitly critiques
Bacon's inductive reasoning and, he claims, comes closer to
its "first topic" than Bacon's discredited natural experiments
come to theirs. Agutter's sermon also emphasizes Henderson's
a-Baconian originality: "Surely God has various ways of commu-
nicating knowledge to man, without waiting for the flow information of the outward senses [sic]," Agutter insists.[41] For all
that, inspiration is forensic and aggressive: Henderson "dis-
carded all the systems of men, saw the clouds of mysteries dis-
pelling, and was able, in his comprehensive view, to reconcile
many apparent contradictions in contending sects."[42] Despite
his evasive irony, Henderson continues to see in necromancy and
Boehmenism empirical matters, susceptible to evidentiary reasoning and potentially to experimental knowledge. His orientation toward final things, conditioned by a convergence of
rational Dissent, Anglican enthusiasm, and high classical scholarship, reintroduces a "professional necromancy," close cultural kin to the professional poetry of Wordsworth, Southey, and
Coleridge, that would be rigorous, learned, and divinely
inspired.

In sum, Henderson's professionalism is based on risk at several
levels: his dangerous practice in Oxford, the risk of resisting a
professional place, the intellectual and moral risks of abstruse,
occult research. For Cottle, this blend is over-rich and dangerous,
and his "Monody" skips over Henderson's necromantic experiments as well as his medical achievements, instead re-describing
the memoir's "sphere more favorable" and suggesting, more
artfully, why Henderson needed to graduate to it. Remunerated or
not, Cottle insists, Henderson has always had a specific calling. His
Henderson is not a doctor but a teacher, and the significance of
the afterlife in Cottle's view is that Henderson's pedagogic work
will be renewed there:

> Then only not a friend of all mankind,
> When to thyself a foe – farewell, GREAT MIND!
> We wander tearful through this vale below,
> But thou are gone where tears forget to flow;
> Where LOVE and JOY eternal vigils hold,
> And scatter healing as their wings unfold;
> Where Souls their radiant course forever run,

And move like Planets round the Almighty Sun.
If Friendship be a flower, whose am'ranth bloom
Endures that heavenly clime; beyond the tomb
I, haply I (low scenes of earth, retreat!)
Am doom'd once more thy honor'd form to meet;
Behold thee stand "girt in a starry zone"
Where Wisdom wells beneath th'Omniscient's throne;
And thou to me with outstretch'd arm shalt bring
Nectar ebullient from that living spring. (97–112)

While it is a habit of modernity to think of "lifespan as a distinctive and closed trajectory," the "Monody" extends that trajectory into infinity.[43] (This is even clearer in Cottle's 1796 revision of the climactic lines, which delete the fountain and declare that Henderson is to "[b]e my Loved instructor once again!")[44] Cottle moves between a theocentric and an anthropocentric vision of heaven, but the poem's conclusion insists on the latter category. Henderson's excellence and his suitability as a teacher will be reproduced in heaven, but only in heaven, the "Monody" anticipates, will the personal finally merge with the professional. Henderson's calling, which could not be institutionally contained on earth, will result in deep personal satisfaction as well as spontaneous access to systematic knowledge "beyond the tomb."

Cottle's vision of heaven offers a tribute to Henderson that forcibly accommodates Henderson's vocational roguishness to a new kind of domestic consolation. In memory of Henderson, Cottle's demotic orthodoxies tame Swedenborg's radically materialist theology, which was publicly defended by Henderson and denounced by Priestley and Wesley alike, while demonstrating that Henderson had really been doing productive work all along. That is, in attempting to honor Henderson's mixed heritage of enthusiasm and science while mitigating his rebellion against work, Cottle helps invent a heaven that is tonally distinct from its antecedents and that is part of a cultural groundswell. The "Monody"'s conclusion serves as a kind of notional testimony, providing good news to that large part of his audience for whom life's most tangible risk is not that the French War or the global economy will be mismanaged by experts but that, as "John the Baptist" ominously puts it, "tho' all shall see the eternal state/Far different scenes will different souls await" (205–206). Henderson's fascination with the corporal persistence of the self after death becomes, in Cottle's hands, a way of extending and recuperating Henderson's career as well as a Bristovian illustration of how Heaven will prove to be a rewarding place for the people who deserve, because of all their hard work, to go there.

In the face of this act of containment, Coleridge's "To the Author" uses the conventional narrative of a "perilous" Parnassian ascent as his figure for the ongoing improvement of Cottle's verse. Coleridge's version of poetic identity is progressive, and he tempers Cottle's literal-minded earnestness regarding the possibilities of the afterlife:

> Unboastful Bard! whose verse concise yet clear
> Tunes to smooth melody unconquer'd sense,
> May your fame fadeless live, as "never-sere"
> The Ivy wreathes yon Oak, whose broad defence
> Embowers me from Noon's sultry influence!
> For, like the nameless Rivulet stealing by,
> Your modest verse to musing Quiet dear
> Is rich with tints heaven-borrowed: the charm'd eye
> Shall gaze undazzled there, and love the soften'd sky.
>
> Circling the base of the Poetic mount
> A stream there is, which rolls in lazy flow
> Its coal-black waters from Oblivion's fount:
> The vapour-poison'd Birds, that fly too low,
> Fall with dead swoop, and to the bottom go.
> Escaped that heavy stream on pinion fleet
> Beneath the Mountain's lofty-frowning brow,
> Ere ought of perilous ascent you meet,
> A mead of mildest charms delays th'unlabring feet.
>
> Not there the cloud-climb'd rock, sublime and vast,
> That like some giant king, o'er-glooms the hill;
> Nor there the Pine-grove to the midnight blast
> Makes solemn music! But th'unceasing rill
> To the soft Wren or Lark's descending trill
> Murmurs sweet undersong 'mid jasmin bowers.
> In this same pleasant meadow, at your will
> I ween, you wander'd – there collecting flowers
> Of sober tint, and herbs of med'cinable powers!
>
> There for the monarch-murdered Soldier's tomb
> You Wove th' unfinish'd wreath of saddest hues;
> And to that holier chaplet added bloom
> Besprinkling it with Jordan's cleansing dews.

But lo your Henderson awakes the Muse –
His Spirit beckon'd from the mountain's height!
You left the plain and soar'd mid richer views!
So Nature mourn'd when sunk the First Day's light,
With stars, unseen before, spangling her robe of night!

Still soar, my Friend, those richer views among,
Strong, rapid, fervent, flashing Fancy's beam!
Virtue and Truth shall love your gentler song;
But Poesy demands th' impassion'd theme:
Waked by Heaven's silent dews at Eve's mild gleam
What balmy sweets Pomona breathes around!
But if the vext air rush a stormy stream
Or Autumn's shrill gust moan in plaintive sound,
With fruits and flowers she loads the tempest-honour'd ground.[45]

As a description of the dangerous, laborious acquisition of professional power, "To the Author" is almost too transparently allegorical. The first stanza calls the pre-"Henderson" Cottle "unboastful" and his verses "modest," and later lines emphasize his restfulness as he pauses at the foot of the "poetic mount" and gathers "med'cinable herbs and flowers." Only after his "perilous ascent" does Cottle's monody on the death of his former tutor "waken ... the muse" and allow Cottle to "soar"; in order to write his best kind of poem, he must evade the "coal-black waters" of "Oblivion," leave the "mead of mildest charm [that] delays th'unlabouring feet," and confront his journey to "the Mountain's lofty-frowning brow." That is, the most laudable poetic activity is here figured as exploratory and dangerous, and in this, the poem's treatment of the poet's task reverses certain vocational commonplaces while retaining others. The gatherer of medicine is indolent, "Truth and Virtue" are "gentle" and static, but "Poesy" itself is vexatious, fecund, and dangerous. The flying poet is, as Chapter 2 will also discuss, conventional, but it remains surprising to see that poet's claims so specifically urged over those of the healer's, to encounter the materially useful servant at the foot of the mountain while the inspired author is found high above. The Hendersonian Cottle is contrasted favorably to the melancholy Cottle whose indolence is generally serviceable but is not noteworthy, not exciting, and cannot be improved.

As sympathetic as Coleridge seems to have been to the professional profile offered by Cottle's monody, and as resistant as he was in principle to Henderson's literal, materialist understanding of the afterlife, Cottle's climactic, saving gesture comes too cheap, and the most telling part of Coleridge's treatment of Cottle is his involvement in the generic question of the elegy. As the poetic form most directly concerned with the question of what is missing, the elegy has always been a promising site for meditations on vocational trouble. We might even say, glancing at the most famous English ones, that the poet's calling is always somewhere at stake in them.[46] In this case, Coleridge's critical interventions do not just revise the "Monody"'s treatment of profession and the afterlife, they do so by improving upon Cottle's engagement with Milton. The precursor monody "Lycidas" divides the fact of the departed poet's talent from the question of its lifetime development. Because Lycidas is "dead ere his prime," it is left to the Miltonic speaker to ponder the long-term uses of "Fame" and the costs entailed by "meditating the thankless muse." The power of Lycidas is emblematic, and his status as an unconsummated poet (and minister – it is always important that Edward King was on his way to take up his first living when he drowned) enables the living poet to go on.[47] What Cottle's "Monody" proposes in response to "Lycidas" is nothing less than a subject so integrated that it retains its vocational talents, and the status those talents confer, on the other side of the grave. By invoking a pedagogically active afterlife for Henderson, Cottle's big finish translates the generic dyad – dead, unconsummated poet and living, reflecting one – into a single, continuous biographical stream. The absence that "Lycidas" works to compensate for is replaced by an always material, immutable presence, neither figurative nor aesthetic, and the disruption of innocence by experience and by death is healed not through the work of elegiac consolation but through a literalizing narrative of reunion and renewed tutelage.

In response, Coleridge's poem focuses its attention on the question of the living monodist. "Lycidas" renews convention when it transforms poets into shepherds, although the passage about neglectful religious leaders is a reminder that, for Milton as for Coleridge, the intellectual authority of the poet is genealogically related to the authority of the cleric. Cottle is more literal-minded in his discussion of the departed Henderson's undergraduate days, readily demanding, for instance, "What if an artificial aid he sought,/Worn out with prodigality of thought?" (65–66).

Coleridge's subsequent move is to propose for Cottle himself the double identity that is divided in Lycidas between the monodist and the loved object he mourns – not only the living poet and the dead one, but also the surprisingly pastoral doctor, who spends innocent, helpful days gathering herbs, and the poet proper, who retains Lycidas' purposeless charisma but also possesses the sublime, soaring bravery of the natural philosopher. In the flying figure of Cottle, Coleridge indicates that the distinction between potential and consummation, talent and effort, need not be figured as the difference between life and death, but may instead be discerned in the lifetime working-out of a vocational impulse. Nor must this structure bear the burdensome lack of progress with which it is threatened by "Henderson"'s climax. Coleridge seeks to attach a notion of risk to the professional account that Cottle establishes in "Henderson." In this way he also rhetorically recuperates some of what Cottle's conclusion has abdicated, the "satisfaction of being open to adventure and risk, including the fear of dissolution that any enlargement of consciousness may bring in its wake."[48]

III "TINTERN ABBEY" AND *NIGHT THOUGHTS*

In a slightly different context, Mark Schoenfield has also sug- gested that the history of professionalism illuminates the "unna- tural" nature of death itself.[49] The connection is partially due to the problems of knowledge, method, and authority I have already discussed, but it is also due to the fact that professionalism des- ignates the relationship of finite individuals to a variety of tem- porally extended institutions. This means that in the context of Schoenfield's argument, death and the afterlife become both legal and "anti-legal" matters. As Schoenfield puts it in his dis- cussion of Wordsworth and copyright, Wordsworth develops a

set of interpretive strategies for his community; these interpretive stra- tegies are often appropriated from the very fields of discourse – law, science, history – that romantic poetry seeks to master. This appropria- tion, in turn, forced Wordsworth's poetry to rely on the very structures it attempts to transcend as the ground of its intelligibility.[50]

While Coleridge eventually learns to mourn a profession of poetry which no one has ever been able to put into practice, Wordsworth, on this account, imagines that the goals of such a profession might also be realized through a set of special relationships to which readers and writers of (his own) verse would be party. Yet in what form are these relationships to be established? According to Schoenfield, the legal and economic worlds produce "the lack which only the poet can fill," but by the end of his career, Wordsworth finds that that lack can only be filled legally and economically, through the institution of copyright.[51] This is the "paradox" Schoenfield describes with particular elegance: Wordsworth can't "transcend" the historical world without addressing himself to it.[52]

It may be, though, that Wordsworth's "interpretive strategies" are the efflux of more than one kind of professional circumstance. In particular, Wordsworth's relationship to medicine, church, and the law cannot fully be described as either competitive or co-optive. As true as it is that the claims of other professionals impinge on the status of the poet, it is equally true, and equally important, that Wordsworth is framed by the same shifting body of interests and assumptions as the professionals are. Here I consider a major example. "Tintern Abbey" participates in an exchange about human mortality that has for its key terms not "sacred" and "secular" but "authorized" and "lay." The exchange is realized in Wordsworth's acts of affinity with two other figures in the poem: his sister Dorothy, and Doctor Edward Young, the author of one of the poem's great eighteenth-century precursors, *Night Thoughts*. Like Henderson, Wordsworth rejects the shelter of established institutions and of consoling versions of the afterlife for the sake of new forms of potentially professional power.

As a text that is directly concerned with the dramatic presentation of poetic argument, "Tintern Abbey" is formally as well as thematically a descendent of *Night Thoughts*, itself an anthology of mid-century providential naturalism as cast in the vocabulary of the sublime.[53] Young's long poem is an extended address directed at a young libertine, Lorenzo, which attempts to win Lorenzo over to a Christian understanding of the immortality of the soul. Young uses a variety of strategies in the poem, but one of his most persistent is his recourse to the harmonies of Nature. The beauties of the night sky, for example, "shed religion on the soul/ [and are] At once the Temple, and the Preacher!"[54] "Tintern" echoes the thematic organization of *Night Thoughts*. Over the course of the lyric Wordsworth develops the belief that Nature is trustworthy, and he prays that Dorothy will, like the speaker, "mature" into a "sober" appreciation of the fact. Much has been said, and more might be, about the differences between an eighteenth-century poem like *Night Thoughts*, with its vigorous commitment to a complex orthodoxy, and the Romantically skeptical "Tintern," which refuses to move from "Nature" to "God," yet both poems dramatize ongoing acts of persuasion that become indistinguishable from the speaker's deep preoccupation with his own death. For literary criticism, then, the important question is not only what either or both poets "believed" about nature, God, or the afterlife, but how the sources of their lyric credibility are to be differentiated. Young's appeal to Lorenzo, as forceful, learned, and intricate as it is, must come from as close to a lay perspective as the poet, an Anglican priest, can get. On the other hand, "Tintern Abbey" attempts to rewrite *Night Thoughts*'s scene of overpowering instruction as a scene of possible, gentle convergence. In order to do so, it must create a different relationship between speaker and auditor. That relationship may be seen as professional once "Tintern" 's lay speaker is contrasted with the clerical speaker of *Night Thoughts*.

Wordsworth identifies an allusion to *Night Thoughts* in one of two authorial footnotes to "Tintern Abbey." The footnoted passage, and the section in Young to which it refers, are as follows:

> Therefore am I still
> A lover of the meadows and the woods,
> And mountains; and of all that we behold
> From this green earth; of all the mighty world
> Of eye, and ear, – both what they half-create,*
> And what perceive; well pleased to recognize
> In nature and the language of the sense,
> The anchor of my purest thoughts, the nurse,
> The guide, the guardian of my heart, and soul
> Of all my moral being.

* This line has a close resemblance to an admirable line of Young, the exact expression of which I cannot recollect.[55]

> [Seek "thy true treasure"] In Senses, which inherit Earth, and
>   Heavens;
> Enjoy the various riches Nature yields;
> Far nobler! give the riches they enjoy;
> Give tast to Fruits; and harmony to Groves;
> Their radiant beams to Gold, and Gold's bright Sire;

> Take in, at once, the landscape of the world,
> At a small Inlet, which a Grain might close,
> And half-create the wondrous World, they see.
> Our senses, as our reason, are divine. (VI 420–426)

There is a special irony in this exchange. Young maintains the figure of "riches" as he works his way up to his conclusion about
"sense." In particular, the act of seeing proves alchemical, giving its
own "beams" to "Gold" and to "Gold's bright sire," the sun. In
Wordsworth's hands, however, the phenomenologies of creation
and perception are firmly and literally applied to the question of
"Nature," whose virtues are compressed into tropes of wealth only
when economic etymologies are meant to compete with affective
connotations. The "interest" of the landscape is now "unbor-
rowed" from the eye, not dependent on it, and the landscape is
"dear" not only in itself but because it has become the sign of the
covenant with Dorothy. Recovered in Wordsworth's management
of the trope of riches is his own integrity as speaker, not because it is
wrong to mention wealth, but because Young's comparison
between the "false" wealth of diamonds and gold and the "real"
wealth of sensory perception is unmodulated, even crass. It evokes,
at best, the unreflecting "appetite of the eye" that Young himself
generally exceeds in his treatments of natural sublimity. More
damningly, Young has descended in this passage to an argument by
analogy that tarnishes his relationship with Lorenzo. His appeal is
based on an interest that Young only shares with Lorenzo when he is
at his most despairing, the interest in personal advantage. (More
often, *Night Thoughts* demolishes the idea of "value.") Young shows
himself willing to speak in less than his best voice and take advantage of his auditor's less advanced sensibility by fooling with the idea
of what "riches" really are. As the comparison with Young indicates,
then, Wordsworth's foot-noted revision of Young, largely by virtue
of what it leaves out, is one of the places in "Tintern Abbey" that
most carefully maintains the intellectual as well as the affective
equivalence between speaker and auditor.

   The question of credibility is not quite the same as the question
of "sincerity," though, and I would like to turn outward, to the
sociology of these poetic voices. The best way to define Young's
voice is to begin with what it is not. Explicitly, the speaker of *Night
Thoughts* is someone who might be speaking from a pulpit with the

weight of the establishment behind him but who chooses to work personally and informally instead. The distinction between Young-the-divine and Young-the-poet is a familiar fact of his biography, and it is tendentiously outlined by Herbert Croft in his "Life of Young": "Young was a poet; and ... poets by profession do not always make the best clergymen. If the author of the *Night Thoughts* composed many sermons [,] he did not oblige the public with many."[56] As Croft's observation suggests, *Night Thoughts* may be a Christian defense of God's goodness by an Anglican cleric, but it does not quite count as clerical work, and Croft uses this kind of accounting to suggest a more general vocational failure on Young's part. Croft begins the tradition of thinking about Young as a self-righteous, preferment-seeking hypocrite, although, as Chapter 5 will indicate, it is possible to treat Croft's attack on Young as an act of identification gone wrong, since Croft is also an Anglican clergyman-of-letters who actively seeks patronage.[57]

At any rate, Croft's account is not quite complete. *Night Thoughts* may not be a sermon but it is in many ways continuous with Young's practice, his training, and his presumed intellectual interests as an Anglican cleric. The poem, as has been demonstrated in various places, is deeply imbricated in the church's anti-Deistic apologetics.[58] Further, one of its main arguments is previewed in the most formidable and most popular of Young's three published sermons, "A True Estimate of Human Life," a text which Croft's biography overlooks. In the sermon as in the poem, youth and old age, poverty and riches, talent and luck, are systematically revealed to be unsatisfactory, so that one conclusive proof of Christian revelation is, as Isabel St. John Bliss says of *Night Thoughts*, "the fact that man, no matter what his rank or degree of fortune, is discontented .... That neither his passions nor his higher powers can find what they seek suggests his immortal nature."[59] As the sermon's even more elaborate period has it, "[Happiness] is that of which our despair is as necessary as our passion for it is vehement and strong."[60] *Night Thoughts* extends the apologetic into other areas, but its theology is generally consistent with that of "A True Estimate."

There are also stylistic continuities between the sermon and the poem. Young's rhetoric is in both cases classical to the point of being mannered. The passage of *Night Thoughts* cited by Wordsworth, for example, contains the chiasmus "Enjoy the various riches Nature yields;/Far nobler, give the riches they enjoy!'' and the lines are controlled by the relationship of a single subject to a series of different verbs that rhetoricians call ''dia-zeugma.'' (The figure allows Young to dramatize the senses' not-unprofessional rhetorical climb from ''inheriting'' to ''half-creating'' the pleasures of the natural world.) The poetic passage on money and the senses may be compared with a thematically cognate section from ''A True Estimate,'' which is similar, and typical of the whole, in its dependence on acts of repetition:

[Men of riches] are so high in their opinion of what they largely possess, that they think to have riches is to have every thing; that they think them the price, and title to, all the world can give, or man enjoy. Hence high expectations and high resentments; and every evil is aggravated by these. (334–335)

Stretches of the passage have strong iambic potential, and the final clause is suitably, dramatically direct. This sermonizer is enthu-siastic, but not to the extent that he forgets the proprieties of his style. His appeal is to reason and to taste as well as to emotion. The same may be said, more provisionally, of the speaker of *Night Thoughts*, and like the poem's melancholy theological argument, its genteel but forceful idiom looks almost like a direct adaptation of Young's clerical writing.

Almost, but not quite, and the measure of difference between sermon and poem is also the difference between the Anglican cleric and the working poet. Carey McIntosh claims that eighteenth-century prose follows a process of ''gentrification and literacy,'' meaning that the concrete and verbal style of the beginning of the century gives way to an abstract, nominal, ''written'' style by the end of it.[61] According to this scheme, *Night Thoughts'* colloquial moments threaten to make it more ''prosaic'' than the highly gentrified prose of ''A True Estimate,'' but while Young's diction is in both cases genteel and ''written,'' the aphoristic, headlong style of *Night Thoughts'* organization contrasts strongly with the highly ordered forensics of ''A True Estimate.'' *Night Thoughts* invites abridgement and excerption. As Marshall Brown, who considers the poem to be an example of the ''urbane sublime,'' observes, ''wherever it is opened – and some early editions are indexed to facilitate browsing – the reader enters into the middle of an elevated, consoling conversation.''[62] The sermon, on the other hand, is an organized, balanced whole, a carefully tooled theological lecture that is in its own way enthusiastic but which also maintains the appropriate distance between the speaker and his matter.

This stylistic difference, and the difference in speaker which it entails, is repeated at the level of the poem's argument. *Night Thoughts* very deliberately distinguishes itself from the professional work of the cleric. Early on, the speaker identifies himself as a priest: "Thou say'st I preach; Lorenzo! 'tis confest./What if, for once, I preach thee quite awake?" (II.62–63). The joke is double-edged. Lorenzo may well be tired of hearing Young going on, and Young wryly comments on the soporific powers of his official homiletics, but *Night Thoughts* is bonus speech, uncontained by the expectations of pulpit oratory, including the increasingly urgent evangelical charge that an elaborate style is inappropriate. While Young proceeds in this passage to dismiss "amusements" and "trifles," he expects to earn the attention of his audience primarily through flourishes of language and reasoning that would not be quite appropriate in the context of the sermon. Theological argument has been digested by this speaker but so have a variety of other experiences and ideas, and the voice which results purports to be more urgent, more compelling, than the voice from the pulpit.

The poem is not everywhere so self-assured about its own powers as a stimulant. *Night Thoughts* balances Young's general Christian faith in the triumph of "Immortal man" against the different fear that his ministrations will fail, and, in failing, will negate the claims he has everywhere made for the self-as-style. Nowhere is this clearer than in a series of lines that appears near the end of Book VIII:

> Since Verse you think from Priestcraft somewhat free,
> Thus, in an Age so gay, the Muse plain Truths
> (Truths, which, at Church, you might have heard in Prose)
> Has ventur'd into Light; well-pleas'd the Verse
> Should be forgot, if you the Truths retain;
> And crown her with your Welfare, not your Praise:
> But Praise she need not fear; I see my Fate;
> And headlong leap, like CURTIUS, down the Gulph.
> Since many an ample Volume, mighty Tome,
> Must die; and die Unwept; O Thou minute,
> Devoted Page! go forth among thy Foes;

Go, nobly proud of Martyrdom for Truth,
And die a double Death: Mankind, incens'd
Denies thee long to live: Nor shalt thou rest,
When thou art Dead; in Stygian Shades arraign'd
By LUCIFER, as Traitor to his Throne. (VIII 1386–1402)

Young begins by reiterating that official clerical speech is no
longer credible among the members of its most important audience, the one that includes Lorenzo, because sermons are bur-
dened by "priestcraft." Everybody understands that priests get
paid to say these things and that they are likely to say only those
things that will help perpetuate the authority of the Anglican
establishment, an observation Young repeats in his later description of Addison's death, where he notes that church-men have
been "taxed with an abatement of influence by the bulk of mankind," and that is part of the literary genealogy of Cottle's
"Monody."[63] In other words, the layman is more trustworthy or at
least more widely trusted than the professional. But Young goes on
to imagine the failure of his lay sermon, and the fate he projects
for it is odd, to say the least. It won't just be killed off by readerly
neglect. In its not-very-comforting afterlife, Lucifer will torment it
as a "traitor," a fate that is inevitable precisely because the poem
participates in the worldliness it critiques. Not only is *Night
Thoughts* bought and sold, but as the parade of noble dedicatees
for each book reminds us, the poem is itself part of Young's
famous, ongoing search for preferment. Its textual afterlife will
embody the guilt of the gentleman poet who is free neither to
write nor to not to write.

In the end, *Night Thoughts* does not so much redeem the Doctor's clerical career as render it moot. His learning, the intensity of
his own experiences, and, in the final analysis, the social status
which is implied by all of these other factors, amount to a personally held authority which cannot be reduced to any of its components or defined by any of them. This status is virtually
independent of the Doctor's profession, which is secondary to his
individual (for the doctor-as-speaker, stylistic) attributes. The genteel intellectual is certified to arrange the moral life of the nation,
including its aristocrats, or so the poem claims. But at the same
time, this intellectual draws his standing from the standing of the
high company he keeps. We learn quite a bit, over the course of the
poem, about Lorenzo's high living and particularly about the fact

that he draws his income from his rents. The speaker of *Night Thoughts* works beyond the pale of ecclesiastical authority, but Young has already acknowledged that the Church is in many ways secondary in the competition between religiosity and the world by which he is himself defined. For better or worse, the pulpit's power of suasion is replaced in this poem by a stylistic force which appears at first to depend on the speaker's individuality, but which proves on further inspection to emerge from an established system of cultural differences.

William Wordsworth cannot absorb Young's genteel stance whole largely because of the kinds of hierarchies in which Young is invested. Young assumes not only the priority of Anglican doctrine and the church establishment, but the inalterability of what he calls "the world" and its flawed institutions. In response to Young's tactical gentility, which is both the purpose and the product of his lay authority, "Tintern Abbey" rejects the prerogatives of the aphorism in favor of the prerogatives of experiment. He confronts danger and manages risk in the name of collective service, not by presenting the poet as a martyr, but through the elementary act of treating potentially a-rational experiences in roughly Lockean terms.[64] Further, like "To the Author," "Tintern Abbey" is powered by a death-defying act of identification. In distinction to the marvelous harangue of *Night Thoughts*, it dramatizes a consultation in which Wordsworth's own interest in an afterlife depends on the reproduction of his experiences, not in the body of a text which is damned and then saved, but in the newly trained mind of his young colleague. When Wordsworth theorizes his afterlife, then, he moves away from Young's overwrought account of martyrdom and harrowing to the professional equivalence of "love" and "service."

Wordsworth's experiments in self-healing are only fully redeemable if they serve as an example, if they are reproduced by Dorothy's own career. The turn to Dorothy that occurs about three-fifths of the way through "Tintern Abbey" has elicited a number of responses that may be sorted into two camps. Either the figure of Dorothy is elevated by virtue of her inclusion into the poem's ameliorating vision, or she is debased by a logic, gendered or otherwise, which demands that the speaker's various self-assertions come at the expense of a passive, listening Other. William Galperin finds in Dorothy a "scapegoat" for the

relationship of the poet to his invisible audience, and Susan
Eilenberg observes more generally that "to occupy the place of
Wordsworth's conversational object, of his second self, is to be
emptied out and left voiceless."[65] In a biographically and historically informed reading that touches on this one at several key
points, Judith Page argues that if Wordsworth does do Dorothy a
disservice, it is in his failure to acknowledge the real differences in
their positions. Wordsworth might return from the French Revolution's dual trial of love and war in order to become a practicing,
powerful poet, but Dorothy will not be able to duplicate these
necessarily masculine experiences. Her fate will instead be firmly
domestic, and Wordsworth's predictions for her future must prove
to be mere projections of what can only, in fact, be true for
himself.[66]

In light of Wordsworth's revisions of Young, I would like to
suggest a different answer to the questions raised by Page. In
attempting to account for the poem's hold over readers, she
concludes, "the male poet denies his sister her own story, but he
does bless her life with the highest love he can imagine."[67] Crucially, "Tintern"'s blessing is essentially vocational. Mary Jacobus
has pointed out the existence of the "loved companion" in precursor texts such as *The Seasons* and *The Task*, in passages that
resonate very strongly with the parallel sections of "Tintern
Abbey." As Jacobus notes, though, Thomson's "Lucinda" "simply
completes a definition of the good life," and Cowper's Mrs. Unwin
is the object of "quiet sincerity," not Wordsworth's more impas-
sioned "tribute."[68] Wordsworth's experience, and by implication
Dorothy's future orientation, are described in language reminiscent not only of religious enlightenment, but more specifically, of
a pastoral commitment. This is the urgency of *Night Thoughts*:

> I, so long a worshiper of Nature, hither came
> Unwearied in that service: rather say
> With warmer love – oh! with far deeper zeal
> Of holier love! (152–155)

Insofar as the highest love "Tintern Abbey" can imagine is also
the form of professional service to which Wordsworth's own story
is always driving him, it appears that he is not so much denying
Dorothy her narrative as indulging in a moment of utopian imagination in which his sister really can complete her own five-year

curriculum, confronting moments of "solitude, or fear, or pain, or grief" that have the same function, if not the same form, as the trials to which Wordsworth has submitted. While he does demand that Dorothy "remember me" as a condition of her deliverance, her presence on the banks of the Wye is also necessary to his self-recognition and to the perpetuation of service and love. Dorothy is an "audience" who is not a "reader," and Wordsworth marks the difference between audiences (Dorothy and Coleridge) who will be able to learn and serve, and the "audience" he addresses less hopefully and less warmly in his prose works.

Wordsworth's turn to Dorothy is another attempt to imagine the institution to which Coleridge also appeals in his revision of Cottle's "Monody." For Coleridge, the most urgent matter is the replacement of a materialist afterlife with a rich, speculative professional biography. Wordsworth faces the same question and focuses more narrowly on the matter of reproduction. Larson has argued that the professional project encompasses two "contradictory" components. Through professional training, professional labor reifies and reproduces itself, but the monopoly on the means of training also proves to be a way of negating the "exchange value" of professional services – the length of training is "arbitrary," and so the price of service no longer reflects social necessity.[69] Crucially, however, the ringing "five years" of the poem's opening is both arbitrary and necessary. While imagining that Dorothy's training will be as strenuous as his and will derive its shape from her recollection of his own introduction to the mission of love and zeal they share, Wordsworth cannot specify a chronology for Dorothy's coming-to-power. The professional form of this biography excludes the client and maintains its credibility in the face of potential marketplace pressures, that is, it refuses to commodify or rationalize the reproduction of power in order to justify itself. In this sense, the professionalism of "Tintern Abbey" is truer to the autonomous ideal than professions that constitute themselves in regard to the market.

"Tintern Abbey" 's attempt to produce specialized, trustworthy speech as an answer to Young's lay stylistics runs afoul of a perceived cultural impossibility. In treating a woman, Dorothy, like a professional gentleman, it sets up the dissonance that accounts for its reflexive doubling-back from potentially "vain belief" to reliable practice. *Night Thoughts* accepts asymmetries at every level – poet vs. preacher, teacher vs. student, speaker vs. audience, middle-class man-of-letters vs. aristocratic lounger – except in the matter of theology. "Tintern Abbey" participates in a response to the professional circumstances of Young's "abated" cleric, but it, too, is predicated on asymmetry. It will not allow audience and poet to become equivalent, and it certainly will not allow a sister to take the place of an apprentice. Yet these are the positions to which Wordsworth is temporarily driven by the dynamics of the scene as well as by his critique of the pre-Revolutionary Establishment. The transformation of Young's wayward "Lorenzo" into Wordsworth's more co-operative "Dorothy" makes the relationship between speaker and auditor familial and interdependent. In so doing, it also reveals the necessary, even visionary gap between theory and practice – between the serene faith in procedure the speaker has acquired over time and the knowingly willful assertiveness to which the presence of his sister prompts him. Dorothy can't be Lorenzo, but as Page's analysis also shows, she can't really be Wordsworth's second self, either.

Young's passage on gold and the senses re-occurred to Wordsworth at at least one other moment in his career, not surprisingly, when he was more explicitly considering the public role of the Anglican preacher. In Book VII of the Prelude, Wordsworth moves from "entertainments that are such/Professedly, to others titled higher" (1805, VII.517–518), discovering among those supposedly nobler but as cheaply distracting pursuits the "brawls of lawyers" (521) and, more inappropriately, the overwrought theatrics of the London cleric:

> Other public Shows
> The Capital City teems with, of a kind
> More light, and where but the holy Church?
> There have I seen a comely Bachelor,
> Fresh from a toilette of two hours, ascend
> The Pulpit; with seraphic glance look up;
> And, in a tone elaborately low
> Beginning, lead his voice through many a maze,
> A minuet course; and winding up his mouth,
> From time to time, into an orifice
> Most delicate, a lurking eyelet, small
> And only not invisible, again
> Open it out, diffusing thence a smile

Of rapt irradiation exquisite.
Meanwhile the Evangelists, Isaiah, Job,
Moses, and he who penn'd in these our days
The Death of Abel, Shakespear and the Bard
Of Night who spangled o'er a gloomy theme
With fancies thick as his inspiring stars
And Ossian (doubt not, 'tis the naked truth)
Summon'd from streamy Morven, each and all
Must in their turn lend ornaments and flowers
To entwine the Crook of eloquence with which
This pretty Shepherd, pride of all the Plains,
Leads high and low his captivated flock.[70]

Wordsworth's professional theoretic may have demanded that "Tintern Abbey" revise *Night Thoughts*, but Young is still a creditable and influential forebear for whom Wordsworth maintains his regard, and this passage defends Young's career in two separate ways. The epithet "Bard of Night," which replaces the simpler "Doctor Young" of the 1805 version of the poem, gives Young pride of place in the sequence, even after Shakespeare. (The reference to Ossian, whose diction is reproduced in Wordsworth's "streamy Morven," follows epic naming with comic deflation). In addition, Wordsworth recognizes that Young's claim on his audience is primarily stylistic. Young's "inspiration," the passage observes, did not produce his "gloomy theme" but "spangled" it over with "fancies." The driving force of *Night Thoughts*, again, is not philosophical or theological innovation but linguistic performance.

The allusion to Young's stylistic power does not diminish his theological or moral authority. *The Prelude* rewrites the same passage that Wordsworth had cited so effectively in "Tintern Abbey," but here the allusion is an element in an ingenious parody of pulpit speech gone wrong: The "small Inlet, which a Grain might close" has become "an orifice\Most delicate, a lurking eyelet, small\And only not invisible" (548–550). In swapping "inlet" for "eyelet," eye for mouth, Wordsworth attacks the vanity of the preacher. Where Doctor Young attends to his own senses and delivers a successful if troubled lay sermon on the complex marriage of heaven and matter, the "comely bachelor" is reduced to an embarrassingly showy bodily disposition that is productive of nothing. Or nothing useful. The cruelest turn in Wordsworth's description is that what should be an organ of spiritual generosity, the mouth of the preacher, becomes in turn a sphinctrate symbol of parsimonious self-regard and an "irradiate" sign of self-indulgence. (Wordsworth must also have in mind Milton's "blind mouths.") The "pretty shepherd" dances his verbal "minuet" in the name of an essentially self-referential desire for the admiration of an audience, not in service to or out of "holy love" for his flock or his church. Further, where *Night Thoughts* had produced an original if flawed idiom in its struggle with the power of style to demand attention, the comely bachelor is a plagiarist – not least, a plagiarist of the author of *Conjectures on Original Composition*.[71]

Edward Young provided Wordsworth with a prominent example of a poet whose professional situation required improvement. Trapped in the it-seemed-to-him failing profession of the Anglican priesthood, Young sought out an idiom that would produce credibility via invention and persistence. As a public character, he could never quite shake the accusation that in attempting to serve his God and his social position at once, he had produced a poem that was dishonest or insincere. Wordsworth improved on Young's phenomenology and creatively rewrote his authorial anxiety, but he knew better than Croft did on the question of Young's heart. What Young had in mind to do, which was to move outside of institutions that were failing, was exactly right. The only question was whether Young continued to owe too much to the principle of subordination on which the functions of those institutions were based.

Neither Wordsworth nor Coleridge could undertake their professional self-construction without at some point coming to terms with their separate, individual Doctors Young. Despite the suggestive accident of their naming, the two doctors cannot easily be collapsed into a single figure, but they do share at least one major trait. Each comes to represent the ways status is realized as an effect of the management of risk. Coleridge's Young attempts, in the face of the baby poet's curse, to heal the wounds that will not heal. Wordsworth's Young abandons the pulpit to pursue an idiosyncratic style that still depends, in the end, on being recognized by a genteel audience. But Romantic professionalism cannot be construed as a simple reaction, as the unchecked embrace of professional, moral, or stylistic danger and independence. William Hazlitt offers a neatly dialectical account of Wordsworth's poetry: It is "levelling," but it demands respect; Wordsworth "is jealous of all excellence but his own" and "scorns even the admiration of himself, thinking it a presumption in any one to suppose that he has taste or sense enough to understand him."[72] Hazlitt's allusion to "taste" and "sense" completes his argument, although in ways of which he may not be aware. Wordsworthian isolation does not reject its audience. It demands that its audience recognize, and defer to, professional talent and training as though these rationally identifiable qualities were constituted organically, even royally – one can no more "admire" Wordsworth than, for Burke or for Samuel Johnson, one can "approve of" the institution of monarchy.

Over the course of the eighteenth century, new possibilities for amassing social credit are generated not only by a growing economy but by the fact that the constitution had been visibly redesigned since the Restoration, and the next section of this book addresses eighteenth-century forms of professional power that precede Wordsworth's combination, as Hazlitt describes it, of political leveling and charismatic self-assertion. In particular, the figure of the wanderer, as developed by writers such as Richard Savage in the early part of the century and James Beattie in the 1770s, becomes a means of imagining poetic self-sufficiency in terms that both refer to and negate the authority of monarchs, aristocrats, and rival professional practitioners. Wordsworth assumes the right to evaluate himself, and he expects his self-evaluation to be honored by others. This kind of assumption has a specific eighteenth-century history, as the following section will argue.

PART II

Genealogies of the romantic wanderer

CHAPTER 2

Merit and reward in 1729

Like accounts of the eighteenth-century professions, which have described both the growth of collective independence and an enduring state of "personal subservience" to patrons, the history of eighteenth-century authorship provides divergent explanations of how a writer's merit – the term itself has contradictory meanings – could be evaluated and rewarded.[1] The traditional, Whiggish narrative traces an arc of emancipation that runs from the impoverishment of the place-seeking Grub Street hack to Samuel Johnson's commercial triumph, finally culminating in the author's withdrawal from the marketplace and Romantic poetry's aesthetic freedom. We have seen how this narrative is adapted by critics who understand Romantic transcendence in material or "class" terms. An alternative stresses the continuity of "clientage not class" for authors over the course of the century, as demonstrated for example by Dustin Griffin, who emphasizes that "virtually every writer of any significant reputation" up to the end of the century benefits from various forms of patronage even as they all seek to publish and profit from their wares.[2] These conflicting accounts provoke a choice between an earlier and a later date for the final passing of a vertically organized, "old" regime, but at the level of individualized poetic experience, they also represent coexisting possibilities. Thus, the autonomy of the poet, construed as self-determination in relation to patrons and to other audiences, proves to be imaginable in advance of those large-scale trends that are generally understood to account for real authorial independence. This imaginary autonomy involves both identification with the sources of patronage and an open-ended movement toward the authorizing effect of "experience," and it connects early-century poets to the professions and to the Lake poets who would succeed them.

63

During the 1790s, the Lake poets were individually aided by the Wedgwoods, the Pinneys, Wynn, Cottle and others, and they welcomed this patronage while also trying to rhetorically frame and manage it. As discussed in Chapter 1, Coleridge makes an important statement of independence in his poem to Cottle. Similarly, when Wordsworth acknowledges Raisley Calvert's bequest in the 1805 *Prelude*, he departs from the kind of praise with which earlier poets would favor their supporters:

> Himself no poet, yet
> Far less a common spirit of the world,
> He deemed that my pursuits and labors lay
> Apart from all that leads to wealth, or even
> Perhaps to necessary maintenance,
> Without some hazard to the finer sense,
> He cleared a passage for me, and the stream
> Flowed in the bent of Nature.[3]

As Kenneth Johnston's account of the Calvert bequest points out, Wordsworth has been involved in a culturally enduring habit, the pursuit of a "legacy" not limited by ties of blood.[4] Yet Wordsworth works against the traditional, vertical relationships that such a practice implies. Calvert is no "common spirit" but he is "no poet," either, and the professionally self-sacrificing Wordsworth, whose life as an author may forestall "wealth" or even "maintenance," is both lucky and deserving when he finds Calvert posthumously working on his behalf. The passage does not end by reiterating the patron's fine qualities but by reasserting the special shape of Wordsworth's career. In an Ovidian figure turned upside down, Calvert is embodied and put to work, clearing the way for a metamorphosized poetic "stream" that pursues abstract "pursuits" and "labors" of its own device. It is a central moment in the poem. As Johnston says, "*The Prelude*'s dominant image for the narrative of the hero's life (walking, wandering) and its dominant image for its own progress (a river or stream) here join forces."[5]

As I have suggested, such "dominant images" flow out of earlier, related attempts to define the poet's independence. In order to see how, this chapter begins with the early-century career of Richard Savage, in whose autobiographical poem *The Wanderer* and related texts debates about professional power, literary talent, and royal authority, as well as arguments regarding origins, merit, experience, and training, are particularly easy to discern. Savage offers a vision of the poet as rigorously prepared and self-evaluating, and he also suggests that the preparation of the poet mirrors that of the monarch, which, in the 1720s, means that it is alternately magical and mundane. Later encounters repeat this pattern, and the chapter concludes by exploring David Hume's, Samuel Johnson's, and James Beattie's separate encounters with the noble/professional matrix. Wordsworth's shift-of-focus in *The Prelude*, from the patron's virtue to the author's giftedness, may thus be understood as one in a long series of attempts to separate the patron's unauthorized judgments from his welcome actions in the name of the poet's professionally constituted "finer sense."

I RICHARD SAVAGE

Historically, most descriptions of Savage's career have been attuned to the sensational elements of his case, which include authorial indigence, bastardy (or, more probably, fraud), and murder. In particular, his life story resonates across the century as an example of the perils, including the psychological perils, of early eighteenth-century authorship. Nigel Cross, for example, places Savage at the beginning of a line of famous indigent poets that becomes fully established later in the century with the supposed suicide of Chatterton.[6] Savage's story was well known particularly because of Johnson's *Life of Savage*, but it was not only the *Life* that kept the tale in print: "The decade of the seventies was the peak of Savage's fame, though afterwards, down to about 1820, his collected works were often reprinted, evidently as a necessary part of the various many-volumed sets of the English poets that enterprising publishers got out for gentlemen's libraries."[7] Admittedly, Savage's poetry was probably not closely read by many of the "gentleman" readers who owned copies of his works. The famous forger W. H. Ireland, for example, includes several poems about the supposed "shameful neglect" of Savage's talent in his volume *Neglected Genius* (1812), but there is little in them to suggest Ireland knew much more about Savage's work than could be found in *Life*. By way of contrast, his volume contains several poems that attempt to mimic the style of Chatterton's *Rowley* poems.[8] But if Chatterton had emerged by the early nineteenth century as the most pressing recent case of the pains of literature, Savage is a forerunner and an essential example of the theme.

Criticism has often acknowledged the representative or emblematic implications of Savage's career, which has been located at the
crux of competing middle-class "professional" and aristocratic
models of authorship. Generally, it has been argued that Savage's
fantasies of aristocratic power would be rendered inappropriate or
beside the point by further developments in the literary field. Linda
Zionkowski, whose claim is that authorship turns from an aristocratic
and leisurely ethic toward a "masculine," work-based one during the
century, observes that "writing in the period from 1717 to 1743,
Savage could not have predicted that the esteem conferred upon
literature by high rank (either the author's or the patron's) eventually would be dispersed through a complex network of booksellers,
readers, authors, reviewers, and critics like Johnson."[9] Similarly,
Dustin Griffin claims that "in Savage's career can be seen a kind of
parable about the conditions of authorship at a time when the
patronage system was beginning to be supplemented by another
economy. Savage was born under one dispensation and grew up
under another."[10] Less concerned with Savage's position within the
chronology of theories of authorship, Hal Gladfelder nonetheless
frames his discussion historically, noting "the affinity between
criminal and gentlemanly idlers, both of whom repudiate the values
of thrift, labor, sobriety, restraint that defined the ideal of the middle
station in the eighteenth century."[11] For Gladfelder, the "middle
station" and its "pieties" haven't changed much, so that Savage's
repudiation of them retains its interest.[12] In his performance of
himself, that is, Savage defines "the artist as antibourgeois," a fact
which is equaled in critical importance for Gladfelder by Savage's
demonstration that authorship *is* performance.[13]

This body of criticism has been acute, but in emphasizing
Savage's notable personal excesses, it tends to behave as though
the kinds of claims Savage would make on the writer's behalf
would lose their interest, as though literary history is reducible to,
and ends with, Johnson's regret over Savage's lack of financial
responsibility. Yet while it is not difficult to identify the places
Savage's direct appeals to patronage repeat a mode of argument
that would soon outlive its usefulness, if it hadn't already, or to
note occasional lapses in his decorum or technique, his attempt to
create a visionary allegory out of his own biography is remarkable,
and his insistence that the poet inhabits a space where other
judgments, including the judgment of posterity, are potentially

irrelevant is not nostalgic but prescient, not only "antibourgeois" but also protoprofessional. These facts are too readily overlooked partially because Savage's acts of poetic self-vindication today seem merely like bad versions of natural and transparent ones. Yet, signaling the irrelevance of both patronage and posterity, Savage's aged Bard will laboriously transform into a figure that is both awesome and uncannily familiar: "The late-dimm'd eye, a vivid lustre sheds/Hairs, once so thin, now graceful locks decline," Savage writes, and the flashing eyes and floating hair of "Kubla Khan's" inspired poet, which also mark both a transformation and a birthright, are typologically if awkwardly expressed.[14]

Savage's self-reflections are occupied with the measurement of merit and the competing principles of origin and experience. Having been "scold[ed]" by his friend Dyer "for continuing to look for rank and position," Savage responds in "The Picture" (1724) that "titles ... / ... claim Homage, when they crown the Wise," but he goes on to wonder:

> ... [W]ho to Birth *alone* wou'd Honours owe?
> Honours, if true, from Seeds of *Merit* grow:
> Those trees, with sweetest Charms, invite our Eyes,
> Which from our own Engraftment fruitful rise!
> Still we love best what we with Labour gain,
> As the Child's dearer for the Mother's Pain. (38–46)[15]

When Savage likens poetic composition to child-birth or gardening, he breaks little new ground, but he goes further in indicating that "*Merit*," and its progeny "Honours," are ultimately to be discovered through the intensity of the poet's love of self. The appropriation of "honour" through "merit" may be seen as a protoprofessional counterpart to the humanist dialectic of "honour" and "virtue," since "merit" is a notoriously slippery term indicating both value-laden achievement and, particularly in theological discourse, an inappropriate expectation of reward for action. In Nicholas Amhurst's "The Convocation," for example, the speaker is untroubled when praising Bishop Hoadley's "*Merit*," but a little later on, during an anti-Catholic attack on "superstition," he recurs to a more loaded sense of the word:

> Fantastick Visions rise before her Sight,
> And all the empty Phantoms of the Night.
> On meritorious Baubles she depends,
> Of Sainted Ruffians, and departed Friends.[16]

Here, the "meritorious Baubles," presumably statues or medallions, are empty signs of a perverted and fearful worship, mechanical and futile emblems of an effort to earn grace.[17] Satan's repeated emphasis on his own "merit" indicates Milton's similar position on the subject. (Later on, on the other hand, Cottle would find Henderson buried in "MERIT'S grave" [3]). Unconcerned by the point that exercises Milton, Hoadley, and Amhurst, however, Savage's belief in the organic production of "true" "Honours" from "Seeds of *Merit*" aligns him with an order that rejects both unjustifiable place-holding and the privileges of birthright. The botanical figure may seem to relate uneasily to the passage's emphasis on "Labour," but "Engraftment" represents transformative work, and here it accomplishes an aesthetic double-play. The engrafted tree, representative of applied effort, is both "fruitful" and beautiful.[18]

Savage's poem *The Bastard* (1728) explores the question of merit by asking how experience both produces and reveals it, but in this poem Savage's description of authorial identity will prove to be too dependent on an aristocratic order. Immediately under scrutiny is a version of "freedom" that the poem will come to find wanting:

> Born to himself, by no possession led,
> In freedom foster'd, and by fortune fed;
> Nor Guides, nor Rules, his sov'reign choice controul,
> His body independant, as his soul.
> Loos'd to the world's wide range – enjoyn'd no aim;
> Prescrib'd no duty, and assign'd no Name:
> Nature's unbounded son, he stands alone,
> His heart unbiassed, and his mind his own. (13–20)

This passage's vocabulary of intellectual and financial independence aligns it with various anti-party screeds that distinguish the true patriot from the corrupt place-servers of Walpole's machine, but Savage, who always goes too far, blows this language out to potentially seditious proportions. Displaced, the bastard is also free from duty and "by fortune fed," a libertine Satan who knows no monarch nor creator. It is not clear whether Savage is consciously parodying some extreme form of Whig deism or whether his speaker is intoxicated by an overlapping set of ideas – the freedom of the bastard aristocrat is the freedom of the self-producing bourgeoisie – but the poem does not take long to get both possibilities under control, primarily by re-casting the first half as "unprophetic" and "misinspired" and finding in Savage's own notorious life-story material for a lesson about the corrective effects of hardship (47). The second half of *The Bastard* thus transforms Savage's 1727 murder conviction and 1728 pardon into a narrative about the bastard's now-to-be-critiqued self-sufficiency and about his need to be accepted into a different kind of family.[19] Rejected by the Countess, to whom *The Bastard* is ironically dedicated, Savage comes to blame the absence of a "mother's care" and a "father's guardian hand" (89, 91) for his predicament, but he finds a new mother in the Queen whose intercession has saved his life:

> Lost to the life *you* gave, *your* son no more,
> And now *adopted*, who was *doom'd* before,
> *New-born* I may a nobler mother claim;
> But dare not whisper her immortal *name*;
> Supreamly lovely, and serenely great!
> Majestic *mother* of a kneeling *state*!
> *Queen* of a people's hearts, who ne'er before
> Agreed – yet now with one consent *adore* (103–110)

The story of Savage turns out to be the story of the British state, an act of identification which aggrandizes the bastard even as it appears to efface him. Once self-condemned to a kind of anarchy, the state has now, by a suggestive mix of consent and adoration, been reborn as a constitutional monarchy, where electoral conflict disappears into a moment of theatricality and appreciation: "One contest yet remains in this desire,/Who most shall give applause, where all admire" (111–112). National history, like the life of the bastard, has been interrupted by civil war, revolution, and dynastic controversy, but Queen Caroline's interventions have served to create a new continuity and a new self-identity. The Hanoverian settlement replaces accreting, negative experience by moving outside of dramatic time to the moment of culmination and applause – the recognition of the monarch brings the story of experience to an end.

The Bastard indicates in an unfinished form how an overheated rhetoric of hard times and lessons learned could coexist with descriptions of monarchical charisma, but in that poem the speaker remains a penitent, and worse, a mere audience, if a special one, for the queen's performance. Savage's subsequent insight is that the poet might become independent of this system of evaluation without giving up his specific vocational claims, and he would develop ambitions that identify poets with monarchs more directly. In some ways, the time appeared to be right for such a maneuver. By the turn of the century, as public discourse shifts from Stuart martyrology to the administrative details of the 1701 settlement, discussions of royal prerogative have become less "devotional" than "legalistic."[20] This legalism, which coexists with the Jacobite aura of devotion that could still suffuse public events, means that the foundation of public order is unusually susceptible to rhetorical adjustment and appropriation. If Parliament could make a king, perhaps bureaucrats could produce and redistribute the monarchical aura that was once in the gift of God alone, and perhaps, as Hume would eventually suggest, this aura could be mysteriously reassembled even in the mundane-looking market for professional services.

Royal autonomy would require various theorists whose rhetoric oscillated between the propagation of fantastic glamor and technocratic, professional management. Bolingbroke, with whom Savage may have been personally acquainted and whose work has been called a "synecdoche" for an aristocratic, nostalgic tradition opposed to Walpole, is the best known and is particularly relevant to Savage's case.[21] Bolingbroke's political maneuverings of the teens and 20s evolve, in the 1730s, into the "illusory consensus" of "Country ideology," finally rising or falling to the abstract depiction of monarchy elaborated in his essay *The Idea of a Patriot King*, and this sequence has been examined from a number of directions.[22] My own interest is in the extent to which Bolingbroke's later formulations are anticipated by a poem like *The Wanderer*, which has already confronted the incompatibility of charismatic leadership with the cultural economies of Hanoverian England. As Christine Gerrard writes, "The *Patriot King* derives much from the language of patriot kingship which was then currently being expounded in equally high-flown terms in poetry and on the stage."[23] What remains to be explained is the particular function of this "high-flown" language, which Gerrard elsewhere notes is an "apotheosis" of the language of the Hill circle, in *The Wanderer*'s meditation on merit and poetic training.[24]

One example of Bolingbroke's language makes his treatment of the aesthetics of kingship clear, and it also introduces aspects of his language that are pertinent to *The Wanderer*'s emerging professional purpose:

A Patriot King is the most powerful of all reformers; for he is himself a sort of standing miracle, so rarely seen and so little understood, that the sure effects of his appearance will be admiration and love in every honest breast, confusion and terror to every guilty conscience, but submission and resignation in all. Innumerable metamorphoses, like those which poets feign, will happen in very deed: and, while men are conscious that they are the same individuals, the difference of their sentiments will almost persuade them that they are changed into different beings.[25]

On the other hand, Bolingbroke's more broadly conceived and evidently autobiographical "patriot" is susceptible to a punishing kind of exile, one of the fates that would commonly be attributed to the poetic genius, with Savage as an early and salient example:

If [the great] retire from the world, their splendour accompanies them, and enlightens even the obscurity of their retreat. If they take a part in public life, the effect is never indifferent. They either appear like ministers of divine vengeance, and their course through the world is marked by desolation and oppression, by poverty and servitude: or they are the guardian angels of the country they inhabit, busy to avert even the most distant evil, and to maintain or to procure peace, plenty, and the greatest of human blessings, liberty.[26]

The great man's splendor is no guarantee of his happiness or success. The passage is an attack on corruption, but it is not just that. "Poverty and servitude" are the consequences of failure because they are the natural weapons of tyrannical wealth, so that hard experience comes to those who have earned it. Even in defeat, however, which is to say even in exile or retirement, the patriot is unmistakable, his charisma always in effect.

Bolingbroke is not only borrowing an already available permutation of the language of kingship, he and Savage are responding to long-term changes in the way authority and status are calculated. What we see in a figure such as the Patriot King, as Michael McKeon puts it, is "how individualistic and class criteria are eating away, as it were from within, at a social structure whose external shell still seems roughly assimilable to the status model."[27] Noting that Bolingbroke's vision follows Harrington by acknowledging "the rule of the private individual," which decrees that leaders are chosen and their merit tested by the ruled, McKeon's analysis underscores the performative aspect of an "aristocratic ideology" that is most emphatic, and most vulnerable to co-optation, when it is most endangered.[28] (The situation is also illustrated by the evidently necessary approval of the nonetheless "kneeling state" of *The Bastard*.) The absorption or adaptation of this broadly defined ideology by other groups recurs in British literary history, and so does the process in which aristocratic power is periodically challenged and refigured. As Andrew Elfenbein has demonstrated, for example, Victorian "Byronism" provides virtual access to an "aristocratic subjectivity" that a professional intellectual such as Carlyle must appropriate, and surmount, on behalf of his middle-class readership; in a different case, as Dino Felluga argues, the lawyer-turned-author Walter Scott helps generate the merely ceremonial gestures that disassociate Royal authority from violence in advance of the nineteenth century's age of reform.[29] The tremendous fame of Byron and Scott gives them a particular kind of significance, and I do not suggest that their interventions are the equivalent of Savage's visions or, for that matter, that the status of the British aristocrat does not change over time. My immediate concern, however, is with a politics of distribution that is refined early in the eighteenth century and that remains pertinent not only for Byron and Scott but, earlier, for the Lake poets. The glorious abjection of the Patriot is a sign of his merit, and it is also the means by which merit is produced. Tribulation brings out what must have already been there, thus creating a new, closed circuit of autonomous value that exceeds the practicalities of service. Such value demands, not fealty, but recognition and reward.

In *The Wanderer*, the connections among wandering figures, disappointing experience, and the mechanisms of recompense are obsessively reiterated. The title character of this dream vision meets a Hermit who has gone into exile in order to mourn his dead wife, Olympia; it emerges that, in a terrifying act of divine instrumentality, Olympia has been killed in order to focus the Hermit's attention on God. The Wanderer also meets a Bard who at first appears in a state of poverty, but it is later revealed that the Bard has been translated into an angelic state after death, in which state he wanders the world in disguise in order to identify various deserving but mistreated characters. The bard is suited for his posthumous role by his earthly sufferings – "The *Bard*, whose Want so multiplied his Woes,/He sunk a Mortal, and a Seraph rose" (V. 282–82) – and he is so profoundly independent that, like Wordsworth in the Wye Valley, he even disdains the evaluation of posterity: "Why shou'd unrelish'd Wit these honours cause?/ Custom, not Knowledge, dictates your Applause" (V. 308–309). The poem's compulsive depiction of neglected merit redeemed by intervention from above makes it easily understood as an expression of Savage's own complaints and desires. However, the intensity with which the poem integrates poetic experience with other vocabularies of order means that it does not just fulfill wishes for Savage. It also identifies, in admittedly garish terms, what the poet's professional utopia might look like.

When Savage initially presents the at-first earth-bound version of the poet-figure, for example, he does so in language that depicts the poet's traditional glamor and also links him to the set of themes that Bolingbroke would codify. Bolingbroke and Ovid converge, as a basic example of "the metamorphoses ... poets feign" is here feigned in the service of "patriotism":

> There sits the sapient BARD in museful Mood,
> And glows impassion'd for his Country's Good!
> All the bright *Spirits* of the *Just*, combin'd,
> Inform, refine, and prompt his tow'ring Mind!
> He takes his *gifted Quill* from *Hands divine*,
> Around his Temples Rays refulgent shine!
> Now rapt! now more than Man! – I see him climb,
> To view this speck of Earth from Worlds sublime!
>
> . . . .
>
> Ye Traytors, Tyrants, fear his stinging Lay!
> Ye Pow'rs unlov'd, unpitied in Decay!
> But know, to *you* sweet-blossom'd Fame he brings,
> Ye Heroes, Patriots, and paternal Kings! (191–214)

The oppositional bite of the reference to traitors and tyrants is made more fierce, but is also made double-sided, by its allusion to "paternal Kings." On the one hand, the adjective might describe the behavior of kings who take responsibility for their subjects, as a remorseful Savage had been taken care of by the machinery of the royal pardon, but it also divides monarchs whose rights are certain from those who take the throne without a "paternal" mandate. This doubled reference reflects back on the evaluative powers of the bard. As the "quill" first "stings" but then "blossoms" into "Fame," the depiction of bardic authority in the passage (a combination of

the acquired wisdom of the nation's best and brightest "Spirits,"
gleaned presumably through study, and a briefly embodied divine
"hand" of inspiration) co-opts the question of the succession in the
name of authorial insight. What is important is no longer who
the proper monarch is, but that the sapient bard will be empowered
to identify and reward royal paternity, in other words, to patronize
the patron.

Like his eighteenth-century and Lake school successors, Savage
transforms descriptions of landscape into commentary on these
mechanisms of reward. In *The Wanderer*, this transformation takes
place by way of an energizing literality. In lines that are echoed
with a difference over the course of the century (and which
themselves echo, with a difference, a Virgilian topos most likely
picked up from Thomson), the hermit-figure who acts as the
wanderer's moral guide explains the source of his own livelihood
in terms that apply to the facts of Savage's own career:[30]

> On me, yon City, kind, bestows her care,
> Meat for keen Famine, and the gen'rous Juice,
> That warms chill'd Life, her Charities produce:
> Accept without Reward; unask'd 'twas mine;
> Here what thy Health requires, as free be thine.
> Hence learn that GOD, (who, in the Time of Need,)
> In frozen Desarts can the Raven feed)
> Well-sought, will delegate some pitying Breast,
> His second Means, to succour Man distrest. (I. 246–254)

God's "delegate" at the time of composition is not in fact an
anonymous "City" but the charitable Lord Tyrconnel, and by
muting the cruelties of his real environment and reproducing his
patron as a faceless, collective power of well-doing, Savage is again
taking over, at least at the level of narrative, the arbiter's role. Dis-
placing the country pleasures of Tyrconnel's estate, where Savage
had lived at his leisure, to an urban landscape, he re-imagines a
London whose commercial and professional classes are now
coherent enough to act in concert on behalf of the charismatic but
"distrest" moral exemplar, the patriot/hermit whose power comes
with a story attached.

Unlike Wordsworth's tribute to Calvert, however, Savage's
metaphorical displacement of the patron's function must be
prepared for ahead of time by more conventional forms of flattery

and praise. *The Wanderer* begins with an address to Tyrconnel that puts financial generosity ahead of poetic inspiration:

> Fain would my verse, Tyrconnel, boast thy Name,
> Brownlow, at once my subject, and my Fame!
> Oh! cou'd that Spirit, which thy Bosom warms,
> Whose Strength surprises, and whose Goodness charms!
> That various Worth! – cou'd that inspire my Lays,
> Envy shou'd smile, and Censure learn to praise:
> Yet, though unequal to a Soul, like thine,
> A generous Soul, approaching to Divine,
> When bless'd beneath such Patronage I write,
> Great my attempt, though hazardous my Flight. (I. 1–10)

Although he quotes them with approval, Johnson could have said about these opening lines what he says about Savage's prose dedication, which is that it is "filled with the highest strains of Panegyric, and the warmest Professions of Gratitude, but by no Means remarkable for Delicacy of Connection or Elegance of Stile."[31] The patron as inspiration or "divine soul" is just the dedicatory trope that Wordsworth would later revise – "stoop to my theme, inspirit every line," Thomson unblushingly implores Bubb Dodington at the opening of "Summer" – but in Savage we detect a frustrated longing, whereas Thomson is just being polite. This is the longing Griffin identifies when he observes that "to be 'entitled' to patronage makes the poet metaphorically possessed of a kind of right or estate to which he holds title, and sets him on a level with his patrons," but we must also recognize the way this longing turns against itself.[32] Since Savage cannot become a Savage/Tyrconnel he contents himself with "Patronage," but the other mechanisms of reward depicted by the poem, both urban and international, indicate the insufficiencies of this personal and contingent means of support.

Savage's notional professionalism is, of course, vulnerable to the charge of un-realism, a condition it shares with the magical rule of Bolingbroke's patriot figures and that is forestalled by the generic realism of texts such as *The Prelude*, and *The Life of Savage* actively presents Savage as a counter-term to Johnson's sad but wise pragmatism. Because Savage is so distinctively marginal, according to William Epstein, Johnson's ability to turn him into a "biographical subject" is a triumph for the "individualizing" power of modernity that Boswell's Johnson would capitalize on: "If Johnson's Savage is a transitional agent of change ... demonstrating that the traditional three estates are no longer the sole patrons and beneficiaries of English biography, then Boswell's Johnson is the modern state itself ... a self-patronizing, self-advertising, self-consuming economy of biography that perfectly encapsulates the secular form of pastoral power."[33] Yet because it is important to recognize the coexistence of traditional and modern modes, particularly at the level of poetic language, I would like to resist the image of literary modernity as a steam-roller with Johnson at the wheel. If Johnson tries to understand Savage as a certain kind of biographical subject, it is partially because Savage has already argued for a different but equally viable mode of authorial subjectivity. While the Foucauldian harmonization of Christianity's pastoral power and modernity's "governmentality" appears to provide a blanket description of a fully matured professional authority to which a figure like Savage, or interpretations of his life-story, can only succumb, Savage enacts the kinds of resistant orientation toward futurity upon which the Romantic, experiential model will come to depend. Savage's agonistic relationship to patronage and the book trade precedes Johnson's discovery of the latter and nominal rejection of the former, and Savage's response to them recodes immediate conflicts over the production and recognition of merit. "Millions invisible befriend Mankind," the Bard announces (V. 343), and Pope's sylphs are suddenly dragooned to minister to the disinherited heirs and noble traitors that share Savage's alienation. There is the way things are, Savage's fantasy announces, and the way things ought to be.

This wishfulness does not take place in a state of innocence about the actual situation of other forms of intellectual work. Alongside the insistence on self-nomination that comes through in the dream-vision of *The Wanderer*, and contemporary with that poem, is an account of Grub Street hackdom that is fascinated by all the ways Savage's attempts at self-construction had failed and that responds directly to the role the professions played as a counterpart to authorial self-assertion. At the end of 1729, Savage publishes his pamphlet *An Author to be Lett*, which its modern editor describes as "a by-product of Pope's war with the dunces."[34] Drawing on Pope's warrant, Savage identifies a group of urban hacks characterized by their poverty, unscrupulousness, and lack of talent. As Johnson was not alone in recognizing, the group portrait included striking details that seemed to describe Savage as well. Richard Holmes notes the level of "self-laceration" contained in the pamphlet, which "is surely a deliberate act of self-exposure, in the hard, unforgiving vernacular of Grub Street."[35] The pamphlet is signed "Iscariot Hackney," "as if," Holmes points out, Savage "consciously reveled in the role of betrayal."[36] At the root of such betrayal, however, is the understanding that it is preordained and necessary. One more act of identification that runs through *Author to be Lett* reveals the extent to which Savage knew he was caught in a series of them based not only on pleasure, but also on a shared pathology that worked below the surface of professional position.

This pathology hinges particularly on Hackney's association with a professional man. He identifies himself at several points with a "Mr. R – m"; "R – m cannot excel me, unless he excels himself," he declares at one point, and at another, to be discussed below, he is even more explicit: "R – m, thou who art my other self!" (8; 10). As Savage's fictional "Publisher's Preface" makes clear, "R – m" is in fact Edward Roome, a journalist and a lawyer, one of the writers who (in the wake of *The Beggar's Opera*) helped convert John Broome's *Jovial Crew* into a musical, and a figure who is prodded at several points in *The Dunciad*. This obscure figure looms so large in Savage's pseudo-autobiography largely because of his appearance. *The Dunciad* describes Roome's countenance as "funereal" (a joke that also refers to Roome's undertaker father), and a popular epigram on the failures of Roome's comic writing, probably also by Pope, concludes "The jest is lost unless he prints his face!" Thus, the physical resemblance between Iscariot and Roome emphasizes, in Grub Street shorthand, Iscariot's laughable, ugly features. Yet Iscariot also indicates that a certain "droll Solemnity of Countenance" makes him pleasing to others, and this is a central element of Savage's frank identification with Roome (3). Johnson, for example, reports that Savage had a "long Visage, coarse features, and melancholy aspect."[37] A wit on earth gets by not only on the strength of what he says or writes, but also on the strength of a kind of pleasing, even amusing bearing that works in excess of the letter, or for that matter the picture. What is true of the apparently charming Savage is true of the grim Roome, or at least it is asserted of him in comically parallel language. His face, his presence, is required to render his material vivid. Savage's

Grub Street is dominated both by print and by personality. In his identification with Roome, Iscariot/Savage comes close to suggesting that personality is more important than print and that in Savage's world of coffee-houses, drawing rooms, and alley-ways there is the dangerous possibility that ugly personalities might yet have sway over the literary world in the place of properly experienced writers or meritorious language.

This bleak irony, which contains the self-mocking reflection that Savage himself may be one of the hucksters in question, is contained in what looks to be part of the same old gag about Roome's resemblance to Iscariot:

I will at least indulge my Vanity in appearing on a large Sheet of Paper, in a Wooden Cut, which ingenious School-Boys may delight to Colour with yellow and red *Ocker*. What a glaring Figure shall I then make in the long Piazza of *Covent-Garden*! I shall be surrounded by venerable Old Ballads; and several of my Family Pieces, such as the *Sinner's Coat of Arms*, and the dreadful sketches of *Death, Judgment,* and *Damnation*! Thence shall I be translated to the naked Walls of Country Ale-houses, Coblers Stalls, and Necessary Houses! – And thou, O R – m, thou who art my *other self*! be this thy Glory! however different our Fortunes, however unlike the Incidents of our Lives; yet whensoe'er the countenance of *Iscariot Hackney* is seen, thy own *dear Phiz* will be called to Remembrance. (11)

There is weight to this particular art of sinking in posterity: the vain hack puts himself in circulation, is depicted in more than one color but mainly as a monster by his "ingenious" critics, finds himself surrounded on various public walls by popular and anonymous prints and ballads, and finally, inevitably, it's off to the privy, for reading or worse.

Through this process of diminishment, the fate of Hackney signifies the local dilemma of the author and criticizes the morally failing although really robust professional reward-structures that co-ordinate Grub Street with Westminster. The lawyer Roome had in fact succeeded in his quest for patronage and by 1729 had become the solicitor of the treasury. However, *Author to be Lett* promises that his reputation will finally be one with Iscariot's. Writing might have furthered his success in law, but the posterity of the privy will remember him as a writer, and as the wrong, the other writer, the one whose quest for a better profession fails. Savage's aristocratic pose collapses here, or rather, he gives it up. Surrounded by emblems of sin, judgment, and death, Iscariot's "phiz" is a comical remembrance of death that also reminds the knowing reader of Solicitor Roome's father, the undertaker. *Author to be Lett* proves to be *The Wanderer*'s companion-piece, a deflating prose-comedy matched to the poem's epic intentions. Where *The Wanderer* shows the sapient bard translated into a state of power, doling out favors that reach across the chasm between life and death while distinguishing carefully between virtuous authors and selfish ones, *Author to be Lett* demonstrates that all hacks, getting by sometimes on their printed writing but other times on their countenances alone, are interchangeable, and they all end up in the same place. It also shows that the condition of the hack is the condition of the professional in general, since Roome's legal success cannot negate the economies of patronage in which he is trapped any more than it can erase the economies of literary hustling from which he has escaped.

II HUME, JOHNSON, AND BEATTIE

For Savage, poetic autonomy is imaginatively generated through qualifying experience, and in this he has anticipated a procedure that would remain of interest for the Lake poets. In his study of eighteenth-century philosophy and Romantic writing, Tim Milnes identifies "the stress-fracture within eighteenth-century foundationalism" as the split that divides a "creationist aesthetic" from its "empiricist" origins; as "inspired" genius takes the place of a now-skeptical philosophy that can no longer derive certainty from experience, Romantic writing, which moves between epistemological inquiry and practical "indifference," offers to assume philosophy's role.[38] The poet's ability to work across the gap that separates episteme and phenomenon, abstraction and technique, establishes a right of self-qualification that is, in the terms I have been developing, inherently professional. Savage meets the question of experience head-on and concludes that the poet's role in the ecology of work is to transform tribulation, experience, into measurable success as well as into abstract knowledge. It is for this reason that, while his pretensions to nobility may at first seem to anticipate Byron more directly than the Lake poets, he may also be associated with the earlier writers. In his emphasis on rigorous preparation and perilous performance, Savage not only demonstrates "strength" but a professionalism that exceeds the jobbery of a figure such as Roome. Like Byron, Savage raises the problem of whether "a lord is a cultural or a natural fact," but like the Lake poets he reinstates authority in the language of aristocratically, but also experientially, self-determined merit.[39]

Here Hume, both a recipient and distributor of patronage, and a theoretical defender (against Bolingbroke) of its role in Parliamentary affairs, provides an important link between Savage and the Lake school.[40] Hume comments in several places on the role of experience in the making of professional power, and when he does so, he triangulates royal power, professional talent, and poetic or philosophical creativity in ways that sharply emphasize the logic that associates as well as divides them. Disparity and forced consensus drive Hume's account of the way practitioners learn their trade and are evaluated, as is displayed in a substantial and revealing comment in *An Enquiry Concerning Human Understanding*:

The ... distinction between reason and experience is maintained in all our deliberations concerning the conduct of life; while the experienced statesman, general, physician, or merchant is trusted and followed; and the unpracticed novice, with whatever natural talents endowed, neglected and despised. Though it be allowed, that reason may form very plausible conjectures with regard to the consequences of such a particular conduct in such particular circumstances; it is still supposed imperfect, without the assistance of experience, which is alone able to give stability and certainty to the maxims, derived from study and reflection.

But notwithstanding that this distinction be thus universally received, both in the active and speculative scenes of life, I shall not scruple to pronounce, that it is, at bottom, erroneous, at least, superficial.[41]

At first glance, the case is clear enough. Since, Hume is arguing, all reasoning has perceptual experience as its basis, the distinction between the experienced practitioner and one who depends on "reason" and theoretical knowledge of maxims is either "erroneous" or "superficial." So is the distinction between maxims drawn from experience and those produced by sheer reason, since in either event, the maxim involved will ultimately have perceptual referents. Hume does allow one measure of difference between reason and experience as the terms are commonly used. Conclusions drawn from what we call "experience" do not require reflection, since the already "experienced event" is of exactly the same kind as those events we are looking forward to, whereas the conclusions drawn by reason require "reflection" and "thought." The experienced practitioner knows about tyranny because he knows about tyrants like Nero and Tiberius, whereas the reasoning one is able to bring to bear "the observation of any fraud and cruelty in private life" on matters of public affairs.[42] Hume is thus able to apply his own maxim, that "custom is the great guide of human life," both to the grizzled veteran, whom it appears to suit, and to the bright but untried beginner who is "neglected and despised."

Hume is conscious that he is working in the realm of practice and that his case will be tested against the perceptions, or pre-conceptions, of his readership, and his discussion quickly moves away from the attention-getting announcement that the distinction between reason and experience is misconceived. As it does so, philosophy itself turns out to be a machine for challenging but then re-instating the equilibrium by which "nature" is balanced with our "natural" ways of talking about things.[43] It is not just that reason requires a separate act of reflection whereas experience, in Hume's technical sense, does not. Slipping from his precise definition to a vernacular one, Hume quickly indicates that reason really does need experience to function well, although the experience he means in this case is different from the "experience" he has been theorizing. It takes "time and farther experience" to learn how the maxims of reason should really be applied: "In every situation or incident, there are many particular and seemingly minute circumstances, which the man of greatest talents is, at first, apt to overlook, though on them the justness of his conclusions, and consequently the prudence of his conduct, entirely depend." For "inexperienced," he finally allows, read "comparative[ly less experienced]," and our usual expectations regarding the sources of proficiency in statesmen, generals, physicians, and merchants remain intact.[44] As always in Hume, when the philosopher turns his eye to practical matters, custom and nature will win out, and it is reassuring in this instance to learn that Hume's description of experience asks nothing of it or us that we have not already anticipated. Reason is at first opposed to experience, the "reason" of the novice is transformed into "natural talent," and finally Hume concludes that reason, or talent, must be perfected through experience. As dangerous as Hume's skepticism was felt to be by some of his philosophical opponents, here he seems to indulge only in minor tinkering with a concept as old as Aristotelian "prudence."

Yet just as the faculty of prudence seems both familiar and virtuous until somebody tries to define it with precision, the apparently unassailable contention that talent is improved by experience is complicated by Hume's treatment of "reason" and "talent" as synonyms, which is necessary within the terms of his project. His major claim is for the overriding privilege of experience, but he has also had to notice that some kind of "talent" exists outside of the experience which informs it. There are so obviously differences in talents among people – we have the idea of "talent" as a variable element in the human character, as Hume might put it – that it is not necessarily a problem of argument for Hume to omit an explanation of the origin of this difference. (An incipient language of physical or nervous "organization" is already present in the tradition via Hobbes.)[45] However, while in other circumstances the evocation of talent might signal a desire for (or a belief in) merit as a principle of social order, when set in contrast to Hume's rigorous, occasionally bloodless series of technical distinctions, the word also discloses the mysterious connotations of its Biblical etymology.[46] In *Matthew* 25: 14–30, the text which enables the change in meaning from "talent" as a form of currency to "talent" as a property of persons, "talents" are at once earned from, recognized and bestowed by a supernatural force. "Talent" precedes everything, especially the formal similarities among people, Hume has made it his business to explain. It's true that, based on the hard accounting of Matthew, the thing we call talent seems to be measurable and improvable, which is probably why eighteenth-century theorists prefer to talk about "gifts" or "genius," leaving talent to the artisans.[47] At the same time, the biblical account is supported by a theistic epistemology of the kind Hume is directly opposing. Although Hume offers to reduce cognition to a set of simple parts, there is always a mechanism working just in the corner of the eye which we can never quite get a good look at, upon which will be based a system of achievements and rewards that should be transparent but keeps baffling the understanding.[48]

Hume's acknowledgment of "talent" might still be accommodated to an egalitarian (not to say Napoleonic) ethos, and the familiar essay "Of the Middling Station of Life" is easily read as supporting that view. The enlightenment project, such as it is, of re-appropriating the charismatic function of the aristocracy on behalf of the middle-class is rarely pursued so explicitly or with such confidence, and Hume here takes the final step of comparing professional leadership directly with kingship: "There are more natural Parts, and a stronger Genius requisite to make a good Lawyer or Physician," Hume affirms, "than to make a great Monarch."[49] Of twenty-eight British sovereigns, he accounts, eight "are esteem'd Princes of great capacity," and he finds that this is a pretty high rate of success, which suggests that being Sovereign is no great challenge compared with other pursuits: "I believe every one will allow, that, in the common Run of Mankind, there are not eight out of twenty eight, who are fitted, by Nature, to make a Figure either on the Bench or at the Bar." Monarchical rule has been put in its place if it hasn't been discredited outright. Even the method Hume uses to make these judgments is designed to shift charisma from royalty to the professional. Kings and Queens are named, toted up, and rather cavalierly evaluated, while doctors and lawyers remain unnamed, known only by mysterious, and tactically commingled, attributes such as "parts," "talent," "genius," and so on.

As in the *Treatise*, however, and more intensely, what acts primarily as a leveling argument also wanders into a different kind of territory; from a treatment of humans as receiving and combining machines, Hume switches to the vocabulary of "fine souls" as he had earlier taken recourse to the idea of an indivisible and mysterious "talent." This shift occurs during another apparently casual move, from professional work to the practice of philosophy and poetry: "Since the common Professions, such as Law or Physic, require equal, if not superior Capacity, to what are exerted in the higher Spheres of Life, 'tis evident, that the Soul must be made of a still finer Mold, to shine in Philosophy or Poetry, or in any of the higher Parts of Learning."[50] The chain of associations is at least partially at odds with beliefs Hume has articulated elsewhere. In other contexts, for example the *Treatise*, he suggests that the activities of the poetic imagination are separate from common processes of ideation, and particularly from the rigors of philosophy: "There is something weak and imperfect amidst all that seeming vehemence of thought and sentiment, which attends the fictions of poetry."[51] Here, though, Hume tries for a different kind of consistency. Blending poetry and philosophy back into "the liberal Arts and Sciences," he gives a run-down of what success requires that would be banal were it not for the implications he draws from them. He is explicit that talent needs to be developed in just the ways professional training offers to do: "Nature" must provide "Genius," "Education and Example" must "cultivate" it from childhood, and "Industry" must be applied. A poet, on this analysis, is just a higher form of doctor or lawyer (the absence of the clergyman is conspicuous), and meanwhile all three are obviously more gifted as well as more industrious than the mere queen or king.[52] Poets and philosophers are continuous with, and yet special and apart from, the lawyers and rulers who appear further down the ladder. They are made of finer stuff, but cultivation is necessary in every case. It is not that Hume is nostalgic for a world in which the mysterious claims of Plato or the Stuarts can be maintained, but that he cannot stay away from this kind of talk about poetry in an Addisonian essay aimed at the genteel consumer of such language.[53] The genre within which Hume is still seeking to place himself demands that he pay at least lip-service to a charismatic figure unsupported by what is specific and unique about his case.

Hume's terminology registers a specific process in the broader history of the British professions. Whereas the practical necessity of obtaining a university education had worked as an economic and social barrier to entry into the upper branches of Church, Medicine, and Law, a number of other only recently "professional" professions, as well as the lower branches of the traditional ones, were flourishing not least because of new, empirical, and much cheaper methods of training via apprenticeship. Holmes, whose thesis I am following here, quotes Dr. Charles Goodall, writing in 1694, in reference to apothecaries: "We have to deal with a sort of men not of academical but mechanic education."[54] As it pertains to actually existing professions, Hume's case is no less democratic than it should be, since it leaves little room for one to make an outright distinction between "academical" and "mechanic" education. Except for the "academic philosophy" which Hume's own reflections represent, all education must essentially be mechanic. Further, as Hume's imagined audience seems already to believe, academic deliberations regarding the conduct of life should be treated carefully, if not suspiciously.

While philosophers and poets might search for a formal equation of royal and poetic power, the King is the nominal head of a real system of patronage, and just as Hume could not maintain the distinctions among professional, poetic, and royal charisma, royal charisma may fail in the presence of the self-sufficient author. That is, an encounter with the crown may bring the crown's ability to magically apprehend merit into doubt, even when author and monarch are nominally in accord. This means, in turn, that professional structures of formation, affiliation and evaluation become relatively more significant. Johnson's meeting with the king is one well-known example. In 1767, Johnson encountered George III during an informal visit to the King's Library, and Alvin Kernan, expanding on a long tradition, finds that this conversation signifies a major alteration in the conditions of authorship: "In the social history of letters, this scene between Johnson and King George in the library divides the old regime of courtly letters in the service of the established hierarchical order from a new kind of letters centered not on a king and his court but on print and the writer."[55] Kernan's reading is, as he explains, based on a kind of historical hindsight. Neither Boswell nor Johnson, "staunch loyalists," consciously understand that "a transfer of literary power from king to author was being symbolically enacted"[56] But enacted it has been, as Kernan has it, if primarily in the telling. Boswell's narrative, which privileges the author's perspective at the expense of the king's, is one of "the numerous events through which a new print-based, author-centered literary system was constructed and made real."[57]

As Kernan acknowledges when he mentions the politics of the two "loyalists," the immediate meaning of the scene, for them, has separate implications for the production of literary texts and the management of authorial identity. Especially significant are the dynamics of affiliation activated by Johnson's literary conversation with his monarch, dynamics which are not immediately affected by the rising dominance of print Kernan describes. Asked about Dr. John Hill, Johnson at first replies that, although "ingenious," Hill had "no veracity"; immediately, though, Johnson "began to consider that I was depreciating this man in front of his Sovereign, and thought it was time for me to say something that might be more favourable."[58] (Johnson is similarly tactful regarding Warburton, Lowth, and Lyttleton.) There is a man-to-man and writer-to-writer bond between Johnson and his writerly inferior, Dr. Hill, and that bond is established largely by the difference between Hill and Johnson, as a category of persons, and the King, who stands above and alone. Johnson's feelings about the monarchy are separate from his feelings about the mechanisms of literary evaluation. The king represents an establishment of which the literary sphere remains, as far as Johnson is concerned, an integrated but separately functioning part. As often as Johnson's independence has been attributed to his success in the marketplace, it is also generated by moments such as this one, when the specialized role of the author and the author's affiliation with others who share his line of work are revealed in the crucible of social difference.

A less widely remarked meeting between George III and a famous author tells a different story about a local moment of deference, condescension and the generalized workings of the literary sphere. This time, the interrelationship of certain kinds of authorial and royal identity, as well as their vulnerability, are more evident. The author in question is James Beattie, whose celebrity is at its height in 1773, the year of his meeting with George III. Beattie's career is a significant reminder that, even later in the century, prudent authors with relatively successful literary careers could find themselves in need of other sources of income. Both Beattie's philosophical disquisition *An Essay on Truth* and the almost exactly contemporaneous first book of *The Minstrel* sold widely and were highly regarded, but, even when coupled with his position as professor of Moral Philosophy at Marischal College, his writing did not bring in a satisfactory income.[59] A search for some kind of patronage was almost automatic, but he was not indiscriminate. At various times, for example, friends would attempt to place him in the Anglican Church, but this was a means of support he would turn down. More satisfactorily, in April 1773, Beattie traveled to London to lobby for the annuity which he would receive in August, and this visit is the occasion of his meeting with royalty.

Beattie's journal account of his interview with George III and Queen Charlotte, accompanied by Dr. Majendie, the Huguenot priest who acted as instructor to the Queen and tutor to Prince Frederick and the Prince of Wales, is at first glance a rebuttal of the fall-of-patronage thesis, since Beattie, like Young, is a successful author who continues to search for other kinds of rewards.[60] Yet just as Johnson's meeting can be held up to the light at two different angles, revealing both the respectful Royalist in the company of his sovereign and the independent man of letters who has precious little need for a king, except perhaps as a matter of lingering sentiment, Beattie's also has a double implication. It begins on an almost painfully traditional note, with the dependent poet waiting around a drawing room, but the king's subsequent condescension betrays another loss of royal power:

The Dr. and I waited a considerable time (for the King was busy) and then we were called into a large room, furnished as a library, where the King was walking about, and the Queen sitting in a chair. We were received in the most gracious manner possible by both their Majesties. I had the honour of a conversation with them (nobody else being present but Dr. Majendie) for upwards of an hour, on a great variety of topics, in which both the King and Queen joined, with a degree of chearfulness, affability, and ease, that was to me surprising, and soon dissipated the concern which I felt at the beginning of the conference.[61]

Worried that his behavior might not have been appropriate, Beattie is reassured by Majendie, who tells him he is sure it was, "as sure ... as I am of my own existence" – a joke, since Beattie's reputation as a philosopher was based on his refutation of Humean skepticism and of "the modern philosophy" as regularly traced back to Descartes' *Meditations*.[62] The doctor's ontological gag puts a fine point on what has been, after all, the lesson of the exercise. Monarchs and philosophers can mingle affably, if not on terms of equality, in the drawing-room/library where principles of common sense are given their due. Royal "ease" comes as a surprise only in the way that certain fables have surprising but necessary happy endings.

All of this congeniality comes at a price. Beattie's detailed exposition of royal commentary tends to diminish the aura of this particular king more than did Johnson's independent but respectful interview, even though the King had sought out Johnson, whereas Beattie appears before him as a petitioner. If it is pleasant to find one's audience with the king conducted politely, and comforting to be informed that the appropriateness of one's behavior has lived up to a Cartesian standard of certainty, there is also, in the scene, a kind of let-down. In contrast to the divisive but widely known pamphleteering of a Charles I or a James I, the best this royal patron of philosophy can do is to agree cheerfully with popular philosophers. In the absence of Johnson's moral example, this cheerfulness takes an especially unpleasant turn. While Johnson had remembered to protect Dr. Hill before his monarch, Beattie and George III gang up on their enemies. The King is happy to note that "the sale of Hume's essays had failed, since [*Essay on Truth*] was published," a deflating observation not least because it grants the marketplace the force of arbitration in the realm of ideas.[63] George III displays neither the supernatural insight exercised by Richard Savage's patron-figures nor the forceful originality of Viscount Bolingbroke, and Beattie's business with the crown lacks the drama of Savage's real-life rescue from the gallows by a bureaucratic apparatus come suddenly to life. Beattie's ethical fire, on display in his *Essay on Truth* and *The Minstrel*, is not able to produce or defend the aesthetically consistent order an earlier generation had still been able to dream of. That is, the interaction of author and king need not be understood as a direct competition, in which Johnson wins one and Beattie loses one for the independent writer. There are senses in which the King's loss is also the author's, particularly when, like Beattie and unlike Johnson, the author has not become so thoroughly associated with the new marketplace as to become an emblem of it. Hume's professional prophecies only grow more convincing as the century wears on.

Marjorie Hope Nicolson finds Savage's to be the most "exaggerated" version of a group of "excursion" poems which also includes the work of Mallet and Thomson, and the trope of poetic flight that defines the genre, illustrating what Margaret Anne Doody has called the Augustan "love of the boundless," has a long afterlife.[64] The poet of Coleridge's "To the Author" owes much to this convention as well as to the ascent of Parnassus and the heavenly translation of Lycidas, and it makes a surprising reappearance in the Preface to *Lyrical Ballads,* as is discussed in Chapter 7. One might also think of *Peter Bell*'s flying boat and the opening sequence of Shelley's *Queen Mab*. It has not, however, been the aim of this chapter to collapse literary/historical moments that differ so widely in terms of formal and thematic expectation and practice, but to begin to discern the kinds of structural connections that are implied by shifting representational strategies. The next chapter draws closer to the Lake poets in time and closer to the more familiar body of their predecessors and influences. James Beattie is widely recognized as a Romantic precursor, but it is less often noted how closely his professional puzzles anticipate Lake school dilemmas, or how energetic are his attempts to make an acceptable, usable art out of them. As Chapter 3 argues, Beattie continues the struggle with professional development and professional evaluation, even though he is himself an established intellectual figure, the Professor of Moral Philosophy at Aberdeen.

James Beattie and The Minstrel

James Beattie is among the most important late-century precursors of Romantic writing. His *The Minstrel* (1771, 1773), an auto-biographical account of the poet's education in nature, was widely influential, and some measure of its significance may be detected in the identification made by Dorothy Wordsworth: "Beattie's Minstrel always reminds me of [William Wordsworth], and indeed the whole character of Edwin resembles much what William was when first I knew him."[1] The occasion of Dorothy's comment is revealing, and not much remarked on.[2] Wordsworth has been quarreling with his uncle about his refusal to enter the Church, and the point of Dorothy's comparison is to exonerate Wordsworth on the basis of his "natural disposition," which is that of Beattie's "strange and wayward wight."[3] "Disposition" here is a natural inclination toward (and away from) certain kinds of work, and in hindsight Dorothy may be granting too much to her family in her defense of her brother. Wordsworth's Beattiean "waywardness" is not merely a languid resistance to professional labor. For the fictional minstrel and the real Wordsworth both, vocational wandering stands for the desire to reconstitute a new profession-alism that saves old arrangements from morbidity and corruption.

Central to this new professionalism is a reconsideration of the making of the individual professional, and like Savage before him and the Lake poets after him, Beattie will suggest that a series of special experiences is required to qualify the poet for his role. One fructifying complication for Beattie is that "experience" itself has become a controversial category by the second half of the century. *The Minstrel* is the basis of Beattie's modern reputation, but in his lifetime he was equally well-known for his criticism of David Hume's philosophical writing. Beattie responds to Hume's skepticism, and to Hume's charismatic hold over the British reading public, by

popularizing Thomas Reid's Common Sense philosophy and
attempting to establish unassailable standards of evaluation. Yet
while it may seem that a providential epistemology such as Reid's
would complement the spontaneous yet inevitable emergence
of Beattie's idealized poet, there is a twist: the actual structures
of professional life to which *The Minstrel* refers belie the possibility of
a universally recognized standard. It is of course logically possible,
even necessary, to distinguish between philosophies of perception
and sociologies of distribution. However, as I will discuss in what
follows, this is just the distinction Beattie refuses to make.

I HUME, REID, AND BEATTIE: WHAT WE TALK ABOUT WHEN WE TALK ABOUT SPACE

Historians of philosophy generally agree that the first detailed
response to Hume's *Enquiry* is Reid's *An Inquiry into the Human
Mind on the Principles of Common Sense,* first published in 1764.
Beattie's *Essay* popularizes Reid's more complex treatment, and to
understand Beattie, it is helpful to begin with Reid. In its outlines,
Reid's procedure is straightforward. Establishing Hume as a proponent of what he calls the "ideal system," Reid argues that
the stance he attributes to the Descartes-Malebranche-Locke-
Berkeley-Hume line of reasoning, that "ideas . . . are the only
objects of thought," and that ideas come only from impressions, is
both undefended and indefensible.[4] Adherents of the ideal system
present themselves as being free of suppositions, and as working
from first principles, yet they are bound to a single premise upon
which they refuse to reflect. Further, that premise is clearly flawed.
From raw sensations, Reid argues again and again, nobody could
ever form an idea. Sensations do not "resemble" ideas, as the
ideal-system philosophers claim, so the feeling of touching a hard
object, for instance, could not lead to the idea of "hardness," of
"the firm cohesion of parts of a body."[5]

   While Reid and Beattie find ideal-system philosophers guilty of a
basic error of reasoning, it is not those philosophers' intelligence
or ingenuity that is ultimately at issue, but their refusal to scruti-
nize their own position and their indifference to the fact that
intellectual dishonesty distorts the proper appraisal of people and
ideas. Were the ideal premise true, Reid allows, most of the
conclusions figures such as Hume have drawn from it, including

the most abstruse and surprising, would stand. Since the premise is intuitively unappealing as well as demonstrably false, however, the philosophical failings of its adherents prove to be moral as well as logical, and Hume is the most dangerous and irresponsible skeptic of them all. He represents a false system of evaluation, both in the sense that he falsely evaluates perceptual phenomena and the basis of human understanding and in the sense that his arguments may be incorrectly appraised by the reading public. Beattie is particularly emphatic that Hume's arguments have already been allowed too much credence in the public sphere, not because they are convincing, but because Hume's reasoning is impenetrable while his conclusions are flattering to the vain and consoling to the immoral: "Moral paradoxes, when men begin to look about for arguments in vindication of impiety and immorality, become interesting, and can hardly fail of a powerful and numerous patronage."[6] Hume's *Treatise*, while appearing to assume a kind of spontaneous formation of consensus in its discussions of "the passions," for example, seems to the common sense philosophers to foment an uncommon kind of nonsense.

In ways that are particularly troubling for Beattie, Hume divides up sociologically and geographically distinct audiences when it is wrong to do so and he collapses them when it is wrong to do so, and it is this subdivision of the question of experience that impinges most closely on the texture of Beattie's professional language. In order to see how this works, I would like to consider an extended example of Hume's phenomenology and the response of Reid and Beattie. Hume's account of space is entirely idiosyncratic, and it is among the arguments most easily disposed of by his critics, yet it also has a measurable and immediate impact on his opponents and thus on the uses of space in Beattie's trend-setting poetry. Reid's extensive description of "the geometry of visibles" is a rebuttal or a modification of Hume's "space," and Beattie's philosophical writing definitively assents to Reid's views. Nonetheless, when Beattie sets out to manufacture a setting for his autobiographical poem, he will be haunted by Hume's notion that space, as plenitude, can become a crucible of character to which providence assigns no meaning and over which it grants humanity no dominion. Savage's free excursiveness, that is, when reiterated by Beattie, is not to be domesticated by mere common sense.

As Hume describes it, our understanding of space (or "extension") is derived from the visual and tactile perception of an
arrangement of minima, which he takes to be colored and tangible
mathematical points. For an ideal-system philosopher, the sensory
derivation of the idea of "space" is uncontroversial, but Hume's
insistence on his theory of "points" as a consequence leads to
complications. In particular, he must take some pains to account
for how and why people could come to have an idea of "space"
that does not contain material points – a vacuum, as opposed to a
plenum – since, according to his analysis, no one can have a direct
impression of such a thing. His argument, awkwardly enough, is
that people do not have such an idea. Rather, they mistake
a "fictional distance," the perceived separation between visible
objects, for the real experience of sight and touch which leads to
the real idea of space; but "as blindness and darkness afford us
no idea of extension, 'tis impossible that the dark and undis-
tinguishable distance 'twixt two bodies can ever produce that idea
[i.e. the idea of extension with nothing in it]."[7] Because the
"imaginary distance" leads to ideas that are similar to the idea of
true extension (they form its negative), we mistakenly imagine
that we have the idea of a vacuum when we are really thinking
about a plenum after all.[8]

The collection of issues that relate touch and sight to extension
is fundamental in the debate over skeptical philosophy, as these
are central to the question of whether external bodies exist or can
be known. In denying the idea of a vacuum, that is, the idea of
nothing, Hume has pressed the ideal hypothesis as far as it can go,
or farther. Thus he logically follows his section on extension with
an initial, brief statement of his position on external objects: "Let
us chace our imagination to the heavens, or to the utmost limits of
the universe; we never really advance a step beyond ourselves, nor
can conceive any kind of existence, but those perceptions, which
have appear'd in that narrow compass. This is the universe of the
imagination, nor have we any idea but what is there produc'd."[9]
Hume's language speaks directly to his prior discussion of space
and, it may be argued, to the condition of the poetic wanderer. He
deflates the power of all universe-spanning thought experiments,
and of the imagination, by reminding his readers that the only
thing to be found in imaginary space is what has already been
presented to the "narrow compass" of the self. Wherever you go,

as Savage's wanderer had discovered, there you are. Even the capacity for visionary flight can only lead one back around to where one has already been.

Before relegating Hume's impoverished version of the imagination and his correlate account of space to the dustbin of pre-Kantian or pre-Coleridgian history, it is important to note that where Hume has already been may be in turn welcoming and uncanny.[10] While Hume is his century's laureate of defamiliarization, his work habitually seeks its ground in the familiar, and this habit manifests itself in unlikely places. In order to discredit the monism of Berkeley and Spinoza, for example, Hume proposes that "perceptions," because they are discrete and individual, cannot properly be conceived of as "actions," which are continuous and relational. The issue would appear to be tangential to Reid and Beattie, except that, in order to make the point, Hume offers the following apparently off-hand example:

> Motion to all appearances induces no real or essential change on the body, but only varies its relation to other objects. But betwixt a person in the morning walking in the garden with company, agreeable to him; and a person in the afternoon enclos'd in a dungeon, and full of terror, despair, and resentment, there seems to be a radical difference, and of quite another kind, than what is produc'd on a body by the change of its situation.[11]

The mind's perceptions have changed, because the body has moved from the garden to the dungeon, but the body itself clearly has not changed, or not in the same way as the mind. Thus, action, at least when construed according to a physical analogy with motion, is separate from perception. Yet, perhaps despite himself, Hume remains interested in the way "the change of a body's situation" has psychological effects, and he quickly goes on to argue that

> You reason too hastily ... when you conclude 'tis impossible motion can ever produce thought, or a different position of parts give rise to a different passion or reflection. Nay 'tis not only possible we may have such an experience, but 'tis certain we have it, since every one may perceive, that the different dispositions of his body change his thoughts and sentiments.[12]

Because our notion of causality is derived from customary connection, either there is no such thing as a direct perception of causality, or else motion may cause thought as well as thought, motion. Hume's broader agenda is to follow Locke in demonstrating that matter might in principle cause thought, thus establishing that there is no a priori way of determining whether the soul is material or immaterial. In his commonsense observation that our moods change with our positions, however, Hume reminds us that what begins as abstruse has immediate, tangible referents, but further, that these very referents plunge us back into a state of uncertainty. The phenomena of body language and of the transfer from the garden to the dungeon only appear to be easy to understand, since they have as their consequence the potential materiality of soul and the reversal of usual causal sequences. Hume has separated the subject of "action" from the subject of "cause," but his examples reveal that action and cause are persistently related and surprisingly reversible, if only by habit, if only through experience. The proposed transitivity of thought and motion is vertiginous; in place of a single-substance universe, Hume has discovered one in which anything can cause anything, and only our customary but inevitable preference for gardens and company over dungeons and solitude is really sure. In turn, this customary preference reflects back on the structure of Hume's argument. As Marina Frasca-Spada explains, Hume's true philosopher, recognizing the organic force of the drive to talk about vacuums, also recognizes the value of sociable and corrective interaction: "We can discuss the idea of empty space, even if we cannot conceive of such an idea, because the erroneous conviction of conceiving an idea is at least as interesting as a true idea"; for Frasca-Spada's Hume, what might be called the language-game of metaphysics is a game about reference, and ultimately about "human nature."[13]

While Frasca-Spada's point about the sociable influence of metaphysical discourse is clarifying, it is not the whole story, since the constitution of the "human," chattering polity which it takes for granted is among the major points of contention among Reid, Hume, and Beattie. From one perspective, Hume's powerful integrations adumbrate an ahistorical public sphere, a virtual reality wherein the philosopher becomes his own audience and brings into being a speculative avant garde that swells to fill the entire universe. Thus, when Hume opposes his "profound philosopher" to the "mere plebeian," his point is that a single person might alternately occupy both roles; appropriately, it is another physical passage, from "shade" to "open day," that "reduces" the philosopher-plebe from one state to the other.[14] Conversely, when resisting the separation of "vulgar" from "philosophical" audiences, the Humean philosopher sets out to "unite the boundaries of the two species of philosophy, by reconciling profound inquiry with clearness."[15] The language of the *Enquiry* reflects its new, popularizing intentions, but the figures express a single if complex idea. Troubled by his own abstract difficulty, Hume fills in the space between himself and his readers on the one hand by imagining out of existence the difference between these subjects and on the other by proposing a plenum throughout which all boundaries touch.[16] What Hume is anticipating, in a piecemeal fashion, is something like Heideggerian "de-distancing," itself an extension of the Cartesian res extensa, now no longer "permanently and objectively present" but phenomenologically contingent.[17] As Frasca-Spada hints and the history of hermeneutics serves to demonstrate, the intersubjective corollary of these spatial metaphors is talk, or social interaction, and as Hume repeatedly shows, the difference between objects and speech, like the difference between thought and motion, is hard or impossible for the skeptic to sustain. To reduce the world to subjective impressions is also to eliminate the barrier between addresser and addressee.

For Reid, on the other hand, what is between here and there is best understood neither as a plenum nor as a vacuum, because this is the wrong way to reason about objects in space and the wrong way to talk about experience. Instead, Reid offers a theory of signs in order to indicate that perception is a matter of interpretation; the ability to interpret signs (such as signs of hardness, or of distance) is God-given and in human terms arbitrary.[18] One such sign, or system of signs, is "visible figure." Berkeley had used the device of visible figure to conclude that objects have no qualities, but Reid appropriates the concept to distinguish between what is actually present in the field of vision and what sure interpretations experience coupled with providence prepare us make about it.[19] Reid's extensive treatment of visible figure and its attendant geometries make for one of his more suggestive rebuttals of Hume, and, unsurprisingly, it is also the occasion for one of his most confident statements about audience. Where Frasca-Spada finds a community of fallible but lovable metaphysicians who are defined by the exchange of ideas and whose correction by Hume is inextricable from Hume's identification with them, Reid discovers a "tribunal" that despotically applies a single arbitrary standard in the judgment of the innocent:

It may be asked, What kind of thing is this visible figure? Is it a sensation, or an idea? If it is an idea, from what sensation is it copied? These questions may seem trivial or impertinent to one who does not know, that there is a tribunal of inquisition erected by certain modern philosophers, before which every thing in nature must answer. The articles of inquisition are few indeed, but very dreadful in their consequences. They are only these: Is the prisoner an impression, or an idea? If an idea, from what impression copied? Now, if it appears that the prisoner is neither an impression, nor an idea copied from some impression, immediately, without being allowed to offer any thing in arrest of judgment, he is sentenced to pass out of existence, and to be, in all time to come, an empty unmeaning sound, or the ghost of a departed entity.[20]

However, the comic element here marks the congenial limit on Reid's anxiety about skepticism and about the philosopher's power over the people. The Humean tribunal cannot really make "visible figure" disappear, or even disappear from conversation, and the tribunal's affectation of an authority it does not have is one major sign of its vulnerability. If anything, Reid's repeated concern is that, if philosophy remains aligned with Humean skepticism, its real powers of consolation will be neglected by "sensible men, who will never be sceptics in common life."[21] Reid imagines a "vulgar" audience for philosophy that is genuinely an audience but is inherently separate from the philosopher. To this extent, Reid's intervention on the part of philosophy, as he presents it, is necessary. He is both its steward and its spokesperson, a philosopher who wants to reconcile the abstruse with what has been commonly understood and experienced.

In other words, in debating space, Hume and Reid are also discussing the status of the general audience in a specialist's age. Although Reid's description of perception may differ from Hume's, it shares with Hume the acknowledgment that what is true on reflection is different from what appears to be true spontaneously, a fact apparent at the level of the sign system and at the level of philosophical practice.[22] As Reid would observe, "It is one thing to have [a] sensation, and another to attend to it, and make it a distinct object of reflection. The first is easy; the last, in most cases, extremely difficult."[23] Consequently, the philosopher's task is two-fold. One part requires attention, applied either through experiment or through the brute force of concentration to sensory experiences that usually go unnoticed. The other part, "reflection," relies on the philosopher's ability to apply logical standards of evaluation to the results of concentration. (The distinction corresponds to the distinction between "sensation" and "perception.") Thus, the philosopher emerges as a specialist in abstruse problems of reasoning and perception whose primary mission is to turn abstract puzzle-solving to the common good, and in this way to effect a bridge between an intellectual elite and other ranks. It is striking, then, that Reid's fascination with the "geometry of visibles" offers to bring him back around to the notional monism of Hume's plenitude of mathematical points. Despite the purported sureness of the natural sign to convey truth about, for example, distance, what lies between the perceiver and the distant object is nothing more or less than a secret act of interpretation of a world of signs that would otherwise be roughly akin to paint on a flat surface. Only the philosopher's insight can account for the depth of the world, and the concert of sight and touch emerges as mysterious and arbitrary. Hume had, probably in jest, characterized Reid as a meddling parson, not a philosopher, but Reid himself proves to be a better guardian of the border between lay and expert inquirer.[24] That border is distinct, definite, and it marks a difference in social function. The ministrations of the expert metaphysician should be made palatable for the audience, but they are not in the end under that audience's evaluative control.

For related reasons, critics have noted that Reid's work has a variety of implications for Romantic writing. For Paul Hamilton, the most important aspect of Reid's thought for Romantic studies is his emphasis on language; because skeptical philosophy, as Reid understands it, abuses what is only an analogy by treating all thoughts as visual images, "the philosopher's task is therefore hermeneutical; he is primarily concerned with providing a convincing interpretation of the language we are obliged to use in understanding the world."[25] While Hamilton goes on to note that it would take an infusion of German idealism to help writers such as Coleridge move beyond Reid's inherent conservatism, he does argue that, because of its programmatic association of language-use and theories of mind, "common-sense philosophy is a much-underestimated part of the explanation of how the Romantic poet could be thought to have a significant philosophical role to play."[26] More recently, Noel B. Jackson has emphasized how, in order to demonstrate that "perceptions" are different both from "sensations" and from the image-based "idea," Reid performs experiments with double-vision that threaten our faith in common-sense perception even as they are supposed to reaffirm that faith: "In so revealing the aberrance of our natural (though occulted) sensations, such experiments open the possibility that our common sense is the result not of a natural order but is rather the product of a prior act of construction."[27] Reid's rhetorical point continues to be that while we can induce aberrant visual effects in ourselves, we are unlikely to be fooled by them, but as Jackson is pointing out, Reid's procedures can't help revealing that what we think we see is not really what we see; the visual field is actually bifurcated, although only a philosopher would go to the trouble of experiencing this fact and reflecting on it. What is "Romantic" about Reid, we may conclude, is also what is professional about him. Although Beattie attempts to resist the conclusion, for Reid the world both gives itself up spontaneously and yet requires specialized, intensive interpretation.

In turn, what Beattie realizes is that the play of motion and locale, with its attendant movement of ideas and influences among writers and audiences, is not culturally neutral. As Anthony Giddens observes: "Because societies differ in their modes of institutional articulation, the modes of intersection of presence and absence that enter into their constitution can be expected to vary."[28] The ways societies are described to themselves also vary along these lines. Hume and Reid, in their different ways, imagine a cosmopolitan world in which a series of spontaneous but predictable encounters, both face-to-face and in print, have a regularizing effect on belief and behavior. In this world, various positions can be adopted and relinquished in the name of adversarial "Entertainment," and it is this latter context which makes a series of relatively congenial exchanges between Hume and Reid possible.[29] On the other hand, Beattie construes the world, at least in his formal argumentation, in agrarian terms. The possibilities of face-to-face contact among different kinds of people are highly constrained, so that no genuine critique or interaction is likely to take place. Even when the plebeian and the philosopher do meet, the circumstances will be ritualized in ways that do not tend toward illuminating argument. Thus, as I will discuss below, Beattie's world is integrated only to the extent that the self-indulgences of philosophers can victimize a range of under-privileged audiences. The distance between the vulgar and the sage is in theory dissolvable for Hume, and in practice its dissolution provides a check on the psychological excesses of the sage and the intellectual naïveté of the vulgar. For Reid, the distance is more sure, and it corresponds both to the verticality of the state and to the articulation of Great Britain's symmetrical institutions, Episcopal and Anglican, as manifest in London, Edinburgh, or Aberdeen.

Plunging into the conventions of sensibility, Beattie counters Hume's fortunately collapsible borders, and Reid's confidence that the court of public opinion will render moot the inquisition of metaphysical lunatics, with a different kind of portrait. Of the skeptics, he writes:

Caressed by those who call themselves the great, ingrossed by the formalities and fopperies of life, intoxicated with vanity, pampered with adulation, dissipated in the tumult of business, or amidst the vicissitudes of folly, they perhaps have little need, and little relish, for the consolations of religion. But let them know, that, in the solitary scenes of life, there is many an honest and tender heart pining with incurable anguish, pierced with the sharpest sting of disappointment, bereft of friends, chilled with poverty, wracked with disease, scourged by the oppressor; whom nothing but trust in Providence, and the hope of a future retribution, could preserve from the agonies of despair. And do they, with sacrilegious hands, attempt to violate this last refuge of the miserable, and to rob them of the only comfort that had survived the ravages of misfortune, malice, and tyranny! Did it ever happen, that the influence of their execrable tenets disturbed the tranquillity of vir-tuous retirement, deepened the gloom of human distress, or aggravated the horrors of the grave?[30]

Beattie's oppressed figure is not only impoverished but "scourged" by an unidentified, malicious "tyranny," and Hume comes to stand not only for skepticism but for cosmopolitan vanity and wealth that does not need (and, we may surmise, had better not expect) the "consolations of religion."

What is particularly important here is Beattie's depiction of a literary culture that parodies the account of psychological caus-ality Hume had refined out of Locke. Whereas Hume claims to be at the mercy of impressions and ideas, the "honest and tender heart" is at the mercy of Hume. Hume is not always understood this way, since as often as Hume the metaphysician shocks the vulgar, Hume the pragmatist inclines toward joining them. As John Richetti puts it, "Hume's thought ratifies common life by traveling through the chaotic alternative life just to the side of it or underneath it. Hume arrives at common life rather than beginning with it."[31] Beattie, however, has detected that "influence," which he might call "fashion," can go awry, so that in one sense there is no "common life," or if there is, it has been perverted by the differentials of power and wealth that he describes. Skepticism penetrates where it is not wanted and where it is most dangerous. The breach in the wall between the brightly lit world of "those who call themselves the great" and the dark and "solitary scenes of life" turns out, unlikely though this appears to be, to be the discipline of "philosophy" itself.[32] Equally surprising is who the wall protects from whom. When Beattie declines to address his opponents "on the principles of benevolence or generosity" because this is "a language ye do not, or will not, understand," he is being insulting in the most appropriate way, since, as he chooses to read it, Hume has done away with "benevolence" in the third book of his *Treatise*. Or at least, according to his own argument, Hume can't exactly choose to be benevolent, and Beattie naturally takes the position that this is a willful refusal and not an involuntary one. All agency belongs to the modern skeptics, who abuse the gift in order to satisfy vanity. Worse, their corruption displaces religious consolation and forces itself on naïve and oppressed solitaries who, because (as Beattie emphasizes) they are incapable of truly understanding skeptical arguments and are instead influenced by passion and popular acclaim, may as well be buffeted about after the fashion of Hume's philosopher. The solitude in which they might retain the consolations of religion is violated by the ideal system that, Beattie suggests, practically as well as theoretically does away with the prophylactic distance between corruption and the isolated but still virtuous corners of the world.[33]

Identification, in other words, especially identification with David Hume, can be dangerous to the oppressed and solitary soul. What Beattie really needs is a super-figure who can combine the virtuous solitude of the hermit (as it had been established over time and particularly in poems like Savage's *The Wanderer*) with an

ability to see into the life of things – a rustic who is not "oppressed" and, perhaps for that reason, is not a dupe. Yet for reasons
I shall explain, this super-figure will prove difficult to describe, or
difficult to sustain. Beattie's version of the minstrel pre-empts the
kind of destructive sympathy that leads the oppressed solitary to
identify with his fashionable oppressors, which means, in Hume's
terms, that he also foregoes the process whereby ideas are transformed into sensations; his solitude is absolute.[34] *The Minstrel* is
thus concerned at one level with the question of experience, of
how certain kinds of input create skeptic-resistant virtue, while at
another level, it is confronted with the insight that all emotional
experience, even the minstrel's, is socially contingent. Hume's
famous account of taste, while arguing for something like an
empirical standard of correctness, eventually gives in and allows
that "we choose our favourite author as we do our friend, from a
conformity of humour and disposition."[35] For Beattie, proper
literary evaluation should be possible, but it is as hard to get as
a satisfactory epistemological position.

II *THE MINSTREL*: THE LONELINESS OF THE LONG-DISTANCE WRITER

To claim that poor standards have benefited one's enemies at the
expense of "the truth," and to offer one's own grounds of evaluation as stable and sure, is to run the risk of appearing self-interested
or "ambitious." As John Sitter has discussed, mid-century treatments of "ambition" are often marked by an ambivalence that
distinguishes them from the more aggressive stance toward commerce and culture evinced by earlier writers, and he identifies the
moment's movement toward "loneliness" as a movement away
from the kinds of direct social engagements that were rhetorically
possible for Savage, but required a different level of mediation for
Beattie and many of his contemporaries. Importantly, Sitter
underlines that this retreat implies a critique of the treatment of
merit that had already been at issue for Savage's generation of
writers: "The best people," he writes, summarizing a common mid-
century attitude, "do not often, perhaps not usually, rise to the top,
because the competition for 'places' in society and in history is
ruthless and demeaning."[36] The point is linked to the diminishing
regard for patronage discussed in the previous chapter; as Paul

J. Korshin observes, "There is always a subtle balance between success and merit and, historically, the support of a patron has frequently been interpreted pejoratively, as an unfair external influence responsible, in whole or in part, for the success of a person whose merit is slight."[37] I would like to argue, though, that the question of evaluation often is neither being abandoned nor repressed but reconceived. Beattie will name two patrons in *The Minstrel*, but the effect, as I will discuss, is to forestall rather than foreground any depiction of Edwin's or Beattie's professional "success." Patrons release Beattie from his account of Edwin's merit-producing experience, but they do not thereby indicate that evaluation and merit are symmetrical. In fact, they prove to be a sign that while the author of *The Minstrel* is aware at every step of the complexities of mid-century professional life, Edwin's independence would in principle be negated by any or all of them.

In his consideration of his own audience, Beattie has a potent model ready to hand: Thomas Gray, a poet often associated with mid-century withdrawal and the rejection of ambition. In an encouraging note to Beattie in 1765, shortly after the two had met for the first time, Gray sketches in a theory of poetic vocation that is pointedly contemporary:

> If either Vanity (that is, a general & undistinguished desire of applause) or Interest, or Ambition has any place in the breast of the poet, he stands a great chance in these our days of being severely disappointed: and yet after all these passions are suppress'd, there may remain in the mind of one, *ingenti perculsus amore* (and such a one I take you to be), incitements of a better sort strong enough to make him write verse all his life, both for his own pleasure & that of all posterity.[38]

Strikingly, Gray stops well short of condemning vanity, interest, or ambition, the unholy trinity of bad poetry, blaming "these our days" for the fact that such apparently natural passions are likely to be disappointed. Once "these passions are suppressed," there is room for the "better sort" of incitement to motivate one who has already been overcome by a literally amateurish impulse. In its variable handling of passions and interests, and its strange glance backward to a pre-Hanoverian age of gold when vain, interested, and ambitious poets were likely to be rewarded for their work, Gray's comment suggestively colors the now-standard characterization of him as "nicely representative of the class and value-system that defined itself against the commercial, public, and professional claims of the eighteenth-century English bourgeoisie."[39] Gently aligning Gray and Beattie with figures who in other places might be defined as dunces or hacks, his weird nostalgia embraces that earlier "class- and value-system" while describing it as being at least potentially corrupt. Love is best, but it is only what is left once patronage, at least as Gray likes to imagine it, dries up.

As the letter to Beattie also indicates, the suppression of certain kinds of ambition may be self-conscious and informed by history, in this case the literary history whereby a golden age of general applause and fulfilled interest has been succeeded by the iron age of the new literary marketplace. Alongside Kaul's direct associa- tion of Gray with a nostalgic and anti-bourgeois ethos, we might therefore place John Guillory's somewhat busier account of how class dynamics are negotiated in Gray's *Elegy*. Although Guillory observes the speaker's insertion of himself, via the poem's use of pastoral modes, into the fanciful role of aristocrat, this insertion takes place at the price of a "repression" that results in mel- ancholia, itself indicative of the coming-together of a middle-class order; the poet's "ambition" for social mobility, through suc- cessful writing as well as through the emulation of prestigious behaviors, and the "Ambition, Luxury, and Pride" of the stereo- typical aristocrat, are mutually implicated, equally shameful, and only partially alleviated by the development within the poem of a "vernacular poetic diction."[40] For the mid-century poet, in other words, part of embracing the old regime is the embarrassment of embracing the old regime, and that shame is central to a middle- class order defined by its own bad faith.

But Beattie, already upwardly mobile and by most definitions middle-class, accepts neither Gray's attitudes nor his practice, and the implications of Beattie's work for the sustenance of a non- aristocratic order are based not on an erasure of self but on a series of self-assertions.[41] While *The Minstrel* may be read as a simple critique of ambition, what is really happening in it is that self- interest is being combined with the public good in a wholly pro- fessional, service-oriented way. Beattie's opening paraphrases Gray's "Elegy": "Who can tell how many a soul sublime/has felt the influence of a malignant star" and, faced with "Poverty's unconquerable bar," has fallen "into the grave, unpitied and unknown!" (I. 3–9).[42] What follows revises Gray by posing a

different set of possibilities. While some people might be defeated
by straightened financial circumstances, it is just as likely that
poverty and obscurity will prove to be facilitating conditions for
the growing bard:

> And yet the languor of inglorious days,
> Not equally oppressive is to all;
> Him who ne'er listen'd to the voice of praise,
> The silence of neglect can ne'er appal.
> There are, who, deaf to mad Ambition's call,
> Would shrink to hear th'obstreperous trump of Fame;
> Supremely blest, if to their portion fall
> Health, competence, and peace. Nor higher aim
> Had he, whose simple tale these artless lines proclaim. (I. 10–19)

"Fame" and "mad Ambition" have no power over Edwin, but this
does not mean that Edwin, or the author for whom he stands in,
have no claim on the nation's attention. On the contrary, Beattie's
career as a writer is shaped by his desire to reach a wide audience.
While he "sweats over his Hume" in composing the *Essay on Truth*,
his advisor John Gregory warns him about the book, "If it is
abstract, be it never so wise and never so deep, people will not read
it."[43] And as detailed at the beginning of the last chapter, while
Beattie sets out in his crusade against Hume in the mode of the
lone prophet, he is more than willing to construe the success of his
treatise in terms of its sales – his battle against fashion is finally
vindicated by the testimony of a silent but paying majority as well as
by the attention of the monarch. The hard-working minstrel has
never been vain, ambitious, or interested – these courtly passions
need not be "suppressed" or burned away by history, because they
have never threatened Edwin's self-control. Correlated with that
stance is the position of Beattie the author, whose professional
premises, oriented around a common sense that must really prove
to be common, stand in an ironic relationship to the rustic, un-
ambitious minstrel as well as to the degraded Humean *ton*. It is the
professional's duty to succeed in the marketplace and to displace
the impostor or the quack. This success, in other words, is controlled not by principles of virtue, but by principles of merit.

Beattie has discovered the generative power of autobiography,
and this is no less the case when the life-story of the rustic bard
proves to be a retrospective of certain established poetic modes or
patterns of allusion. An "abundantly allusive poem," as its single

most sympathetic critic has described it, "much of [*The Minstrel's*] appeal for eighteenth-century readers was associated with their recognition of echoes in the poem of many various sources."[44] *The Minstrel* is crucial for just the reason it remains easily overlooked. By locating the psychology of the untutored minstrel in a body of writings dependent on print culture for its circulation, Beattie presents a rebuke to aristocratic culture which is the inverse of Gray's. Where Gray familiarizes new material on the way to creating a new vernacular, Beattie demonstrates that the eighteenth-century language of poetic experience is already common property. At the same time, in defamiliarizing it through the mechanism of autobiography Beattie also initiates the "process of singularization" whereby the poet, beginning as one of us, becomes estranged from the crowd.[45] Common sense is reproduced at the level of textual allusion, and the common property of the English reader is re-inscribed into the texture of a life-story that makes the speaker a spokesperson even as it separates him from his clientele.

That this separation is both absolute and relative is a fact that shapes *The Minstrel* as it shapes Beattie's practice. In a world of aristocrats, Beattie is ready to distinguish himself by trading one set of affiliations for another. While he was prepared to be personal in critiquing Hume, Hume was in fact personally known and well-liked by Beattie's circle, including Reid, who had submitted his own anti-Humean *Treatise* to Hume for advice. Beattie writes:

> I have heard from very good authority that Mr. Hume speaks of me and my book with very great bitterness (I own I thought he would rather have affected to treat both with contempt); and that he says I have not used him like a gentleman .... The truth is, I, as a rational, moral, immortal being, and something of a philosopher, treated him as a rational, moral, and immortal being, a sceptic and an atheistical writer .... To say that I ought not to have done this with plainness and spirit, is to say, in other words, that I ought either to have held my peace, or to have been a knave. In this case, I might have treated Mr. Hume as a gentleman, but I should not have treated society as a man and a Christian.[46]

Beattie casts himself as the hard-working proprietor of truth and virtue and re-casts his ad hominem attacks on Hume as the free exercise of reason, opposing his own brusque, confrontational rhetoric to a false and oppressive gentility that is a mid-century form of fashionable libertinism. The tactic goes hand-in-hand with an appeal to the protocols of British liberty. In the republic of letters, Hume may be a senator, but in Great Britain only knaves speak other than frankly, even to their supposed betters. What in Gray looks like nostalgia for a genteel form of corruption is cast off by Beattie, whose emphasis on his own rational and moral immortality does appear to partake of some kind of "commercial, public and professional claim," combined with an approach to religion that is nearly enthusiastic. Beattie's writing signals the arrival of two separate orders, the one in which truth has to be constantly redefined even by those who argue for what has everywhere been understood, and the one where aristocratic habits of deference have been eliminated in favor of an argumentative free-for-all.

In his *Essay on Truth*, then, Beattie echoes the conversation about experience and merit in which the professional middle-classes are elevated above monarchs, not by making professionals into heroes at the expense of real kings, but by aligning Hume and his supporters with an unidentified tyrant against the besieged, oppressed solitary. A version of the gesture is reproduced in *The Minstrel*, which consistently opposes itself to a kind of tyranny which has no immediate referent but which combines the vocabulary of mid-century satire with allusion to Beattie's recent escape "[f]rom Pyhrro's maze, and Epicurus' sty" (I. 357).[47] For example, in contemplating the linnets' song, the narrator raises a possibility that would seem to be fairly remote, and that signals a kind of hysteria in excess of the likelihoods involved: "Oh let them ne'er, with artificial note,/To please a tyrant, strain the little bill,/But sing what Heaven inspires, and wander where they will!" (43–45). In his agrarian independence, Edwin's father "envied not, he never thought of kings" (111), and while in the rhetorical war against "ambition" this kind of thing seems neutral enough, it is only the beginning of a series of images in which the virtuous characters of the poem are distinguished from kings and tyrants.[48] "Tyranny" is no longer an attribute of royalty, and more intriguingly, "kings" are to be differentiated from the unnamed Hanover whom Beattie would so comfortably importune a few years later, and whose reign is a sign of the essential beneficence of the mixed constitution.

From a long view, Beattie's adaptation of "patriot" talk is in sync with the currents of 1770s political language, which had further regularized and distributed out the coded rhetoric of Savage's time. No longer freighted with its highly specific if competing party valences, this kind of language could now be used to dissolve ideology into purportedly common-sense political solutions, to signal "measures not men, the end of party under a patriot king."[49] Beattie's un-specificity, it follows, is doing cultural work of its own. Just as his meeting with the king, while undertaken within the most traditional possible frameworks of deference and charisma, only reinforces the absence of Royal charisma, *The Minstrel*'s capacity for arranging tyrants, kings, and patriot princes indifferently into figures for court corruption and into a hypothetical portrait of royal "virtue" means that while the institutions of Church and King count heavily, the person of the King himself keeps fading into the background. This is a major symptom of the absorption of tales of divine election into tales of hard-earned personal merit. The patriot king becomes a placeholder, guaranteeing the function of a rising technocracy that itself, as represented in epistemological writing, will generate only those outcomes to which all reasonable people can agree.

   Yet it would be wrong to argue that Beattie's critique of luxury and ambition, however stern, is merely consistent. Insofar as Beattie is directly concerned with the full variety of the century's theories of "experience," it is unsurprising that in one way or another *The Minstrel* would attempt to oppose itself to the line of Locke and Hume on these grounds, and Beattie begins by suggesting, in congruence with the tenets of Reid's *Inquiry* and his own *Essay on Truth*, that experience is a trustworthy antidote for skeptical reason and for the social ills that attend it. The short version of the argument which Book I of *The Minstrel* enacts is quickly apprehended, and its outlines are comfortably Wordsworthian. Exposure to sublime nature apparently provides Edwin with an expansive soul, and it also provides some assurance of the orderliness of the universe. This broad deism is tempered by the Christian doctrine of Edwin's village teachers, which transforms the complex ecclesiological rapprochement of the early part of the century into an enduring body of folk truths. Beattie counters Hume by turning to direct apprehension as a source of generally available knowledge, and he counters the entire apparatus of Humean fashion by locating true philosophy in the spontaneous feelings of the untutored. Unfortunately, the letter of *The Minstrel* will also tend to demonstrate what Hume had known all along, that the certainties experience can provide, or even reaffirm, are limited.

Like Wordsworth, Beattie is attentive to the positive social relationships that he believes are fostered by country life, as well as to the kinds of beneficent effects the forms of Nature have on her "votaries" (I.353). Early on, the role of nature in a providential economic order is outlined in terms that recall, but do not reiterate, cognate moments in Savage's *The Wanderer*:

> Liberal, not lavish, is kind Nature's hand;
> Nor was perfection made for man below;
> Yet all her schemes with nicest art are plann'd;
> Good counteracting ill, and gladness woe.
> With gold and gems if Chilian mountains glow;
> If bleak and barren Scotia's hills arise;
> There plague and poison, lust and rapine grow;
> Here, peaceful are the vales, and pure the skies,
> And Freedom fires the soul, and sparkles in the eyes. (I.46–54)

An important difference between Savage and Beattie is that while Savage marks the distinction between "country" and "city," all of his landscapes produce luxury. The charity of the unnamed city supports the hermit, while another important example, broadened out into a lesson about providence, involves Libyan orange groves: "Ev'n Scenes, that strike with terrible Surprize,/Still prove a God, just, merciful, and Wise" (V. 177–184). Beattie is likewise interested in the providential landscape, but his is an altogether more penurious and geographically exacting muse. The moral regime he seeks to describe is more hostile to luxury than Savage's (and then some); as a consequence, his depiction of divine/natural balance exacts a violent toll on the beneficiaries of Chile's mountains of "gold and gems." The blushing, unseen gem that may betoken a kind of middle-class bad faith in the "Elegy" here receives a different kind of come-uppance. It is nearly a Reidian sign, spontaneously apprehensible as an indication of impending "plague and poison, lust and rapine."

Yet if Beattie's providential theodicy, as thus described, appears seamless, it is striking that it takes place among spaces that are nearly Humean, by which I mean not the "true space" of Hume's most abstract reasoning, but the "truthful spaces," the garden, the dungeon, and the vacuum-that-is-not-one, that emerge in the *Treatise* when Hume, in thinking about motion and causality, realizes once more how forcefully sociability and habit can impinge on epistemology.[50] To begin with, Edwin's exploration of the countryside is of the kind that Wordsworth would later characterize as a fearful flight, rather than a loving seeking – motion, causing thought:

> But why should I his childish feats display?
> Concourse, and noise, and toil he ever fled;
> Nor car'd to mingle in the clamorous fray
> Of squabbling imps; but to the forest sped,
> Or roam'd at large the lonely mountain's head,
> Or, where the maze of some bewilder'd stream
> To deep untrodden groves his footsteps led,
> There would he wander wild, till Phoebus' beam,
> Shot from the western cliff, releas'd the weary team. (I.XVII)

The "concourse, noise, and toil" and the "clamorous fray/of squabbling imps," would appear to belong to some mock-pastoral depiction of London, Milton's "hubbub wild" growing into Book VII of *The Prelude*, but the satiric language is here applied to childhood, and to Edwin's rural demesne. His consequent roaming, a child's exile, comes to its conclusion within the "maze" of a "bewilder'd stream" that uncomfortably echoes "Pyrrho's maze" and throws into relief the uncertain grounds of experience and belief with which the poem continues, despite itself, to be concerned. Beattie's immediate sources abound with mazes, including the mazy streams of Thomson, the "mighty maze" of human life which Pope would claim has a plan, and, intriguingly, the corrosive maze of scholastic reasoning from which Adam must emerge to "absolve" God of his fall. In seeking to collate the providential message of nature with poetic autobiography, *The Minstrel* gets entangled in a version of Gray's vocational melancholy, or in a version of those perplexities of Reid's which Beattie had tried to paper over. Hell isn't the city, but other people, wherever they are found, and in this way a sociological problem is transformed into a psychological one. The cure for melancholy offered by Hume and Reid is at least temporarily denied Edwin.

The final sequence of events in Book I emphasizes the distance between Edwin and the narrator, and in doing so it deepens the possibility that the fable Edwin's life is meant to develop cannot be congruent with Beattie's real-life vocational circumstances. It is also symptomatic of Beatties' refusal of Hume's social cure for

Edwin's strict experiential regime. The narrator assures us that
Edwin's "wild harp" will eventually gain "elegance" through the
application of "time and culture," and this training process is
compared to the coming of summer after a long Lappish winter:

> Thus on the chill Lapponian's dreary land,
> For many a long month lost in snow profound,
> When Sol from Cancer sends the season bland,
> And in their northern caves the storms are bound;
> From silent mountains, straight, with starting sound,
> Torrents are hurl'd; green hills emerge; and, lo;
> The trees with foliage, cliffs with flowers are crown'd;
> Pure rills through vales of verdure warbling go;
> And wonder, love, and joy, the peasant's heart o'erflow.

The first transformation, of the landscape-as-setting into the
landscape that, in its seasonality, may serve as an emblem of the
poet's growth, assimilates discipline into spontaneity; "From silent
mountains, straight, with starting sound,/Torrents are hurl'd"
(I.527–528), Beattie writes, and his note re-emphasizes the sud-
denness of the change: "Spring and autumn are hardly known to
the Laplanders ... [T]heir fields, which a week before were cov-
ered with snow, appear on a sudden full of grass and flowers"
(274). While the figure insists on the abruptness of the transformation, the narrative has already insisted on the difficulty of the
training process and its tendency to consume time as well as space.
The emergence of the green hills is the mark of an origin that
wishes it could appear natural and "cultured," but towards which
the narrator can only feel nostalgia.

At this point, the poem arrives at its final stanza, thus moving
with a jolt from training to evaluation and patronage:

> Here pause, my gothic lyre, a little while,
> The leisure hour is all that thou canst claim.
> But on this verse if Montagu should smile,
> New strains ere long shall animate thy frame.
> And her applause to me is more than fame;
> For still with truth accords her taste refined.
> At lucre or renown let others aim,
> I only wish to please the gentle mind,
> Whom Nature's charms inspire, and love humankind.

As William Forbes explains, "in the first edition, this poem was
dedicated to a male friend, although the name be left blank. In the

second edition, Mrs. Montagu's name was inserted in the con-
cluding stanza." A footnote identifies the excised male: "Our
common friend, Mr. Arbuthnot."[51] The replacement of Arbuthnot with Montagu is readily explained. Arbuthnot had been a
supportive friend, but Montagu was more recently and in every
sense a patron, who was especially energetic in helping to circulate
Beattie's works and in earning for him such emoluments as the
1773 pension. Just as important, however, is the shift in perspective signaled by the "pause" of the "gothic lyre." The poem has
opened in the first person, its disquisition on poverty and fame
serving as a kind of prelude to the story of Edwin, and to this extent
the narrator is established as a discernible, separate character. The
change finally signaled by the turn to Montagu is that while the
narrator has been trying to imagine independent grounds of
evaluation, via Edwin's training in nature, at the end of Book One
he appears to give up the attempt.

   In electing Montagu arbiter, Beattie may also be giving in to the
"conversational ideal" that Montagu represents and that combines uneasily with his own discursive skepticism.[52] Just as Edwin's
achievements will ultimately be confined to the notional, Beattie's
narrator remarks that the tale of Edwin is for the "leisure hour,"
and aims only to "please the gentle mind." Such statements,
which have corollaries in Beattie's private comments, are usually
used to justify the claim that *The Minstrel* provides a kind of escape
from the less congenial rigors of *The Essay on Truth* and Beattie's
morally charged professorial duties. This act of surrender may be
read as a sign of the importance of the larger discursive project,
and as Beattie's own modest ordering of the arts. It was always the
hope of the common sense theorists that "taste refined" would
work in concert with the perceptions and judgments of Nature's
children, a hope which is in practice deeply conservative. Opposed
to the scurrilities of fashion are the respectful intuitions of
the vulgar and the cultivated, but equivalent, insights of the
aristocrat. The poem has moved from the model of rugged, rural,
self-sufficient common sense to the model of cultivation and
sensibility with which Reid and Beattie had had to struggle. Yet in
his search for a usable example, Beattie is forced to shift frames of
reference, one might even say genres, entirely. The figure who
needs no patronage because the landscape is so liberal is suddenly
nudged aside by the patron the author needs.

However, my claim here is not that "the social" suddenly erupts, without Beattie's volition, to undo the structures that Beattie has tried to set up. On the contrary, it is a blatant act of authorial will and self-assertion for Beattie to call the gentle mind in as witness to the usefulness and propriety of what has gone before. The dedication to the patron is Beattie's opportunity to escape from the Humean solipsism that Book I is always on the verge of encountering, and it is also his opportunity to call on a different structure of remuneration and evaluation than the anti-aristocratic, fully market-based one that subtends so much of the rest of the poem. It is in giving in that Beattie here finds himself, and finds a gentle, intimate audience to counter the anonymous one whose spiritual health he has taken into his care, but with which he can never fully believe it is possible to converse.

III JAMES BEATTIE AND PROFESSIONALISM

The appearance of Montagu is not the end of the story. In *The Minstrel,* "the progress of genius" involves two unlike parts. Book I details the youthful Edwin's enlightening solitude. In Book II, published in 1773 after Beattie's reputation as a public moralist had been secured, Edwin is brought into contact with a hermit-figure, experienced in the ways of a corrupt urban culture, who provides Edwin with the bad news about human nature and human society: "For virtue lost, and ruin'd man, I mourn," he exclaims, and throughout, the hermit opposes the childish fantasies of the dreamy poet to the real hard work of social experience: "Fancy enervates, while it soothes the heart" (II.167; II.361). As David Hill Radcliffe describes it, "the two parts of *The Minstrel* can be construed either as a progressive sequence or as an unresolved opposition between Lockean and Aristotelian educational paradigms," that is, it is possible to read Edwin's tutorial in the second book as either a topcoat on the virtuous primer that gets laid on in the first, or as a rational corrective to the mis-teachings of nature.[53] Ann Yearsley, perhaps with a satirical agenda of her own, would claim to understand the hermit's culture and discipline as the factors that allow Edwin, finally, to speak.[54] Yet as the discussion of Hume in the previous chapter has already suggested, what the poem attempts to explain is, perhaps inherently, inexplicable, so that it is possible to find in the incompatibility of the two books another version of that insight about the relationship of talent, experience, and practice.

The second book is largely taken up with a denunciation of an unspecified, but nominally medieval, court culture, and we have already seen how Beattie has linked an unsurprising Country/ Patriot critique to his attack on Hume. Beattie's criticism of monarchical culture is elaborated in the *Essay*, where he argues that

> In courts, it seems requisite, for the sake of that order which is essential to dignity, to establish certain punctilios in dress, language, and gesture: there too, the most inviolable secrecy is expedient: and there, where men are always under the eye of their superiors, and for the most part engaged in the pursuits of ambition or interest, a smoothness of behaviour will naturally take place, which, among persons of ordinary talents, and ordinary virtue, must on many occasions degenerate into hypocrisy. The customs of the court are always imitated by the higher ranks; the middle ranks follow the higher; and the people come after as fast as they can. It is, however, in the last mentioned class, where nature appears with the least disguise: but, unhappily for moral science, the vulgar are seldom objects of curiosity, either to our philosophers, or historians.
>
> The influence of these causes, in distinguishing human sentiments, will, I presume, be greater or less, according as the monarchy partakes more or less of democratic principles. (302–303)

No position Beattie holds is incompatible with his acceptance of Montagu's aid or the King's pension. On the contrary, Beattie is a model of the independent northerner who gets attention by writing down only what he thinks, and who remains situated across the border despite various invitations to come south. (For example, his relationship with Montagu takes place at Sandelford or in correspondence, almost never at Montagu's salon in London). For Beattie, the system has worked, and his success redeems the system, marks the difference between the Franco-Humean dystopia that Bolingbroke could have loved and the United Kingdom whose moral and intellectual health he seeks, in print and in the classroom, to defend.

Yet the professional trajectory that appears to work out so neatly for Beattie and that may, with some adjustments, be read into the life of the hermit turns out to be impossible for Edwin. The second book, like the first, ends when praise of a patron interrupts a sequence detailing Edwin's professional development, and the Aristotelian and Lockean modes are here in full combat. Over the course of a dozen stanzas the hermit details the benefits

"Science," "Philosophy," and "Reason" have brought to an otherwise benighted populace, and Edwin "proceeds the path of Science to explore" (II.497). It temporarily appears as though there will be a confluence of Edwin's initially visionary nature and the utilitarian impulse which seems to have humanized his soul:

> Fancy now no more
> Wantons on fickle pinion through the skies;
> But, fix'd in aim, and conscious of her power,
> Aloft from cause exults to rise,
> Creation's blended stores arranging as she flies. (II.500–504)

The creative faculty is on the verge of taking on its full-blown cognitive and judgmental role, fusing and "arranging" experience in order to develop "new arts on Nature's plan" (II.509). One of Romantic writing's recurring dreams, that the writing of poetry will be superseded by more tangible kinds of service, is here embraced.

Yet if poetry intervenes in the supersession of poetry, its claims prove vulnerable, not to the viewpoint of the hermit, but to the fragmentary form of the poem itself. "The muse," we are told, still has Edwin's "fond and first regard," and Beattie goes on to anticipate the "sweet delirium" that Edwin will experience once his homely vernacular training is enhanced by the study of Virgil and Homer (II.517; 533). At this point, however, the narrative of Edwin's life comes to an end. Critics have thus been divided about whether we are to understand Edwin's future as poetic or prosaic, and whether we are to read Book II as a warning about poetry, a warning about the hermits of the world, or as something that does not quite cohere at the level of the lesson. Noting the formal elements of this interruption, Greg Kucich observes that while the eighteenth-century poets who wrote Spenserian fragments often took advantage of the incompletion of *The Faerie Queen* in order to avoid finishing their own epics, for Beattie, incompletion, licensed by Spenserian precedent, is functional: "The open indeterminacy of Edwin's conflict justifies a fragmented narrative structure that reinforces the new kind of divisive psychological experience controlling *The Minstrel* . . . . Where Spenser's 'broken text' implies the necessity of endless pilgrimaging in a fallen world, Beattie's even more radically inconclusive ending suggests the modern poet's perpetual conflict about his own aesthetic mission."[55] It is important to extend the point. "The modern poet's perpetual conflict" takes a variety of forms, and here the matter is not just whether it is more important to intervene or retreat, but what kinds of cultural apparatus would make intervention, or retreat, possible. For what service, finally, have Edwin's experiences prepared him?

The interruption of Book II is occasioned by a two-and-a-half stanza elegy on the death of John Gregory, a relative of Reid's and the long-time friend and supporter of Beattie's who had originally put Beattie in contact with Montagu. The elegy on Gregory is doubly significant, and the first point of significance is the generic role of the elegy itself. As Chapter 1 argues, the management of death is among the topics toward which poetry about the professions is especially inclined, and in the conversation between Coleridge and Cottle, the nature of teaching was a special matter of debate; Cottle's Henderson was an orthodox, helpful tutor, who willingly repeats his role in the afterlife, whereas Coleridge's Cottle, on the model of Lycidas, is a sublimely brave explorer who instructs by example. The conclusion of *The Minstrel* anticipates this dialogue, just as the poem's Spenserian sermonizing anticipates the form of Coleridge's "To an Author": "He sleeps in dust, and all the Muses mourn,/He, whom each virtue fired, each grace refin'd,/Friend, teacher, pattern, darling of mankind!/He sleeps in dust" (II.552–555). In contrast to Cottle and Coleridge, and this is significant given the orthodox version of divine order, human freedom, and consolation which *The Minstrel* presents as fact, Beattie takes no recourse to the language of the afterlife, professional or otherwise, when contemplating his absolute loss. Mourning becomes abdication, and this point bears directly on the didactic aspect of the poem; Gregory's death is a forceful negation not just of "the soft amusement of the vacant mind," but of the letter of the hermit's doctrine. No amount of highland stoicism imbibed by Edwin can prevent Beattie, in his own person, from crying out that, in Gregory's absence, he has no source of comfort left. Montagu is surely misinterpreting the poem on purpose when she writes that "I like much the conclusion, although it does not belong to the subject . . . . It is the sweetest office of the Minstrel, to sing the praises of a dear departed friend."[56] On the contrary, the subject has always been the office of the minstrel, while to sing Gregory's praises is, unsweetly, to bring the Minstrel's officiating to an untimely but necessary end.

The elegy also brings death to the minstrel by bringing a kind of space into the poem which will not support Edwin's dual pattern of growth. In this narrative, the natural spaces of Edwin's village and the surrounding scene are replaced, in Book II, by the single "flowery nook" where Edwin undergoes his intellectual training by the hermit (II.219). Once this tutelage begins, description is replaced almost entirely by rhetoric, as the hermit's voice, in conversation with Edwin, overtakes the earlier part of the poem's descriptive agenda. As I have suggested, even the inspiring world of natural signs that dominates Book I raises paradoxical questions about the relationship of space to psychology. Beattie's official position must be that nature teaches Edwin what Edwin already knows, but the minstrel's refusal of the social and the persuasive force of the hermit's satirical utilitarianism combine to suggest that the poet's mind is dangerously receptive, even to contradictory impressions, as those impressions are fomented by the movement through landscape which organizes the poem. Edwin's judgments should be spontaneous and sure, but they merely succeed each other. Thus the scene formed by the procession and the grave, what might be called a "representational space" called up from the generic conditions of elegy and opposed to the visual and rhetorical elements of much of the rest of the poem, arrests Edwin's development just when the vulnerability of that process to accident and chance is becoming most clear.

Where Montagu's "gentle mind" has been made to stand for the intimate, private relationship between an individual writer and a single, approving patron, the elegiac stanzas that conclude the poem suggest shared, collective grief: "With trembling step, to join yon weeping train,/I haste, where gleams funereal glare around,/And, mix'd with shrieks of woe, the knells of death resound" (II.546–549). The death-knell replaces the lyre, which in the previous stanza had been "warbling at will through each harmonious maze," for the mazy puzzles the lyre had been about to transform into music – in short, those questions of human evil with which *The Minstrel* supposedly grapples – reassert themselves in light of what has happened to Gregory, whose death leaves Beattie "to unavailing woe" (II.560). It is true that the procession of muses which Beattie briefly pictures, and seeks to join, quickly disappears, and Beattie appears once more to have rejected the social cure in favor of melancholy, a decision for which he is unapologetic: "'Tis meet that I should mourn: flow forth afresh, my tears" (II.567). Even in grief, however, by remaining at the gravesite Beattie remains in company. That is, while he is apparently frozen in a neurotic act of ever-unfinished mourning, he is also, finally, inhabiting a space, with a history, that enables the poet to give himself over to affect instead of argument.

It is not my intention to build a reading of *The Minstrel* only out of this kind of paradox, but also to indicate how these tensions are produced by the professional situation that would make them meaningful to the Lake poets. By affiliating his patrons with the fragmentation of *The Minstrel*, Beattie performs an act of double-rejection. He brings the story of Edwin to a close, while at the same time, he finds out how patronage and professionalism are equally fatal to the kind of independence he wants to imagine. This may be made clearer by a brief consideration of which cultural forces, exactly, each of Beattie's patrons represent. Wealthy and privileged, Montagu's activities demonstrate the persistence of the patron class in its purest form, but as an active manager of her husband's coal mines and as an important publishing critic, she complicates any equation of aristocracy, or femininity, with ease.[57] The gentle mind for whom Beattie has nominally given up his broad audience is both industrial and polemical, a productive and famous literary figure whose applause is never simply private. On the contrary, Montagu's approval always contains a public component. Her service to him largely amounts to the gathering of lucre and renown.

Gregory presents a different kind of case. He is a physician, and beyond that, he is a lecturer in medicine at Edinburgh and a figure who becomes famous for his role in establishing the ethical basis of modern medical practice. Probably best known to literary scholars for his "Letters to my Daughter," one of Mary Wollstonecraft's polemical targets, Gregory's observations on professional training are more interesting than his orthodox views of female education. Firmly holding that the discipline of medicine did not yet have a comprehensive view of its own subject, he encouraged his students to attend carefully to lay advice, so that his professionalism was a challenge to the specialist mysteries of the monopolistic practitioner as such.[58] Further, Gregory perceived the humane aspects of Humean sympathy that Beattie was anxious to deny, going so far as to adopt some version of it to ground his comments on the relationships of doctors to patients.[59] His version of medical practice is a mirror-image of Beattie's version of the skeptical philosopher: "Disorders of the imagination may be as properly the object of a physician's attention as a disorder of the body ... but it requires great address and good sense in a physician to manage them properly" (104). Reid saw no hope for the real lunatic and assumed that the metaphysical lunatic would have to be self-curing. Gregory has noticed what might be called the secondary mechanism of intersubjective influence that Beattie found so destructive, the mechanism whereby emotional causes and effects are willfully transferred, but he demonstrates that it can be used for good as well as ill.

It is easy enough to conclude that the physician's self-mastery in the face of disease is really the point, but at least one element of Gregory's argument makes it inadequate to stop there. In the same passage, Gregory goes on to lament that victims of "nervous ailments" are often treated badly by physicians when they are poor, but "foster[ed] with the utmost care and apparent sympathy" among rich patients, "there being no diseases, in the stile of the trade, so lucrative as those of the nervous kind." He thus demonstrates how the modern professional will be positioned outside of class differences according to an ethic of service. Rich and poor, in being treated alike, are similarly brought to acknowledge the "proper authority and dignity" of the practitioner, even when this acknowledgment is tacit. The point is related to the equitable, rational fee structure which Gregory has in mind. We do not have to forget that the doctor gets paid, and differently by different people, according to their means. Gregory only wants to insist that payment is separate from professional sympathy.

A glance at the working lives of Beattie, Montagu, and Gregory, two Scots and an Englishwoman whose relationships are held together at least in part by a recognizable, late-century combination of literacy and piety, provides a reminder, if one were needed, of how complex the status structure is to which Beattie responds. Nonetheless, certain symmetries may be described. To the extent that Montagu and Gregory each pursue highly specialized vocations, medicine (classically) and estate management (less so), they represent the rise of those forces that would coalesce into the form of the modern professions. To the extent that each remains embedded in the systems of patronage, piety, and deference that underlay arrangements of "clientage not class," their careers are allied with an aristocratic ethos. In accepting their aid and in singing their praises, Beattie is visibly the bard of both the aristocracy, in his attention to Montagu, and professionalism, in his elegy to Gregory, but insofar as Montagu brings the minstrel's childhood to an end, and the death of Gregory similarly brings the entire poem to a halt, both potentialities, patronage and the professional marketplace, appear to be rejected. It would be possible, given the sense of these particular endings, to associate Edwin's career with Gregory's, but there is too much that distinguishes them. In particular, the complex of associations in which the money-earning physician must help, but also control, rich and poor clients alike separates him from the absolutely independent bard of Beattie's dreams.

Finally, I have only skirted around the issue of Beattie's own relationship to professional identity. As a professor in Scotland, Beattie was in a position to experience real professional growth, but he was also implicated in a system that was based largely on patronage.[60] While his academic success following his rural boyhood in Laurencekirk is a reminder of Scottish education's relative openness to merit, church and university were dominated, in Beattie's experience, by the Moderates of the "Scottish Enlightenment" who were largely drawn from connected, professional families and whose fashionable acceptance of writers such as Hume irritated the more orthodox.[61] Patronage in the Scottish church, organized around the institution of the lay gift that had replaced the influence of the presbytery, was also a matter of controversy.[62] Reid, for example, was initially rejected by the parish to which King's College presented him out of "an aversion to the laws of patronage," although his biographer assures us that the parishioners came to love him; on the other hand, it is evident that he spent more time on his philosophical disquisitions than on his ministry.[63] Beattie's resistance to Hume, that is, cuts close to his own professional life, and it is not going too far to speculate that this is one of the reasons *The Minstrel* remains trapped in Edwin's childhood. In the imaginary highlands of the poem, the "wayward wight" requires only the recognition of the hermit to sustain his claim to uniqueness, or at least adequacy. The adult world, as the hermit not-so-incidentally teaches, may be a less sensible place. Beattie's hatred of fashionable sophistry has an evident personal component.

One final fact about Beattie's professional life should help explain why I prefer to take Beattie, rather than Gray or Goldsmith, as the central mid-century precursor of the Lake school's form of professionalism. Neither Gray's ensconcement at Oxford nor Goldsmiths' entrepreneurial exertions are irrelevant to the Lake poets' self-conceptions, and Goldsmith's early consideration of church and medicine is yet one more reminder that the full-time writer and the learned professional often stem from overlapping populations. Beattie's encounter in this regard is akin but more acute. As a young man, he had been destined for the Presbyterian Church, but he became a schoolteacher, and eventually a man of letters, instead. During the 1770s, while his reputation as the arbiter of "Truth" was firm, among the best ways his supporters south of the border could find to reward him was to offer him various places in the English church, but he consistently rejected these. Among his stated reasons are two which stand out. The first is his fear that if he were to accept preferment, it might appear as though the *Essay on Truth* had been written out of self-interest; and "if my book has any tendency to do good, as I flatter myself it has, I would not for the wealth of the Indies do anything to counteract that tendency."[64] The bard of truth must continue to distance himself from certain kinds of ambition, but this does not mean he refuses attention or reward. It only means that certain mechanisms of reward reflect merit adequately, while others have become suspect.

The second reason is related to the first:

It has also been hinted to me by several persons of very sound judgment that what I have written, or may hereafter write, in favour of Religion has a chance to be more attended to if I continue a layman, than if I was to become a clergyman.[65]

In fact, these two reasons are actually one. Because the Anglican Church appeared to have become primarily a means of distributing patronage, if Beattie were to enter it, the gesture would automatically be understood by the cynical as self-interested, and not, for example, as the spontaneous expression of a vocational calling or as the thoughtful assumption of a different kind of pastoral mission. For the same reason, as explored at some length in Chapter 1, the clerical profession in the mid-eighteenth-century has had its influence "abated among the bulk of mankind," which is why, it will be recalled, Young's *Night Thoughts* is presented as lay speech even though its acknowledged author is Rector of Welwyn. In life as well as in *The Minstrel*, Beattie's most profound if also most typical professional gestures involve the rejection of poor alternatives. It had become clear that some version of professional identity on the model of Gregory and Reid, and even on the model of Montagu, was historically imminent, and that this model had the attractive element of allowing for a self-sufficient and coherent structure of rewards.[66] What Beattie understood, however, was that this professionalism would always remain indebted to the kinds of contingent interactions that he had diagnosed in the case of Hume. Montagu and Gregory are trustworthy, but trust can never go beyond individuals. Thus, while Edwin's professional development appears to create a specialist who may speak for all, a common-sense sage whose vocation would inevitably be to teach about man, nature, and human life, his experience of experience marks just the skepticism he had hoped to defeat.

I have used the term near-enthusiasm in the course of this discussion in order to distinguish Beattie's mild, experience-bound providentialism from the more frankly visionary tradition that connects Smart and Blake to the late seventeenth century. The convergence is evident enough in the Romantic debt to Beattie, which may be coupled with Geoffrey Hartman's infinitely suggestive observation that "Wordsworth's poetry ... carried the Puritan quest for evidence of election into the most ordinary emotional contexts."[67] In the next section of this book, I will consider the possibilities for the metaphorical, poetic itinerancy that the Lake poets discovered in the wake of Savage's appropriation of everything and Beattie's rejection of everything. In order to do so, it will be necessary to consider another professional issue. At stake is the competition between the institutions of the Established Church and the evangelists, Methodists and dissenters, whose social claims grow in urgency as the century comes to a close.

PART III

Romantic itinerants

CHAPTER 4

Authority and the itinerant cleric

When Richard Savage and James Beattie confront the institutions of patronage, they address elements of professional identity, such as the self-evaluation of merit and the proper use of experience, that they would want to quarantine from patrons and the market-place alike. By the 1790s, when the Lake poets begin writing their own wandering verse, itinerancy and vagrancy connect new versions of the poetic career to specific late-century concerns, re-focusing the wanderer trope and involving it in different fields of reference. Thus, critics such as Gary Harrison have associated Romantic "wandering" with homelessness, a special problem in an era of warfare and economic upheaval; as he puts it, the "increasing numbers of discharged soldiers and destitute beg-gars" in the late eighteenth century means that the "ennobling poverty" of the traditional minstrel "threatens to become dis-abling indigence" at the level of the poetic character.[1] Others have emphasized that the actual mobility of the Lake poets and their doubles is a marker of class privilege, since, in the 1790s, "deliberate excursive walking" is a new activity for the "relatively well-to-do and educated."[2] All suggest that the poets, with Wordsworth as the defining example, experience a paradoxical form of authorship wherein poverty and obscurity, and success and honor, are closely related. The long developmental tale of *The Prelude* may be said to recuperate the poet's suspect wandering by closing it out with a suffusing statement of vocational purpose: "[W]hat we have loved/others will love, and we may teach them how," the poem finally states, and the mission that joins Wordsworth and Coleridge separates them from the mere beggar as well as from Beattie's less conclusively drawn minstrel.[3]

What appears to be directly referential, however, the population of late-century texts by late-century vagrants and by affluent speakers who share and transcend their condition, involves other acts of mediation, and it is to one such that I now turn. Over the course of the decade, as Wordsworth, Southey, and Coleridge, having rejected potential places in the Anglican Church, sought to establish their professional identities, a counterpart of their efforts was provided by the itinerant preacher, a figure who had several implications for dissent, Methodism, "enthusiasm," and the conditions of evangelical speech and pastoral care. A central agent in the ecclesiastical landscape, the itinerant preacher embodied a kind of traveling authority that could be at odds with old institutions or could promise to rejuvenate them. The itinerant's efficacy rebuked the system of rewards upon which those institutions were organized, and so, unlike the gentleman and the beggar, and unlike the related case of Edward Young, he or she directly represented the potential for professional reform. Itinerant clerics and Lake poets each respond to failures in eighteenth-century institutions by pursuing self-authorized professional work, and both recreate an informal but highly specialized series of qualifying experiences.

All three Lake poets were close observers of ecclesiological debate, but more important than the writers' direct familiarity with itinerancy is the effect itinerancy has on the ecology of the professions.[4] As Jon Mee has demonstrated, "the need to distinguish pathological from noble enthusiasm was always at work" in Romantic poetics, and a related set of distinctions is necessary regarding the itinerant preacher, who is the physical embodiment of enthusiastic practice.[5] As Abbott points out, the clergy, like other professionals, are engaged in the interprofessional competition over local tasks, and Corfield notes an element of intraprofessional rivalry that should also be borne in mind: "Unlike the lawyers who increasingly spoke of one 'legal profession' with its two complementary branches, clergymen did not see themselves as part of a single clerical profession. Instead, there were numerous religious disputes, some measured, some very acrimonious."[6] Or, as Deryck Lovegrove writes of clerical itinerancy in general, its true significance "come[s] not so much in geographical mobility and the capability of rapid extension, as in the melting down of professional attitudes and structures, and in the maintenance of the subsequent state of flux throughout the critical wartime period."[7] Itinerancy is a structuring principle and a potential weak point in the other learned professions, as well, and its broadest implications go beyond the status of the clergy. The itinerant quack is one character against whom the legitimate medical practitioner is traditionally measured, as Southey would later dramatize in his 1837 *The Doctor*, while the Assizes represent both the national authority and the carnivalesque spectacle of the law.[8] For the itinerant minister, however, mobility itself becomes an extension of the individual's potential to resist or to reorganize traditional structures of training, evaluation, and reward. As he or she is closest to the desire for an invisible or self-guaranteeing certification, the itinerant preacher provides the clearest analog for the concerns of the Lake poet.

The fit between preachers and poets is no less revealing because there is some dissonance between the poets' gentlemanly expectations and the preacher's un-genteel persona. Although intrigued by the enthusiastic discourse with which evangelical itinerancy is marked, and discontent with the state of the Church, none of the Lake writers could fully embrace itinerancy as they believed it was practiced. Coleridge's 1795 description of Robespierre as a blend of "enthusiasm" and "gloom" speaks to widespread satirical images of the evangelical preacher and, in his or her itinerant guise, to the possible danger such free-roaming characters pose to any stable social order.[9] Forecasting the reasoning of his *Lay Sermons*, written more than a decade later, Coleridge indicates where he thinks the border lies between a destructive and a benevolent itinerancy: "He would appear to me to have adopted the best as well as the most benevolent mode of diffusing Truth," he writes, "who uniting the zeal of the Methodist with the views of the Philosopher, should be *personally* among the Poor, and teach them their *Duties* in order that he may render them susceptible of their *Rights*."[10] Individually applied, mobile zeal could make for an effective ministry, but the actual Methodist has no systematic, "philosophical" principles, and this absence corrupts his evangelical just as it pre-empts his pastoral mission.

Underlying the poets' response to traveling enthusiasts, as expressed in this instance by Coleridge, is the friction generated by the nearness of the inspired and un-housed itinerant preacher to the generically attractive roving bard. Physical wandering, the compulsive exercise of a strange power of speech, and resistance to the existing systems of intellectual work and patronage all associate the poet with the itinerant preacher, who is a competitor and a double in the search for new ways to minister to the populace. These effects move between life-practice and literary representation. The itinerant is defined not only by a series of culminating moments of practice, his or her sermons, but by the movement across the landscape that links them. Yet this movement is only contingently tied to the salvation of others and is undertaken by travelers whose own salvation has already been established elsewhere. It is either meritorious or simply useful, not, in itself, transformational.[11] The effects of travel are equally oblique for the Lake poets, who are generically and biographically tied to wandering but discover that traditional schemas such as the pilgrimage or the metaphorical "life-is-a-journey" are no longer aesthetically productive. As Geoffrey Hartman has observed, at least for Wordsworth a goal-oriented pilgrimage yields to a "negative way" – the Romantic wanderer is neither pilgrim nor revolutionary, but "typifies a new vision" in which "the natural and the supernatural" are joined together by the actions of a third term, the imagination.[12] I argue, however, that the poet is never entirely separate from a landscape that continues, as in Savage and Beattie, to represent both his experience and training and the conditions of his work. As Beattie had discovered, once the landscape in the poem becomes just another expression of cumulative experience, a peculiarly Humean phenomenology threatens the stability of intellectual and public order just as it threatens the distinction between cause and effect.

As the following chapter details, the question of itinerant work provides a series of test-cases for the Lake poets' adoptions of the conventions of the traveling bard. The writers strive to readjust the connection between the fore-grounded poetic professional and the also-professional background, discovering along the way that itinerancy provides a negative of ideal professional autonomy. In turn, Chapter 5 argues, these experiments lead them back to a central predecessor who is a failed professional, a wandering poet, and an enthusiast all at once – William Cowper.

I ITINERANTS AND ROMANTICS

The eighteenth-century history of professional authority is partially recapitulated in the history of itinerant preaching, which starts out as an act of reform within the establishment but does not remain there. Beginning with John Wesley's 1735 ministry in Georgia, and continuing with the open-air preaching that the Wesleys and George Whitefield undertook at the end of the 1730s, itinerancy was one of the main vehicles of Methodist preaching. By the 1760s, dissenters had also adopted itinerancy, while other groups, notably the Countess of Huntingdon's Calvinist connection, continued to grow in importance.[13] In all of its guises, the practice met immediate resistance. Stereotypical condemnations of "Methodees" as hypocritical, greedy, and prurient complemented establishment hostility toward itinerant preaching, which, in its use of lay practitioners and its independence from the parish system, posed an evident threat to the order of the Church. The lay itinerant's supposed opportunism and ignorance were all the more problematic because they conflicted with a properly functioning division of labor. As the bookseller James Lackington writes about an acquaintance who has taken up a circuit, "I am only sorry as lately he was an honest tradesman, that he should have so much spiritual quixotism in him, as at thirty years of age to shut up his shop and turn preacher, without being able to read his primer."[14] The forces that swell the ranks of readers and writers also threaten to overturn barriers of entry in other areas of intellectual work.

By the 1790s, Methodism's break with the Church and dissent's escalating use of itinerancy generate an increasingly hostile and broad-based response.[15] A writer in the *Anti-Jacobin Review* responds to the latter phenomenon with pristine paranoia and emphasizes the dangers posed by itinerancy's general structure:

The dissenters have endeavoured to disseminate their political principles and to overturn the established constitution of church and state. Being baffled in these daring attempts by the good sense and rising spirit of the nation, they have lately pursued another course: they have attempted to promote their designs by means of religion, and by sending forth missionaries of their doctrines, under the name of dissenting ministers, in different parts of the kingdom .... There is, therefore, the strongest presumption to conclude, that associations are formed for the purpose of maintaining itinerant preachers, who, with their religious doctrines, propagate sentiments of disaffection to the established government.[16]

This statement bears little relation to the actual aims of dissenting itinerants in 1798, and the politically motivated, conspiratorial

"Jacobins" here described are essentially fictional. However, this writer unveils an important set of concerns and signals a shift in the connection between wandering and the establishment. While Richard Savage had been able to comment freely on ecclesiastical controversy, his work as a satirist and a polemicist was only obliquely reflected in the narrative form of *The Wanderer*, a poem which unfolds as a cry for professional independence but also sustains at least a working regard for the then-new settlement. By the end of the century, the most recent version of that settlement is under attack, and the evaluative and political stakes of the wandering figure as a sheerly literary device have been renewed and re-emphasized. Free dissemination is now being framed as, inherently, the dissemination of ideas that are enthusiastically subversive of a consensual order, one based on the "good sense" of the layman working in concert with the traditional organization of church and state.

Wesley's pre-revolutionary defense of the preparation of his own itinerant preachers strikes at the heart of traditional professionalism, at least as institutional conservatives wanted to perceive it. Himself an able logician and classicist, Wesley dispatches the ideal of the "learned gentleman" without mercy:

> Some of those who now preach are unlearned. They neither understand the ancient languages nor any of the branches of philosophy. And yet this objection might have been spared by those who have frequently made it; because *they* are unlearned too (though accounted otherwise). They have not themselves the very thing they require in others.[17]

Wesley's argument is genuinely radical in its suggestion that entire structures of deference and trust are based on a widespread fraud. The supposed credentials of the nation's intellectual leadership are false, he declares, propped up not by actual attainment but by what amounts in the end to utter cronyism:

> Men in general are under a great mistake with regard to what is called "the learned world." They do not know, they cannot easily imagine, how little learning there is among them. I do not speak of *abstruse* learning, but of what all divines, at least of any note, are supposed to have, viz. the knowledge of the tongues, at least Latin, Greek, Hebrew, and of the common arts and sciences.[18]

"How few men of learning, so called, understand Hebrew"? he goes on to wonder, before calling into question the average learned gentleman's facility with classical literature or "the general principles of logic."[19]

In contrast to "the learned world," the unlearned itinerants of the Wesleyan connection, who are only a little less ignorant of logic and languages than most of their fraudulent establishment counterparts, are far more knowledgeable about their main concern, the saving of souls. This successful specialization separates them from the unlearned learned gentlemen whose specific training is as weak as their general knowledge:

Indeed in the one thing [Wesley's lay ministers] profess to know they are not ignorant men. I trust there is not one of them who is not able to go through such an examination in substantial, practical, experimental divinity, as few of our candidates for holy orders, even in the university (I speak it with sorrow and shame, and in tender love) are able to do. But O! what manner of examination do the most of these candidates go through? And what proof are the *testimonials* commonly brought ... either of their piety or knowledge, to whom are entrusted those sheep which God hath purchased with his own blood![20]

"Experimental" religion, religion that is to be judged by its actual effects, is the measure of the preacher as it should be the measure of other professional practitioners. Wesley is quite aware of other kinds of learned men who might, but generally do not, "profess" falsely. More than once, he would compare the ordained priest to a physician who has trained at Dublin and been examined by his peers, but who subsequently fails to cure any of his patients.[21] In noting the technical excellence of medical training at Trinity, and suggesting that the Dublin physician is unlikely to be as ineffective as he claims Anglican preachers have become, Wesley offers a test for all professions: systematically apply means to ends, like good foreign medical schools and truly converted preachers do, or fail, like the patronage-ridden institutions of the old regime.

"Enthusiasm" cannot be reduced to "Methodism" any more than the complex entity of eighteenth-century evangelicalism can be accounted for only in terms of Wesley's ongoing, essentially consistent vindication of its Methodist form. Wesley's mid-century rhetoric, however, is a scholar's defense of the inspired amateur, and it is telling not only for what he eliminates but for what he tries to retain. Drawing on the post-Baconian, post-Lockean bent of intellectual inquiry, Wesley's comments and his organizational

practice indicate that preaching and salvation depend on modifying, but retaining, the official division of intellectual labor. That
his experimentalism runs roughshod over centuries of elaborate
debate about the "assurance" of salvation is, among other things,
a rhetorical tactic that sustains the breadth of his appeal by sim-
plifying his central claim.[22] At the same time, institutional order
remains important for him. Defending the special role of the
Anglican priesthood, he would spend his life monitoring the
border that separates the preacher from the ordained minister,
although this institutional conservatism, which grounded the
effort to keep Methodism within the Church of England, would
last for only a few years after his death.[23] His attack on the failings
of the Hanoverian Church was, as his critics had always charged,
uncontainable, and Romantic itinerancy echoes this regard for
the talented outsider as it is combined with the learned perspective of the founder whose real training and experience have been
both experimental and literary.

   To consider Coleridge and Southey in the 1790s is to be struck
by the parallels between their life-stories and the progress of itinerant preaching, parallels that emerge because the field of religious work (and of professional work more generally) and the
individual careers of the authors are under the same set of
demographic and political pressures. In 1795, as Coleridge was
reaching the height of his radical activities and emphasizing the
opposition between intellect and conscience and establishment
politics, the Wesleyan conference was breaking with the Church of
England. (Huntingdon had seceded fourteen years earlier.) From
1797 to 1800, as undenominational itinerancy became active
throughout England, Coleridge and Southey, whose own radical
projects had been tempered by widespread conservative reaction,
published substantial collections of poetry, including Coleridge's
Poems on Various Subjects and Southey's *Poems*, both of which served
to redefine the radicals as itinerant poets and directly engaged the
question of poetic wandering.[24] At the turn of the century, as
dissenting evangelism became more organized, Coleridge and
Southey sought to consolidate their own slowly stabilizing personal and professional identities, Coleridge through a series of freelance literary commitments, Southey in the production of *Madoc*
and in the study of law.[25] Both the radical intellectual poet and the
itinerant cleric were, in the middle of the 1790s, alienated from

establishment authority, and each worked through the latter part of the decade to solve the problem of their own authorization.

What it means to be established and what it means to pursue a religious calling are both subjects that emerge when Coleridge and Southey consider their professional options. In Coleridge's case, the threat of poverty and the possibilities of itinerancy are intertwined. In January of 1796, while acting as a lay preacher on the *Watchman* tour, he could write that "My poor crazy ark has been tossed to and fro on an ocean of business, and I long for the Mount Ararat on which it is to rest."[26] His fatigue and ill health on the tour are offset by the energizing experience of meeting, conversing with, and preaching to a multitude of more or less receptive strangers, and "business" is just the ocean which keeps the ship of his literary career afloat. Exactly a month later, however, back at his mother-in-law's house in Bristol (just prior to the move to Nether Stowey), Coleridge laments to Cottle:

I think I should have been more thankful, if [God] had made me a journeyman Shoemaker, instead of an 'Author by Trade'! – I have left my friends, I have left plenty – I have left that ease which would have enabled me to secure a literary immortality at the price of pleasure, and to have given the public works conceived in moments of inspiration, and published with leisurely solicitude.[27]

The journeyman shoemaker is enviable precisely because he does not journey, and Coleridge opposes the necessity of writing for a living to that "leisurely solicitude" which is the only real path to "immortality." His despair is brought on, for the most part, by his domestic situation. He is not only banished but fettered, restrained from the kind of spiritual mobility that the writing of poetry requires:

So I am forced to write for bread – write the high flights of poetic enthusiasm, when every minute I am hearing a groan of pain from my wife ... My happiest moments for composition are broken in on by the reflection of – I must make haste! – I am too late! – I am already months behind! – I have received my pay beforehand! – O way-ward and desultory Spirit of Genius! Ill canst thou brook a task-master! The hand of obligation wounds thee, like a scourge of scorpions – .[28]

Defining creativity in terms of "flight" and "enthusiasm," Coleridge finds himself grounded. He must write himself into an independence, but the only way to do that is under the hand of the taskmaster whose scorpion-like scourge is the enemy of wayward "Genius." Worse, the "scourge" is here wielded, at least figuratively, by Cottle, the patron who has paid Coleridge "beforehand." The image thus expresses Coleridge's complicated position within the framework of industrial patronage and marketing.

Even when, in 1798, Coleridge's financial position has become more secure, he is troubled by the double-edged possibilities of forced motion. Writing to Wordsworth after receiving the Wedgwood settlement, Coleridge says of the visiting duties of the minister that:

I perceive clearly, that without great courage & perseverance in the use of the monosyllable, NO! I should have been plunged in a very maelstrom of visiting – whirled round, and round, never changing yet always moving.[29]

Perpetual motion is autonomy negated, particularly because the "maelstrom" Coleridge fears is driven by the status-destroying proximity of the practitioner to the client.[30] Threatened by the demands of his audience, Coleridge contends that only the "courage and perseverance" to insist on professional autonomy, which here means the right to command his own time and that of his patrons, could have made the job of minister worth having. A doctrinal problem is in this way combined with an organizational one. As Daniel E. White has shown, Coleridge's post-Anglican Unitarianism distances itself from property-and-trade based forms of "old dissent"; practically speaking, it may be added, this ideal audience is subsumed in the larger, old-dissenting one, since Coleridge meets precious few "Eolian" philosophers on the *Watchman* tour.[31] Because Coleridge's actual clientage is not "philosophical" enough, his relationship to it reproduces the structures of patron/audience and client/preacher, not professional philosopher and client audience, that it is supposed to cure.

Professional work presumes a certain level of mobility, both to facilitate training and experience and to allow for the establishment of a practice within inter- and intraprofessional marketplaces, and in this way, mobility can lead to domestic fixedness.[32] The sequence also applies to itinerant preachers, whose supposed threat to order is not only that they wander, but that they might found chapels and marry into communities – although the entrepreneurial motivations of itinerants can only be speculated about, mobility can lead to new establishments, or to new professional structures that encroach on the old.[33] From the point-of-view of the practitioner, the flip-side of entrepreneurial reward is the element of risk. Wandering labor may lead to a new home, but it may result in, or be the result of, homelessness. It may impoverish or establish the itinerant preacher and the un-established poet alike, just as the experience of enthusiastic transport may reveal a providential fittedness of things or prove to be unsettling and uncanny. Upon emigrating to North America in 1794, for example, Joseph Priestley opposes his forced journey and the disruption of his domestic arrangements to the stability of scripture and of the City of Heaven: "All the connexions we form here, the most endearing and important ones, are slight and transient," he offers, whereas the city of God in Heaven is "as much more fixed and stable, as it is in itself of more value."[34] Endemic fluctuations among security, vocational displacement, and vocational permanence connect the Lake poets' circumstances to a thoroughly diffused language of itinerant work.[35]

For Southey, who never takes up an actual ministry, alternative kinds of service will remain a potential way of revising institutions that demand it and of anticipating forms of autonomy that are otherwise hard to imagine. A 1793 attack on "ambition," launched while Southey is still at Oxford, expresses his revivalist anger at establishment quiescence, but at first he contemplates reform instead of dissolution:

Prebendaries Deaneries and Bishopricks may be hunted by the fools and rogues in black who wish them. I shall feel prouder in a coarse country jacket digging in my own garden than if tricked out with lawn sleeves or the purple tiara and more like a minister of Christ when easing the woes of Poverty and smoothing the bed of Death than of bellowing blasphemy on the 30th of January, or supporting Intolerance on the wool sack.[36]

Southey, Edmund Seward and Richard Lewis had argued with their friends that Church incomes should be limited, an argument they won, Southey explains, largely because they were "all three designed" to become clergymen.[37] In this case, Southey's disgust at a martyrology that includes Charles I, executed on January 30 and commemorated in the Book of Common Prayer, evinces both a radical's attitude and a Puritan's. This attitude complements the secular version of English Jacobinism that generally accounts for

Southey's youthful subversiveness, but the two are not synon-
ymous. It may be a joke, but it is a self-aware and revealing one, that
he signs the letter quoted above "yr enthusiastic friend," aligning
himself with forces both inside and outside the Church that
oppose an intense experimentalism to the established order.
Southey's humble parish cleric and Wesley's itinerant preacher
each reproach the established Church order, not only because
they both take over the Church's work, its pastoral and evangelical
functions now being wrested from the feckless placeholder, but
from the point-of-view of the practitioner's identity. The practitioner foregoes certain kinds of rewards (on the one hand) and an
inappropriate but officially certified training (on the other) in his
or her development of a new, enthusiastic kind of ministry.

In his unaffected pastoral behavior, Southey's ideal cleric
admittedly looks more like Goldsmith's "village preacher" than
an evangelical itinerant. Southey's fantasy of self-sufficiency will
ultimately lead, however, to dreams of mobility and domesticity
that echo Priestley's heavenly consolation and remove the professional, domestic establishment from its middle-class context.
Southey's version of agricultural independence anticipates the
other Lake writers' similar fantasies of a cottage existence, and it
gets its fullest expression in his and Coleridge's proposed Pantisocracy, where a community of laborers, working by hand in the
daytime and with their minds at night, aim to be set free from
contemporary vocational politics by a massive relocation across the
Atlantic. The revolutionary ideal of Pantisocracy allows Southey
and Coleridge, in Nicholas Roe's words, to "transpose ... one
major Romantic topos, the millennium, onto an equally prominent Romantic theme, the reclusive life of retreat and retirement," but, crucially, their "retreat" is a retreat toward a new kind
of work. The millennial and the domestic are already implicated in
the writers' response to institutional failure.[38]

Although Southey's place on the vocational map has shifted by
1798, his understanding of professionalism, vagrancy, and dissent
continues to shape how he imagines his working life, and in ways
that exhibits failed as well as successful acts of professional identification. In an important series of remarks, he begins by drawing
an unsurprising distinction between the impoverished vagrant
and the professional gentleman that seems to allow men-of-letters,
at least by association, to take on the burden of middle-class

leadership. Commenting on the inhumane administration of the Poor Laws, Southey argues that "affluent" members of society should take greater responsibility: "Clergymen might do much – and medical men, & it would be well if the parish offices were accepted by persons more respectable."[39] At first sight, this new paternalism seems to fit in with the claims of an educated class that is naturally quick to equate affluence with respectability, and it is an especially Southeyan brand of prescience to categorize the responsibilities of the professional gentleman and the moral failings of the poor in such terms.

It becomes clear, however, that the relationship of this individual Romantic writer to the professions cannot simply be a matter of direct affiliation. Southey is himself training for the law at this time, and he is involved in the measurement of at least two separate kinds of "independence," neither of which can be reconciled with his announced belief in professional rectitude. Not quite a month later, he is specific about professional ethics, and he is opposed to them:

You ask me my opinion on how a lawyer should act. They tell me he should undertake any cause, because if he refuses to be the advocate he makes himself the judge. My dear friend this may be true — but I never go to my head for an answer when my heart is ready with one. [C]ertainly I would not plead in a bad cause. I *feel* it would be wrong. I have no love for the profession — but I have a strong love of independence, & would labour for it.[40]

While the collective identity of lawyers demands a suspension of individual judgment, Southey depends on his "heart" to keep him "independent" from the corporate body. At the same time, while the practice of law threatens one's moral or ethical independence, it does offer to provide financial security and with it, intellectual freedom. As Southey puts it, a career as a lawyer will provide financial "independence and leisure" for his "favorite studies."[41] Professional life should provide shelter for a private man of letters who is at best individuated, at worst alienated from the facts of his public career – a familiar plan, and one that is here made possible by the patronage of a school-friend, Charles Wynn, as well as by Southey's educational background. Even if Southey-the-poet, or Southey-the-lawyer, were to take an active role in local administration, it could only be as an enthusiastic individual, not as the representative of an established profession.

Inhabiting this letter of the law as an unrealized possibility is another, alternative profession. Still reflecting on his own discontent, Southey notes that:

> [O]f all the modes of life[,] that of a clergyman would best suit my habits & feelings. I should have been happy & useful in the church had my creed permitted it. [W]ere I again at liberty to choose my way of life I should not hesitate at becoming a dissenting minister.[42]

Having begun this disquisition by depicting a modern order wherein the professional classes administrate the lives of the vagrant poor, Southey ends by contrasting the financial security of those classes to the dissenter's ministerial "liberty," interpreted here as the freedom of life-choice which has been curtailed for Southey by his marriage. Professionals have both responsibility and leisure, yet, Southey discovers, the cost of this independence is (or would be) a fixation of identity to which the free dissenter, he allows himself to imagine, need not submit. A dissenting ministry, in this vision, would close the gap between the collective responsibilities of the professions and the complex privations of the individual practitioner.

Southey's opposition of dissent and freedom to professional independence, articulated so that the poets' enthusiasm is contained or framed by his professional and domestic circumstances, evokes metaphors that have been widely used to account for "modernity" itself. In doing so, it also outlines the resistance the Lake poets will express toward emerging professional forms. In J. G. A. Pocock's standard account, capital mobility, which amounts to a new "mobility of property," follows the financial revolution of the late seventeenth century and allows for greater vocational specialization. Because this process results in a paid soldiery, it also dislocates "virtue" from the virtues of the warrior/aristocrat, and for Pocock the sequence begins the genesis of modern "liberalism."[43] Jurgen Habermas's version of the modern/liberal order is another that reiterates the equation of modernity with mobility. For Habermas, "the traffic in commodities and news created by early capitalist long-distance trade" expands until it overcomes "the vertical relations of dependence" characteristic of feudalism; new social forms based on communicative reason, rather than on ties of clientage, indicate the endpoint of modernity's "unfinished project."[44] What these separate kinds of accounts have in common is their persistent central image. Pre-modernity, based on a stable kind of property that produces a vertical order, is grounded, while modernity, searching for an abstract and horizontal harmony, keeps moving around. "All that is solid melts into air," Marx says, and in this dissolution is both the promise and the threat of a modern condition.

Because "specialization" may lead to an alienating individualism, and communicative reason may result in a dehumanizing abstraction, these theoretical touchstones also reveal some of the ways the social norms through which modernity becomes naturalized have been vulnerable to critique. As one important comment on Habermas argues, the formalism of circulating discourse might represent, not the possibility of open deliberation, but the dislocation of real "experience"; "proletarian" experience cannot be represented in the bourgeois public sphere, while bourgeois experience is inherently attenuated by its dual relationship to the materiality of industrial production and to the abstractions of the commodity form.[45] Treatments such as Siskin's and Pfau's are among the more forceful arguments that follow suit in re-defining Romantic, liberal freedom as merely contingent, and the condition that Celeste Langan has called "Romantic vagrancy" is symptomatic of this supposed emptiness. For Langan, the poet's walking, like the circulation of the commodity, signals a "simulation of freedom": "Coming and going becomes, *in itself,* the pure form of freedom, an absolute unmarked by origin and destination, by interest or antipathy."[46] Coleridge, as an itinerant preacher, had directly expressed the potential emptiness of the freedom to circulate, and, as my reading of Beattie suggests, *The Minstrel* investigates a similar problem. Vagrancy may be Romantic, in this sense, across the long century, and from the point of view of the Lake poet it represents not one but two separate dilemmas. It threatens to bring about an empty or enervating class distinction, as in the plight of the bourgeois poet whose livelihood is now linked to the condition diagnosed by Langan and others, and it also threatens to overturn the means of evaluating status and education entirely, as in the itinerant preacher whose self-justification announces a separate disregard for the dialectics of aristocratic and professional orders.

In their move from their antiestablishment youth to détente and eventual co-operation with the establishment, Southey and

Coleridge experience the conceptual history of itinerancy back-
wards. Initially, they embrace extra-institutional itinerancy as a way
to dissolve the grip of the old regime, but they subsequently find
that it leads to or can lead to absolute vacancy. Yet, in turn, the
abstract ideals of motion give way to real conditions that may make
new versions of professional practice possible. To quote Mee,
"Habermas's notion of the bourgeois public sphere ... had an
alter ego in the heterotopia of chapels, field meetings, and the
huge circulation of popular religious pamphlets and sermons." [47]
Within this heterotopia, itinerancy had the status of real work and
could be seen as establishing a new and independent professional
order. Savage's flying poet and Beattie's wandering one are
designed to transcend the vertical relations that, on Habermas's
analysis, must ultimately succumb to the circulation of discourse,
yet neither Savage nor Beattie represent anything like liberal
rationalism, and in this sense the counter-public sphere described
by Mee takes on the characteristics of Savage's Grub Street or
Beattie's Aberdeen. These are locations at the periphery from
which enthusiastic, self-authorizing truth may emerge. Similarly,
in the Lake poets' account of the enthusiast's ministry, the
meaning of motion is wrested away from the backdrop that signifies bourgeois anomie as well as triumph. The threat that itinerancy merely equals a sterile modernity is offset by the possibility
that it allows for a new and honorable kind of professional effort.
Attempts to discover this kind of work lead to Coleridge's
Unitarian ministry and to his rejection of it, and they lead to
Southey's resuscitation of a genteel professional dream in the
name of intellectual freedom as well as his eventual return to the
literary marketplace. The next section of this chapter explores a
set of literary examples of the theme.

II ROMANTIC ITINERANTS IN 1796

This section considers a pair of early poems by Coleridge and
Southey that explicitly imagine the professional poet as an itinerant. Wandering, in the context of debates about clerical itinerancy and the century-long use of the trope, is an especially fraught
metaphor for professional independence, and through it the
poets explore the standoff between the rejection of established
practice and the acceptance of usable gentility that also effected

Wesley. Although wandering figures are endemic in the writing of the Lake poets, the poems addressed here are especially revealing because of their manifest biographical content. In Coleridge's *Poems on Various Subjects*, the opening "Monody on the Death of Chatterton" conflates a disastrous poetic itinerancy and a disastrous encounter with the literary marketplace. Southey's *Poems* was also published in Bristol, in December of 1796, and its climactic piece, "Hymn to the Penates," manages the feat of imagining Southey as an itinerant, a ghost, a lawyer, and a radical poet simultaneously. In these texts the poets are each saying farewell, Southey because he is anticipating law school, Coleridge because he is at least notionally looking ahead to Pantisocracy, and their meditations on the wandering poet are marked by an elegiac sense that poetry has already failed. Nonetheless, they also suggest how poetic success might be defined in itinerant terms.

In "Monody on the Death of Chatterton," Coleridge examines the career of one of the most famous victims of the eighteenth century's literary marketplace and uses the occasion to work through a negative account of the poet's professional position. In doing so, he reiterates the dissatisfaction that had marked his own lay itinerancy. The English landscape that is supposed to provide sustenance and formative experience instead attacks and diminishes Thomas Chatterton, who, in the absence of a qualifying structure, is unable to transform his own trials into the basis for a positive, continuing office. Coleridge's final attempt to recuperate this figure comes at the cost of abandoning one version of the professional ideal. To leave the open market in literature and ideas, he concludes, is to be protected from the "scathing lightning" that besets Chatterton, but it is also to discard those productive, social tasks that Chatterton had once been able to perform. While the poem appears to offer a sentimental argument about neglected literary genius, it involves a critique of the professions in which itinerancy is a noble alternative to established working arrangements.

The opening stanzas of the poem dramatize what Coleridge's audience would already know, or think they know, about Chatterton, who had been rejected by patrons and had supposedly committed suicide out of disappointment. "Patronage" means more than one thing, however, and as Paul Magnuson has

discussed, the earliest version of the poem demonstrates that
literary patronage and the corruption of Church preferment are
equally on Coleridge's mind when he first drafts the "Monody."[48]
While some of this manifest content is canceled in later versions,
beginning with the 1796 version I am primarily addressing here,
Coleridge maintains contact with the matter of labor through the
convention of the wanderer, whose displacement is explicitly
vocational:

> When faint and sad o'er Sorrow's desert wild
> Slow journeys onward poor Misfortune's child;
> When fades each lovely form by Fancy drest,
> And inly pines the self-consuming breast;
> No scourge of scorpions in thy right arm dread,
> No helmed terrors nodding o'er thy head,
> Assume, O DEATH! the cherub's wings of PEACE,
> And bid the heart-sick Wanderer's anguish cease! (1–7)

These lines reflect back on Coleridge's own lay work and on his
attempts to establish himself domestically. In an echo of the
February 1796 letter discussed above, the "scourge of scorpions"
that had recently represented the compromise of literary piece-
work makes an appearance here, but only to be conjured away by
Coleridge's defense of Chatterton's suicide. Death does not wear
the aspect of "terrors" but is bid to assume angelic "wings of
PEACE." Chatterton is depicted as having passed through discontent, and he has discovered the freedom of the death-wish that
negates domestic attachment and defeats a range of hostile institutional forces.

Although it begins by justifying Chatterton's suicide, the poem
also tries to show that his life was of some use, and given the
sequence of ideas that holds together the following stanza,
Coleridge might have in mind Percy's claim that "minstrel" and
"minister" have a shared etymology.[49] Describing Chatterton's
career, the poem refers to an early moment when his sublime
confidence, perhaps ominously, marks a difference between his
attitude and the humility and caution displayed by a figure like
Beattie's Edwin:

> Sublime of thought and confident of fame,
> From vales where Avon winds the MINSTREL came.
> Light-hearted youth! aye, as he hastes along,

> He meditates the future song,
> How dauntless Aella fray'd the Dacyan foes;
> And, as floating high in air
> Glitter the sunny visions fair,
> His eyes dance rapture, and his bosom glows!

Chatterton's early state of strolling inspiration lends a Kubla-like visionary gleam to the rapture that precedes "future song," but, it emerges, the inclination here is really towards earthly service. Responding to Chatterton's radical reputation and the association of the Beattian minstrel with an anti-court ethic, Coleridge designs a Chatterton who is a friend to more than the preceptor of the rural poor.[50] In the very act of seeing, hearing, and noticing the lives of the "friendless," he ministers to them personally and successfully:

> Friend to the friendless, to the sick man health,
> With generous joy he views the *ideal* wealth;
> He hears the widow's heaven-breath'd prayer of praise;
> He marks the shelter'd orphan's tearful gaze;
> Or, where the sorrow-shrivell'd captive lay,
> Pours the bright blaze of Freedom's noon-tide ray:
> And now, indignant, "grasps the patriot steel,"
> And her own iron rod he makes Oppression feel. (41–48)

This writing has migrated from Coleridge's "Lines on the 'Man of Ross,'" where it describes the charity of a famous inn-keeper, but here its emphasis on the fight against oppression and the transmutation of the "'Man of Ross'"'s "modest wealth" into "*ideal* wealth" lend new and appropriate force to the mission of the poet, which is spiritual and political rather than philanthropic.[51] Notably, the depiction of Chatterton's ministry re-emerges in a surprising form at a later compositional stage. In 1839, when the flying bard would seem to be more old-fashioned than ever, Coleridge rewrites the ministry stanza that had briefly fallen out, recalls "Kubla Khan," and gives his minister wings:

> His eyes have glorious meanings, that declare
> More than the light of outward day shines there,
> A holier triumph and a sterner aim!
> Wings grow within him, and he soars above
> Or Bard's, or Minstrel's lay of war or love.[52]

The excursive potential of Savage's wanderer separates Chatterton's mission from the antique-epic pretensions of Gray, Beattie, and, probably, Scott. Unfortunately, this fierce, cheerful ministry is always shadowed by the poet's impending doom.

The question of Chatterton's suicide is central in shifting the meaning of his plight away from the merely sentimental or melancholic to the contexts in which he undertakes his work. A comparison with *The Wanderer* is instructive. Gothically tempted by a personified "Suicide," Savage's Hermit is saved at the last minute by a dramatically thundering voice that instructs him in the poem's great aristocratic/professional lesson: "Honour, the more obstructed, stronger shines/And Zeal, by Persecution's Rage refines .... From Patience, prudent, clear Experience springs,/ And traces Knowledge through the Course of Things" (II: 243–248). Chatterton, however, is granted only the domestic power of "AFFECTION" to slow his suicide in the face of "insult" and, worse, "dread dependence on the low-born mind" (71, 86–87). While Savage's hermit is supported by a divine voice that creates a Stoic order of knowledge for him, effacing the domestic (personified as the dead Olympia) and working in concert with the providential support of "the city," Coleridge's Chatterton, whose resources remain strictly personal, cannot transform trial into Science. Enthusiastic ministry in the absence of a public structure of support, however controversial or heterotopic such a structure may be, cannot be sustained, and the emptiness of a content-free circulation is here laid bare.

In 1796, Coleridge's poem will find a way to redeem Chatterton's failed service, but before it can do so, this landscape has to be transformed from an expressivist representation of Chatterton's psychological ills to a site of potential self-destruction that is realistically depicted and highly allusive. The transformation involves a change in the dynamics of identification which drive the poem. As Magnuson also observes, Chatterton's situation in the poem's tenth stanza reprises the death-scene of Gray's Bard, who protests the defeat of Wales at the hands of Edward I by plunging into the Conway River.[53] In an enthusiastic moment, Chatterton nearly re-enacts the Bard's death, but without the nationalist's virtue, and only in miniature:

> And here, in INSPIRATION'S eager hour,
> When most the big soul feels the madning pow'r,
>   These wilds, these caverns roaming o'er,
>   Round which the screaming sea-gulls soar,

> With wild, unequal steps he pass'd along
> Oft pouring on the wind a broken song:
> Anon, upon some rough rock's fearful brow
> Would pause abrupt – and gaze upon the waves below. (100–107)

Coleridge revises the equation of Chatterton with Gray's Bard not only because the Bard is a public, patriotic figure while Chatterton's sufferings are private, but because the Bard is in the grip of the history of nations while Chatterton is in the more immediate grip of the history of markets. While treating Chatterton's private demise in public, bardic language, Coleridge finds himself hazardously placed between Chatterton and Gray, challenging a system of literary rewards and punishments that, according to the poem's narrative, has already killed at least once. That is, while setting out to treat Chatterton the way Gray treats the Bard, Coleridge also exposes the risk of becoming, not Gray or his Bard, but Chatterton. Robin Jarvis has argued that there is an "iconic relation between the steady alternating rhythm of blank verse and the signified content of pedestrian travel," and these lines offer a convincing, if inverted, example.[54] Chatterton's "wild, unequal steps" lead to a "broken song" and reflect outwards onto the heterometrics of the poem's now-vestigial Pindarics. It is of equal interest that, as Jarvis notes, Coleridge "preferr[ed] to compose ... 'walking over uneven ground,'" as opposed to Wordsworth, who liked a smoother path.[55] As Chatterton moves further away from his pastoral mission as "friend to the friendless" and becomes more deeply involved in the scene of too-intense inspiration and incoherent composition, his unequal steps also make him ever-more-clearly a double of the poet himself.

The final stanza of the poem, which settles into a series of smoothly stepping couplets, grants both Coleridge and Chatterton their individually appropriate placement in the terrain.

> Yet will I love to follow the sweet dream,
> Where Susquehannah pours his untam'd stream;
> And on some hill, whose forest-frowning side
> Waves o'er the murmurs of his calming tide,
> Will raise a solemn CENOTAPH to thee,
> Sweet Harper of time-shrouded MINSTRELSY!
> And there, sooth'd sadly by the dirgeful wind,
> Muse on the sore ills I had left behind. (136–143)

Coleridge will re-adopt a pensive attitude, but rather than suffering through a process of failed inspiration, as in the depiction of Chatterton's cliff-side contemplation of suicide, he will instead become nature's audience, "sooth'd" by the "dirgeful wind." "MINSTRELSY"'s harp, we learn, is a thing of the past. On the banks of the Susquehanna, the new cliff is safe for bards and would-be-bards alike, but this safety has been purchased at the cost of two tremendous dislocations, the movement through space that Pantisocracy requires, and the movement through time, into the future, that is required to imagine the Pantisocratic community. The end of Chatterton's ministry signals the end of his confrontation with the literary marketplace, since Pantisocracy is communal and self-sufficient. For Coleridge, however, much has been lost, since a redemptive, interactive version of authorship-as-ministry has been offered by the poem only as an ideal that is negated, frankly, by Chatterton's sales failure and by Coleridge's proposed transatlantic retreat. This last itineration avoids the negations of the clerical maelstrom, but divided from Chatterton's inspired enthusiasm, the mere philosopher has nothing left to do but muse and mourn.

Southey's "Hymn to the Penates" (1797) also places the poet in a series of landscapes that represent professional training and support as well as the hardships of circulation. Recalling Edmund Seward and reiterating Southey's discontent about his professional career, it, too, reproduces the figure of the religious itinerant in the figure of the wandering poet. The context for the poem is Southey's return from Portugal and his intention to set aside literature for his legal studies. The Penates, or "HOUSE-HOLD GODS," thus begin the poem by representing both a sentimentalized longing for home and for the economies of the professional gentleman, whose establishment is earned through hard but regular, guaranteed, work. Significantly, this return is not only not "naturalized," it is explicitly made alien by the generic markers and patterns of the poem itself. Part of what makes the poem unusual is its conflict between what the "Monody on Chatterton," referring to Chatterton's Rowley forgeries, calls "the mask" of "hoar antiquity," and the "Hymn"'s inability or unwillingness to devise such a mask. Beattie and Chatterton had developed different but, as far as the Lake poets seem to be concerned, equally usable ways of turning autobiography into romance.

Southey's attempt to adopt other modes, particularly Akenside's classicism, to the valedictory and occasionally elegiac function of the "Hymn," becomes a sign of vocational failure, a fact Jeffrey seems to have understood in citing its gentility as a disqualifier for "Lake school" simplicity in the *Thalaba* review. As in the case of John Henderson, however, failure equals protest, and here that protest will turn directly on the enthusiast's wandering work.

The poem begins by imagining an ending:

> Yet one Song more! one high and solemn strain
> Ere PAEAN! on thy temple's ruined wall
> I hang the silent harp: there may its strings,
> When the rude tempest shakes the aged pile,
> Make melancholy music.[56]

The allusion to Paean, Apollo's healing aspect, refers to a similar citation in Akenside's "Hymn to the Naiads" and reaffirms the linkage between medicine and song. ("Why not physic?" Southey would demand of Bedford, who entered Gray's shortly after he did.[57]) Southey associates the Penates with meditation, privacy, and self-communion, "delightful hours/that gave mysterious pleasures, made me know/All the recesses of my wayward heart" (24–26), which suggests, at least at first, that he is returning to himself by leaving off his full-time, commerce-driven writing. As the passage also indicates, the Penates are not simply a principle that is internally possessed, since the heart is separately "wayward." The Penates can illuminate it, but they are not equivalent to it and they are not sufficient to fix it.

Southey is leaving a state of nature to enter the urban, professional world, and his refusal of nature's gifts makes all the more striking the fact that much of the hymn, while echoing sources in William Cowper as well as in Akenside, also directly anticipates "Tintern Abbey," written a little less than two years later:

> As I grew
> In years and knowledge, and the course of Time
> Developed the young feelings of my heart,
> When most I loved in solitude to rove
> Amid the woodland gloom; or where the rocks
> Darken'd old Avon's stream, in the ivied cave
> Recluse to sit and brood the future song,
> Yet not the less, PENATES, loved I then
> Your altars . . . (49–56)

Wordsworth would re-articulate these sentiments in a narrative of development that contains "the course of Time" within five years and makes it perceptible within the boundaries of a single geographical location, the Wye River valley. Southey's "Hymn" does not look ahead to the way "Tintern Abbey"'s scheme of remembrance and return sets up the paired faculties of memory and imagination, but it does provide something that is even more unexpected. Its speaker internalizes the professional/domestic complex in the way that Wordsworth would internalize the blended landscape. Nature is always with Wordsworth, even in the city, but the Penates are always with Southey, even in nature. The already-professional runs towards his own renewed professionalism, as the Penates, which have been possessed in "solitude" and "gloom," stand to be repossessed, re-sung, at the climactic professional moment ("Yet one song more!") for which they have always been waiting.

At the same time, the Penates are alien and literary in just the way that Wordsworth's nature designedly is not. Southey's turn from the harshness of urban life, unlike Wordsworth's, cannot depend on the providential internalization of the beloved object. Instead, Southey indicates the limits of the Penates' consoling power, since they will become the center of another act of longing as well as a perpetual stay and support. Ultimately, like Chatterton's cenotaph, the Penates function as a fantasy within a fantasy:

> Nor did I cease to reverence you, when driven
> Amid the jarring crowd, an unfit man
> To mingle with the world; still, still my heart
> Sighed for your sanctuary, and inly pined;
> And loathing human converse, I have strayed
> Where o'er the sea-beach chilly howled the blast,
> And gaz'd upon the world of waves, and wished
> That I were far beyond the Atlantic deep,
> In woodland haunts – a sojourner with PEACE. (74–82)

"PEACE" here is imaginable only within the realm of the already lost utopia of Pantisocracy, and at this point in the poem, the very literariness of the Penates theme appears to be at the center of Southey's problem. The principle that should stand for inner content and outward prosperity turns out to be alienable, an object of nostalgia toward which the poem can only perpetually travel, so that Nicholas Roe finds in the poem "a myth of the poet's development … that is … forever out of reach."[58]

However, Southey does not stop here. Having offered the Penates as a symbol of economic man, of man-at-home, he contemplates another potential meaning of these enigmatic figures. In fact, he speculates, they may be "THE SPIRITS OF THE DEAD"(163) who act as guardian angels. The eruption of this idea, which is also central to the reward structure of *The Wanderer* and to the discourse surrounding John Henderson, indicates that the reforming powers of professional enthusiasm may be retained even as Southey moves towards what the poem represents as his conventionally professional destination. Just as Agutter had been doctrinally careful in his sermon on Henderson, Southey enunciates an institutionally generated diffidence: "No mortal eye may pierce the invisible world," he allows, "No light of human reason penetrate/That depth where Truth lies hid" (164–166). Nonetheless, his "heart with instant sympathy assents" to the idea that the dead are with us always:

> I would judge all systems and all faiths
> By that touchstone, from whose test DECEIT
> Shrinks like the Arch-Fiend at Ithuriel's spear,
> And SOPHISTRY'S gay glittering bubble bursts,
> As at the spousals of the Nereid's son,
> When that false Florimel, by her prototype
> Display'd in rivalry, with all her charms
> Dissolved away. (168–174)

The glittering panoply of Miltonic and Spenserian references has the stylistic effect of obscuring Southey's actual position, which is in favor not so much of common sense philosophy as of experimental religion. These are beliefs that move, even when they threaten schism, and they inspire Southey with the unorthodox view, for example, that "the halls of Heaven" are not as pleasing to the disembodied soul as "its earthly haunts" are, "[w]hen with the breeze it wantons round the brow/Of one beloved on earth" (175–179). Southey is well aware of his fellow Bristovian, and it is likely that "Hymn to the Penates" echoes the Hendersonian complex directly. As in Agutter's portrait, and Cottle's, Southey's angelic image borders on the enthusiastic and on the extra-institutional while being careful not to cross that border.

Because Southey's "Hymn" is professionally aggressive and heterodox when it compares the pleasures of heaven to the joy of haunting the earth, it is appropriate that the sequence gives way to an elegiac paragraph on Edmund Seward, Southey's college friend. Seward was known for his moral rigidness and abstemious diet, and he is something like a Southeyan version of Henderson: "[M]erely from the resolution of abridging the luxuries of life water is his only drink, tea and dry bread his only breakfast."[59] Seward is also, unlike Henderson, an enthusiastic if politically conservative clergyman, and so embedded in Southey's poem of withdrawal into the old professions is another reference to the calling that demands both experimental authority and the renewal of exhausted institutions.[60] Southey gives Seward a monitorial mission, and he looks ahead, as Cottle had looked ahead, to reunion: "[M]e didst thou leave/With strengthened step to follow the right path/Till we shall meet again" (204–207). He ends the passage comforted by the belief that Seward's "eye's celestial ken/Pervades me now" (209–210). The wandering pastor, translated into a speculative and immaterial state, takes up his rightful place, "pervading" Southey and sponsoring his correct feelings and his conduct.

This pervasion, a function of the enthusiasm and rectitude that suffuse the itinerant Southey "amid my wanderings," (248) empowers both radicalism and its abandonment. After denouncing "WEALTH" and "POWER," Southey turns his back on youthful activism, which is inseparable from his foresworn literary labor:

> Meantime, all hoping and expecting all
> In patient faith, to you, DOMESTIC GODS!
> I come, studious of other lore than song,
> Of my past years the solace and support:
> Yet shall my heart remember the past years
> With honest pride, trusting that not in vain
> Lives the pure song of LIBERTY and TRUTH. (280–284)

The author, who has been in the past both intellectually "solace"'d and materially "support"'ed by his writing, is now perfectly divided from the law student. The "pure song" lives on because works like *Joan of Arc* are free to circulate regardless of the specific fates of its authors. (Ironically, Southey's *Wat Tyler* would embarrass him by circulating without his permission in 1817.) Seward's enthusiasm has been internalized and politicized, projected outward (as the text of Southey's radical writing) and projected backward (as the content of Southey's wandering past), but, like Coleridge's Pantisocratic fantasy, the future presided over by the Penates invokes a compromise that the poet-speaker who wanders in the hills has yet to face. The Penates represent both the ideal of the comfortable lawyer and the ideal of the clerical enthusiast who has rejected such comfort. The enthusiast is radical and a reformer who lives on in print, or, as print, long after the actual writer has capitulated.

My argument for the importance of enthusiastic itinerancy in this pair of poems is largely grounded in a clash between subject-matter and style. Clement Hawes, who treats eighteenth-century enthusiasm as a class-bound and "subterranean" form, notes that, even for a visionary like Christopher Smart, enthusiasm may be tamed by the author's education. *Jubilate Agno*, he points out, is "a refinement, a sophistication – even a gentrification – of that more plebeian millennial mode."[61] This is all the more true for poems like the "Monody" or the "Hymn," which self-consciously reinterpret the middle-class modes of melancholy and retirement. My point, however, is that the discourse of the autonomous practitioner, with the field preacher as its primary manifestation, remains in contact with the different versions of professionalism it both includes and critiques. Similarly, as Mee demonstrates, Coleridge's move to "domestic" and "supernatural" verse at the end of the 1790s "negotiate[s] a route between the twin poles of enthusiasm, that is, the implosion of the unsociable self and its infectious dissemination into the crowd."[62] Coleridge is impressed both by enthusiasm and by its institutional implications, and the conveniently titled sequence that runs from the prophetic "Religious Musings" and the vocationally stolid "Reflections Upon Leaving a Place of Retirement" to the prototypically withdrawn "Frost at Midnight" might be read to substantiate the point. My effort has been to get closer to the root of this enthusiastic writing in order to suggest that it is marked by the matter of who is to be honored for doing what kind of work. While criticism has been tremendously insightful about Coleridge's theological and philosophical peregrinations, and, in a less ramified way, about Southey's shifting political allegiances, the imaginary institutional framework for all of this motion, including the pressure of itinerancy and the more general question of the profession, is central.

III WORDSWORTHIAN ITINERANTS

Wordsworth's habit of mind is to start from a predefined sense of social standing and work his way back to profession. However,

while critics have been inclined to equate Wordsworth's position
with that of his complexly defined class situation, Wordsworth
himself discovers that class and profession are mutually modifying,
and he begins from the premise that wandering can be the center
of poetic practice if a balance is struck between the genteel tourist
and the untrammeled innovator. In a sequence of poems that
includes such diverse texts as *Descriptive Sketches*, the Salisbury Plain
poems, and "The Idiot Boy," he redescribes the relationship of
the poet to the client, and to his own systematic training, as a
version of the adventures of the ministering wanderer.

Along with *Evening Walk, Descriptive Sketches* is generally recognized as the opening move in Wordsworth's career, and the two
poems, written in meditative and hyper-descriptive couplets, have
always been understood as transitional, whether the direction in
which they are heading is taken to be an idealist or an ideological
one. Their attempt to borrow some of the attitudes and language
of eighteenth-century descriptive verse, for example, has been
defined as a frustrated effort to express "a complex of relationships" that unites consciousness, objects of perception, and ideal
relationships of "inner and outer" and that would later emerge for
Wordsworth in a full-blown transcendentalism.[63] More recently,
readers have found in this poetry an unfolding "politics of the
picturesque," so that the relationship of the poet to his or her
physical environment is recognized as an expression of social
affiliation. Pfau, for example, argues that the poems use picturesque conventions to aestheticize the suffering object and produce
an "imaginary" subjectivity for the poet, a move that does not
achieve its full cultural effect until it is generically naturalized, by
way of "lyric transport," later on.[64]

The endemic voyeurism of *Descriptive Sketches* is manifest in the
distinction between such figures as the Grison gypsy, whose sufferings are described in dramatic detail, and the traveler who
imagines her trials. The gypsy is subjected to a breakneck series of
perils that cannot possibly inform, because of their pace, which
combines stasis and random action, as well as because of their fatal
consequence:

> Low barks the fox; by Havoc rouz'd the bear,
> Quits, growling, the white bones that strew his lair;
> The dry leaves stir as with the serpent's walk,

And, far beneath, Banditti voices talk[.]
. . . .

Ascending, nearer howls the famish'd wolf,
While thro' the stillness scatters wild dismay,
Her babe's small cry, that leads him to his prey. (231–241)

The open-ended and slow-paced journey of the travelers, on the other hand, offers the possibility of a growing understanding as well as of a notionally shared suffering, but the characters here are undirected, and, unlike Beattie's Edwin, they are also unmotivated. The conclusion of the 1793 version pulls the speaker and his companion (Robert Jones, a future clergyman) toward the allegorical train of the miserable:

To night, my friend, within this humble cot,
Be the dead load of mortal ills forgot,
Renewing, when the rosy summits glow
At morn, our various journey, sad and slow.[65] (810–813)

These wanderers undertake their journey in a different kind of space, and for that matter in a different kind of time, than the Grison gypsy, yet this difference presents itself not as a solution but as a problem for the professional poet. Wordsworth and Jones neither work nor take pleasure during what is presented as a touristic experience, and so their gestures of empathy are empty. In eighteenth-century descriptive verse, the topos of the sufferer and the gentleman who perceives suffering goes back to Thomson, whose own description of tormented Alpine rustics is aimed at those who "little think . . . while they dance along,/How many feel, this very moment, death/And all the sad variety of pain."[66] Here, the speaker's recognition of human suffering re-marks a status boundary that has already been established, while the characters' helplessness to alter, comment on, or truthfully represent such suffering grows into a powerful if unintended illustration of Thomson's message. Wordsworth and Jones are itinerants in the worst possible sense. Their failure to cohere with the landscape is not offset by any real capacity to act on, or even to interpret, their surroundings.

In "Adventures on Salisbury Plain," Wordsworth finally exploits the body of figures that clusters around the itinerant, and he is therefore able to reinstate the subject of work. To do so, he has to go as far outside of the institutions of gentility and education as he can get. As is true for "Monody on the Death of Chatterton" and "Hymn to the Penates," what is achieved here is a negative and experimental version of a ministry that proves to be literally but ironically construed. To the enthusiast's standard progress, in which personal conviction of sin is succeeded by salvation through rebirth and by a lifelong process of sanctification through good works, "Adventures on Salisbury Plain" opposes a conviction that is halted in its tracks and that reproduces itself mainly because it is helpless to do otherwise. Such a reading of the poem is, to an extent, congruent with influential recent treatments which examine what David Collings calls the poem's "deconstruction of culture" through its revelation of the "naked sign."[67] However, I argue that the arrested or perverted career is itself a meaningful structure, since it is another one of the ways that the figure of the poet explores the promise of itinerancy but also confronts its liabilities.

The odd fit between the poems' Spenserian stanza and its "social-realist narrative of British poverty and war" is also part of Wordsworth's attempt to produce an un-literal politics, and the Beattiean connection to the stanza has been especially carefully noted.[68] Emphasizing Beattie's affinity for Whig cultural traditions, John Williams observes that it is "by no means surprising to find that when Wordsworth moved from composition of the [radical *Letter to the Archbishop of Llandaff*] to the composition of a poem, he modeled it in the first instance on James Beattie's *The Minstrel*."[69] On one level, the poem's concern with freedom is indeed produced by explicit debates of a kind to which Beattie's poem alludes only distantly. In this landscape, no one is free to decide where they belong or where they are going to go. The sailor's wife, first encountered on the wain the Poor Law "overseers" have placed her on to remove her from their parish, is a type of the sailor, the soldier's widow, and the other vagrants produced by the narrative, all of whom have been driven out into space not by providential order but by the specific, human crimes attendant on greed and war (735). Beyond the poems' anti-Ministerial politics, however, is an experimental rewriting of the connectedness of vocation and motion that addresses long-term structural concerns. Whereas Beattie had worked to separate modes of movement – exile for the hermit, radical autonomy for the minstrel – in "Adventures on Salisbury Plain" Wordsworth is more interested in collapsing them.

The integration of figure and ground is fundamental to the poem's replication of lay itinerancy, because the blasted landscape itself inverts the schema of conviction, conversion, and ministry upon which the itinerant mission depends. Like the helpless vagrants of Thomson and of Wordsworth's pastoral and in contrast to the optimism of Savage, the sailor, like the soldier's widow who shares his condition, encounters a waste-land that, despite the evidence of agriculture, seems to suppress productive work. Human activity has robbed the landscape of its beneficence:

> No tree was there, no meadow's pleasant green,
> No brook to wet his lips or soothe his ear.
> Vast piles of corn-stack here and there were seen,
> But thence no smoke upwreathed his sight to cheer.
> He mark'd a homeward shepherd disappear
> Far off and sent a feeble shout, in vain;
> No sound replies but winds that whistling near
> Sweep the thin grass and passing wildly plain,
> Or desart lark that pours on high a wasted strain. (55–63)

The real shepherd in the scene recedes into a background that reveals both human activity and its absence, and the activities of sound in the passage repeat this backward movement. The sailor's "feeble shout" is answered by alien, uncomprehending nature, the "wasted strain" of the desert lark and the "plain"'t of the plain itself, and such inhuman or ineffective, ultimately non-representational sound, establishes a pattern for the poem and its depiction of a failing public sphere that fosters bad or incomplete acts of communication and exhortation.

Although displaced from family and home, the sailor is carefully placed in the professional ecology of the late eighteenth century. He has been forcibly pressed into service in the American war, and, overtaken by the military ethos, he expects and hopes to be rewarded within the economy that has claimed him. "Death's minister," he grotesquely imagines heaping his wife's lap with a "bloody prize." Predictably, however, Old Corruption proves to be even more potent than the sailor: "he urged his claim; the slaves of Office spurned / The unfriended claimant; at their door he stood / In vain," like a penitent; or like Beattie, waiting for the king, or like any writer or dependant trying to catch the attention of a potential patron (90–93). Thwarted by this system of rewards, the sailor takes his ministry of death outside its military context, killing a man in a robbery on his way back home. Then, as a fugitive, he has a re-death experience that triggers further events of the poem: "He looked, and saw on a bare gibbet nigh/A human body that in irons swang" (114–115), a sight particularly impressive in light of the sailor's guilt: "Nor only did it at once renew/All he had feared from man, but rouzed a train/of the mind's phantoms . . ." (120–122). However, already convicted of his own sin, the sight of the executed felon brings on a peace that really does surpass understanding: "His soul, which in such anguish had been toss'd,/Sank into deepest calm; for now retires/Fear" (128–130). The confrontation with the sheer materiality of the dead body alleviates the sailor's fear of punishment, and his identification with the dead acts as a counterpart to the experience of rebirth which makes the itinerant's work possible. In the poem's final version, the narrator acknowledges that the sailor, desolate and "tried" to the point of hopelessness, is unsuited to console the vagrant, so that he has to fall back on "Proverbial words" that do not reflect his inner state (*Guilt and Sorrow* 457).

The sailor drifts towards a fleeting series of redemptive moments: his consolation of the soldier's widow, his final encounter with his wife, and, in particular, the anti-sermon he delivers to the abusive father he and the widow encounter on the road. Even this anti-sermon begins unpromisingly. "Calling him vagabond, and knave, and mad," and accusing him of obvious criminality and an interest in "plunder," the abusive father treats the sailor the way any secure patriarch would treat a meddling outsider, especially one like the sailor, who comes humbly on foot and is visibly marked only by his sufferings (635–636). Before the sailor can continue, his own position inside and outside the family dynamic is reaffirmed by the sight of the boy's wound, which triggers another trance, and the father and the son are "reconcil'd" even before the sailor gathers himself to speak (655). His lesson, then, comes as a belated comment on whatever conclusion the father has already drawn, and it offers not a transcendent message but a harsh pragmatics that make sense in the context of "Salisbury Plain"'s hostile and alien environment: "It is a bad world, and hard is the world's law," he declares, before defining the familial "bond of nature" as no more than a bleak, tribal compact against "num'rous foes" (658–663). That is, whereas the itinerant's sermon comes out of the speaker's enthusiastic conversion, this sermon describes the sailor's own threat and his own failures, since he has both neglected to cling to his family and he is, or has been, among the wolves that prowl for blood. Pastoral care and evangelical persuasion have each been negated by a body of experiences, or experiments, that prepare the sailor only to bring bad news.

The "correspondent calm" the sailor earns by delivering this speech foretells his final address, since his climactic sermon is, in "Adventures," delivered by way of his own hanged body (666). Conviction, followed by execution, is the preordained life trajectory for guilty sailors and for people like them. As a spectacle for "dissolute men, unthinking and untaught," the meaning of the sailor's body will only be understood when, as is inevitable, "some kindred sufferer," which is to say some kindred inflictor of suffering, will be reminded by it of his own guilt and doom (821–825). The sailor finally becomes a productive part of the poem's unproductive landscape. Although he has been relocated to the city of commerce and law, he is the sole producer of knowledge and value there, just as the first hanged man provides the only true signpost in the wastes of Salisbury plain. Yet the "kindred sufferer" can only react appropriately to the hanged body because he is already lost. This is an enclosed system of identification and punishment, and it may be right to argue, as John Rieder has, that the speaker himself stands apart from the poem's characters, the "broader perspective available to the poet" devoted to contemplation of the impoverished objects of politics just as the deeply educated Wesley would stand distinct from lay itinerants and their falsely learned critics.[70] In the fate of the sailor, however, we may also begin to read one of the fates of the poet. All three Lake writers would return to the wandering scene, often in ways that continue to make the poet's identification with the wanderer figure explicit. The gentleman poet does not confuse himself with the indigent sailor, but the indigent sailor does pose a dilemma. If the professional poet is not to be a minister of death, of experience that can only teach the world's bad law to the already damned, what kind of minister is he going to be?

Potential answers dominate the writing of the years 1798–1799, which includes the preliminary version of *The Prelude*, "The Ruined Cottage," and the lines that would be offered as the Prospectus to *The Recluse*, as well as Coleridge's conversation poems, "Kubla Khan," and "Christabel," and Southey's work on

Thalaba the Destroyer, Madoc, and a number of ballads. In a broad sense, the question of the poet's ability and preparation are central to all of this writing. That said, the line of development with which this chapter has been most directly concerned culminates in a perhaps surprising place. Wordsworth's "The Idiot Boy" is the most fully specified version of the narrative that poses the wanderer directly against the established professional, and it offers a special version of the poet's formative experience. Johnny Foy, whose pony-backed itinerancy is both the consummation of and a parody of the melancholic or manic wanderings of other Romantic figures, expresses the extra-institutionalism of the new professional and the secret at the heart of the professional's perfectly abstract knowledge. This abstract knowledge balances the grim pragmatic experience that is the basis of "Adventures on Sailsbury Plain."

The plot of the poem and the contemporary argument surrounding it are quickly recalled. Betty Foy sends her son, Johnny, to get the doctor for her neighbor Susan Gale, who is ailing. Johnny, the "idiot boy," is placed on the family pony and sent out into the woods. When Johnny does not return, Betty Foy attempts to find him. In the process, she wakes up the doctor, but in her excitement she neglects to tell him about Susan Gale. Eventually, she finds Johnny beside a waterfall. Meanwhile, Susan Gale, upset about the absence of the Foys, forgets her ailment and effects a recovery. She goes after Betty Foy, and the three characters enjoy "a merry meeting/As ever there was in Christendom."[71] Southey would attack the poem in his review of *Lyrical Ballads,* and John Wilson would complain at length that the subject-matter was too "disgust"ing to merit Wordsworth's expert treatment of it.[72] Coleridge would awkwardly defend it as a "fine poem" but go on to allow the two primary objections to it: the figure of Johnny is "*ordinary*" and "*morbid,*" and the mother's behavior is so extreme as to lapse into "burlesque."[73] What all of these critics are concerned about is the besetting subject of decorum, which for Wilson (and Jeffrey) precedes the individual poet and for Coleridge must be rediscovered through the empirics of a principled practical criticism. All critics, that is, sense "The Idiot Boy"'s experimental aim, which is to cancel out in advance the misguided evaluations of the reader in the name of authorial expertise.

Wordsworth's challenge has all along been to establish that the author alone may institute the protocols of poetic writing, and his main defense of the poem, which he launches in his response to Wilson, hinges on the professional poet's special ability to manage experience through reflection. An "idiot" born "in a poor man's house" "cannot be boarded out," Wordsworth explains, and so the poor learn not to be repulsed by conditions like Johnny Foy's.[74] Unfortunately, readers like Wilson, lacking the appropriate experience, misunderstand the texture of rural life. Perhaps consequently, they are also poor readers. They are disgusted by "the *word* idiot," to which they attach physical and verbal deformities that, as Wordsworth insists, are nowhere described in his actual poem.[75]

Wordsworth's defense is humane and perceptive regarding both the "idiot" and those who do not have the luxury to shun him, but before he can exercise his humanity, it is necessary that he place himself within the proper sphere:

People in our rank in life are perpetually falling into one sad mistake, namely, that of supposing that human nature and the persons they associate with are one and the same. Whom do we generally associate with? Gentlemen, persons of fortune, professional men, ladies persons who can afford to buy or can easily procure books of half a guinea price, hot-pressed, and printed upon superfine paper . . . . We err lamentably if we suppose them to be fair representatives of the vast mass of human experience.[76]

The working-class objects of his regard are forced by circumstance into an analogous, practical training that has the incidental effect of allowing them a glimpse into the life of things, but only Wordsworth, who has cultivated his own habits of reflection, is qualified to sort out words and things, or different words and different things:

Few ever consider books but with reference to their power of pleasing these persons and men of a higher rank few descend lower among cottages and fields and among children. A man must have done this habitually before his judgment upon the Idiot Boy would be in any way decisive with me. I *know* I have done this myself habitually[.][77]

Wordsworth's egalitarian spirit is predicated on his gentility and on his willingness to experience the world and reflect on it systematically, activities which allow him to understand a stratified society in the abstract. As he talks his way into the company of "Gentlemen, persons of fortune, professional men" and "ladies," he is also preparing to present the occupational efficacy of poets in particular:

I would fain hope that I have [reflected faithfully in my poems the feelings of human nature]. But a great Poet ought to do more than this .... He ought to travel before men occasionally as well as at their sides.[78]

When Wordsworth notes that books are both written and reviewed from the perspective of "men of higher rank," he is not proposing that cottagers and children should be the real, preferred audience for literature. Rather, he is demonstrating that poets should be entrusted with critical judgment, even or especially about their own products, because only poets, as part of their special function, are capable of translating the "pure" language of the lower ranks of society for the higher ranks that "can afford to buy or can easily procure" expensive books such as *Lyrical Ballads*.

What remains to be established, however, is just how appropriate "The Idiot Boy" is as the occasion for the poet's declaration of professional autonomy. Modern criticism has on the whole been better prepared than Wordsworth's contemporaries to accept the value of Johnny Foy's experiences and to take the author at his word about this character's "closeness to God."[79] On Duncan Wu's convincing reading, for example, Wordsworth's description of human equivalence may be understood literally, and Wu finds the poem illustrating the "audacious" idea that even an idiot can have moments of "pantheist" illumination.[80] Further, Wu points out that Johnny is associated, in terms of the chronology of composition, with the Pedlar of "The Ruined Cottage" and with the speaker of "Tintern Abbey," so that he may well be construed as a version of figures who are more transparently meant to stand in for authorial experience.[81] Others have also been assertive in placing Johnny's experience near the center of the poet's. Mary Jacobus finds that Johnny's viewpoint "is analogous to the poet's" and "makes us see afresh what is familiar," while Ross Woodman, who thinks that "The Idiot Boy" is Wordsworth's "most revolutionary poem," finds in Johnny the lost child, a figure of pre-revolutionary innocence, that grounds all of Wordsworth's work.[82]

As the letter to Wilson reminds us, however, there is no mechanism that can perfectly level out the differences among the author, the idiot, and the audience, "experience" least of all. The coalescence of boy and landscape proves to be, not a sign of identification with the poet, but a necessary sign of the space that separates them. While the professional poet discovers the incompleteness of his training in his inability to fully account for Johnny's experiences, Johnny's autonomy makes him perfectly free from the dynamics of fear and loss that beset Wordsworth's other doubles and stand-ins. He is an abject figure whose appearance in the landscape at first associates him with death, but this association will prove to be the source of his power:

> And while the pony moves his legs,
> In Johnny's left-hand you may see,
> The green bough's motionless and dead;
> The moon that shines above his head
> Is not more still and mute than he. (87–91)

"Still and mute," Johnny looks like the perfect opposite of the itinerant who travels and exhorts, and the stillness is a special kind of optical effect. A single aspect of the scene is brought to life (the pony's legs) while others (the figures of Johnny and the moon) are left inanimate, thus destroying the stable opposition of fore-ground and background. The phenomenology that Beattie cat-ches from Hume remains potent here, since the two-dimensional scene allows for little difference between motion and field, or motivation and effect.

Unmotivated and unwilled though they are, Johnny's frozen travels will be profoundly effective. At first glance, the itinerant Johnny is determinedly antiprofessional. At the level of plot, his adventures "as if by magic" cure Susan Gale, who forgets about her ailment in her concern for Johnny (426). The *Lyrical Ballad*'s characteristic slyness at the expense of the adult rationalist is nowhere clearer than in the doctor's rejection of Johnny's viewpoint:

> "He's not so wise as some folks be."
> "The devil take his wisdom!" said
> The Doctor, looking somewhat grim,
> "What, woman, should I know of him?"
> And, grumbling, he went back to bed. (267–271)

The doctor is already irrelevant, and his dismissal of Johnny's "wisdom" is as comically damning as his "grumbling" retreat from a scene of obvious distress. In this sense, the doctor also becomes a stand-in for the critic, Jeffrey or Wilson, who fails to recognize that professional/authorial knowledge has priority over the routine procedures, aesthetic as well as organizational, of the old establishment.

This does not mean, however, that a community of understanding has been formed between Johnny and the poet. The professional poet is also prevented from directly appropriating Johnny's adventures:

> I to the muses have been bound,
> These fourteen years, by strong indentures;
> Oh gentle muses! let me tell
> But half of what to him befel,
> For sure he met with strange adventures. (347–351)

The fourteen-year term of indenture (half of Wordsworth's life, in 1798), unlike the five-year period of "Tintern Abbey," may at first appear to represent a broken contract, in that the muses are reluctant to deliver what their apprentice asks of them. However, the request is inappropriate, since the idiot boy signifies a mystery, the primordiality of pre-significatory experience, to which the apprentice poet will not be privy until the poem's conclusion. Johnny's pre-linguistic burring is the homologous, contentless speaking-in-tongues at the center of the mystery, the counterpart to the death and stillness that bring life, and Johnny guarantees a raw core of subject matter that will filter over to the poet, a body of experience that the poet will need to purposefully re-code. This process excludes the doctor not because he is a professional, finally, but because he is the wrong kind of professional. Johnny's idiocy, like the damned ministry of the sailor in "Adventures on Salisbury Plain," signifies his distance from the institutions of his culture and the possibility of institutional rejuvenation.

Finally, Wordsworth's speaking persona finds a way of translating without explicating the secret speech of the savant who travels ahead of his audience:

> (His very words I give to you,)
> "The cocks did crow to-whoo, to-whoo,
> "And the sun did shine so cold."
> – Thus answered Johnny in his glory,
> And that was all his travel's story. (459–463)

This sublimely impenetrable moment resists routine and distinguishes the poetic professional from the mere country doctor. Stigma is recuperated, through its very opacity, for the purposes of the working poet, who is content in this case to reproduce the mystery as sheer data. "If you think\Perhaps a tale you'll make it," Wordsworth challenges his audience in "Simon Lee," and the principle here takes on an even more aggressive form. The inversion of the landscape, like the inversions of the eye, can only be re-naturalized by the proper practitioner, who withholds interpretive closure in a performance of solidarity with the itinerant whose circulation is not "pure form" but pure potential. The professional power of the lay itinerant gets doubled up, representing both the poet, experiencing, and the concretized experience of the poet.

Later in their careers, the Lake poets' stance toward the establishment would evolve, and the prospect of Catholic emancipation and the repeal of the Test and Corporation Acts would make the nonconformist itinerant a figure to which they would be explicitly opposed. Nonetheless, the paradoxical marriage of the free wanderer and institutional fixity would continue to provide a source of identity and critique. In the *Biographia*, for example, Coleridge would reiterate both the eighteenth-century dream of professional gentility and the necessity of defending the Established Church when he argues that the position of "Anglican clergyman" is perfect for the man of letters (who, it will be recalled, must "never pursue literature as a trade!"): "The church presents to every rational man of learning and genius a profession, in which he may ... unite the widest schemes of literary utility with the strictest performance of literary duty."[83] Further, the clergyman unites pastoral work with local mobility. The individual cleric moves easily through the high and low ranks of his society while the Church itself exercises a civilizing and "continuous agency" through its network of parish priests.[84] So, as Jon Klancher argues, "the cleric moves ... *almost* as if he were a circulating text ... [but] he bears within him the National Church, the institution that is neither church nor state, yet embodies the authority of the one and the personal freedom of the other."[85] Even the institutionally minded Coleridge of the *Biographia* and *The Statesman's Manual* contends that the church/state establishment, so conceived, is not sufficient to provide intellectual or moral leadership, and an

otherly principled circulation, resistant to mere commercial
reproduction, remains a necessary part of the solution.

Southey would be similarly wistful a few years later. On the
institution of the itinerant friar, disestablished by Henry VIII, he
would argue:

[W]e have felt, and still feel, and perhaps shall one day feel yet more
severely, the evil consequences of having disbanded the whole auxiliary
force of the Church; who did *for* it what the Methodists and other pro-
selytizing sectaries are now doing *against* it; and performed duties which
the parochial clergy had never been numerous enough to discharge in
all places, had the zeal in every case existed, and which, however zealous,
it is not possible that they should discharge in populous places. Their
institution, by rendering poverty a part of their religious profession,
effected in their behalf the general point of making it perfectly compatible
with general respect.[86]

The distinction between the professional and the mendicant has
hardened, at least in Southey's public, polemical statements, but a
sense of the wanderer's formal powers, including his or her power
as an example, remains. Aligned with the anti-enthusiastic reaction, Southey, like Coleridge, retains his belief in the power of
circulation to reaffirm as well as to blow up constitutional ties.

As a final example, one might consider that great Wordsworthian avatar the Wanderer, transformed from "Armytage" and
"The Pedlar" in succeeding versions of "The Ruined Cottage" into
one of the moral spokesmen of *The Excursion*. In the Wanderer's
meeting with the Pastor, the itinerant and the institution stand
nearly twinned:

> Nature had framed them both, and both were marked
> By circumstance, with intermixture fine
> Of contrast and resemblance. To an oak
> Hardy and grand, a weather-beaten oak,
> Fresh in the strength and majesty of age,
> One might be likened: flourishing appeared,
> Though somewhat past the fullness of his prime,
> The other-like a stately sycamore,
> That spreads, in gentle pomp, its honied shade.[87]

The Pastor, whose wealth and gentility enhance his standing and
reaffirm the link between old estates and the continuing Anglican
mission, is likened to a "stately" tree that encompasses the scene
with its shade – an easy metaphor for the aesthetic necessity of an

established church as Wordsworth perceives it in 1815. However, the Wanderer, whose itinerancy leads him to spread religious truths across the landscape, is "fresh in the strength of majesty and age," unlike the Pastor, and it is he, not the Pastor, who is granted the status of the Burkean, state-defining oak. In this most orthodox-seeming of poems, the extra-institutional Wanderer remains the source of national strength and well-being, a fact to which the Poet, the central character of the Anglican epic, is called on to bear witness. "Every office has a history," Everett Hughes reminds us, "in which the informal and unique have become formal and somewhat impersonal."[88] For the Lake poets, itinerancy remains the sign of an informality that really wants to, but is fortunately unable to, become "official."

CHAPTER 5

William Cowper and the itinerant Lake poet

I COWPER'S PROFESSIONAL CONVERSION

In my last chapter, I discussed the Lake poets' response to the figure of the itinerant preacher. This chapter addresses a specific poetic predecessor whose involvement in evangelical religion and professional identity is especially intense. Critics have always been aware that William Cowper's experiments in informal diction and his execution of a long meditation in blank verse, *The Task*, make him one of the Lake poets' central influences. He also shares with them the dilemma of thwarted professional authority. Like his (and their) predecessor Young, Cowper is involved in the question of authorized and unauthorized speech, and like Young, he is particularly interested in situations that allow for extra-institutional acts of religious persuasion. Where Cowper's professional life and his literary doubles evoke a paradoxically reluctant form of such language, however, the Lake poets would discover a source of poetic and professional confidence. In a group of texts that includes *Peter Bell*, *The Rime of the Ancient Mariner*, and *Madoc*, the conversion experience that is persuasion's origin, and that is central to Cowper's authorial identity, is imagined as having the potential to found new institutions and new professional roles rather than subordinating itself to old ones.

At first glance, the process that goes into making a professional has little in common with the Pauline thunderbolt of religious rebirth. As we have seen, however, professional formation occurs over the course of a Humean duration that justifies the practitioner both cumulatively and at every individual moment. It is its own mystery, especially when self-justification goes beyond mere practice and attempts to sustain charismatic or aristocratic claims on the basis of talent and experience. Conversion, despite its apparent emphasis on a binary before-and-after, similarly takes place in more than one temporal frame, as indicated for example by William James' speculation that "instantaneous conversion" begins in a "subliminal" region before erupting into the conscious mind.[1] Shaun Irlam's account of an "'[e]nthusiastic' hermeneutic vision," wherein conversion involves an ongoing perception of time and space as the "self-different" grounds of ultimate intelligibility, may in this way be generalized and extended.[2] As the enthusiast reads what Irlam describes as a semiotically enriched and a merely secular time/space at once, he or she holds in mind what has preceded rebirth along with the controversial possibility, defended for instance by Wesley, that a process of "perfection" extends beyond salvation and into the future.

Of the figures considered in this study, Cowper's encounter with the professions is most closely associated with, and is most seemingly opposed to, the processes of spiritual rebirth. In 1763, after years of waiting, the thirty-two-year-old Cowper was finally offered the Parliamentary clerkship of journals, a position his uncle Ashley had at his disposal and for which Cowper, called to the bar nine years earlier, should have been able to qualify. Opponents of the appointment demanded a public examination, however, which Cowper was not willing to undergo, and this led to his withdrawal from consideration. The situation demonstrates how technique-based and less rationalized means of distributing work, rather than forming a simple historical sequence, coexist and compete. Ashley Cowper's free handling of his patents had already been censured by the Lords, who evidently believed that the point of the system of places was to funnel jobs to qualified people, and while Cowper's examination was not automatic, the demand for it had to be abided by once it was made.[3] On the other hand, the intention of Cowper's opponents was not to open the position up to free competition, but to preserve it for the (highly qualified) son of the man who had previously held it. Cowper was caught in a net of professional loyalties and affiliations that were expected to produce a measurable outcome by a variety of personalized, informal means. Conditioned to expect the ease of a family-held sinecure, he was caught unprepared.

Cowper's fear of the examination and his inability to negotiate Parliament's administrative politics did not just dissuade him from taking the clerkship. They drove him to a breakdown and to a series of suicide attempts which led, ultimately, to his confinement at the hospital in St. Albans. This is where he underwent the final stages of what had always been, his autobiographical *Adelphi* would later claim, a necessary and divinely ordained process: a terrifying "conviction of sin and expectation of judgment" were succeeded by a well meant but inadequate intention to "lead a better life," and, finally, by a transformational and "experimental," that is, experiential, "assurance of faith" in the "sufficiency" of Christ's atonement.[4] *Adelphi's* focus on the clerkship breakdown suppresses some aspects of Cowper's biography and, necessarily, fails to anticipate others. He had suffered from depression before, particularly in relation to a failed courtship; in the decades to come, he would grow distant from the evangelical mission, and his crippling melancholia would periodically return. It remains fair to say, however, that the breakdown-conversion sequence associated with the clerkship is pivotal in the development of Cowper's authorial identity. Before, he had been a satirical gentleman poet, idling in the Middle Temple and living out a dwindling patrimony among a set of distinguished wits. After, he becomes the lay hymnist of Olney, permanently supported by the generosity of various patrons and ultimately writing what would be his most important and influential religiously themed verse. In *Adelphi*, Cowper would explicitly argue that a providential economy had taken the place of a corrupt professional one. Having given up the final sinecure in his possession as an act of conscience and thus reducing himself "to an income scarce sufficient for my maintenance," he reports that "the Lord has since raised up such friends as have enabled me to enjoy all the comforts and conveniences of life."[5]

While it may appear, then, that the enthusiastic, retired author emerges as the alternative to the failed professional, critics have also recognized that Cowper's authorial mission continues to reflect back on its originary disaster. For Julie Ellison, Cowper's "inability to enter gainfully into the masculine public culture of London professionals " leads to a "mediated" interest in the periodical press and its powers of expression, and Conrad Brunstrom argues that Cowper's "recurrent fear of public exposure" is balanced by an "equally strong" intention to fill a public, speech-oriented role.[6] In addition, "speech" and "representation" are closely aligned in a system that perceives electoral and professional patronage as compatible aspects of a single regime. Although Cowper's *Adelphi* loyally smears the motivations of his uncle's enemies, Charles Ryskamp points out that Cowper would in other ways be "ambivalent" about the established system of "'place' and 'interest,'" sometimes denouncing corruption but other times seeking patrons and sinecures.[7] Whatever this ambivalence tells us about the author's personality, it has a broader context. As Tim Fulford has shown, Cowper's hostility to post-Walpolean jobbery, combined with his attraction to Chathamite assertiveness abroad, amount to a recognizable form of "patriotism" that separates the two; as Fulford concludes, the Country position has been "reconstituted … more vulnerably" by a new poetry of retirement that depends on a disenfranchised, not an independently genteel, poetic speaker.[8] Again, Cowper's status as, in his own words, a "non-propertied gentleman" who cannot vote, is specifically produced by his retreat from London's professional world and his move to the country, with its more rigid property qualifications for the franchise.[9] While Beattie could continue to draw on the model of the independent lay reasoner, whose freedom from the ills of unreformed politics and from the spoils-system of patronage is equally absolute, Cowper remains aware that assertions of individual authority can be fundamentally based in a failure to engage with established institutions, sometimes for better, other times for worse – but always under the onus of the new vulnerability Fulford describes, and for which, as I shall discuss, a dangerously revolutionary enablement is a possible successor.

Cowper's enthusiastic ambivalence is manifest in his poetry at various points, but the fault line is located between lay and authorized expression. In poems such as "Table Talk" and *The Task*, he enunciates the idea that neither poets nor lawyers can be depended on to do what he is in fact doing, arguing in public for his particular account of spiritual truth. This discomforting position fits in with a ready-to-hand, classical vocabulary of poetic prophecy that is a source of nostalgia and some anxiety. In *Table Talk*, for example, Cowper evinces longing for the "inspired" state of "British bards":

> [I]n a Roman mouth, the graceful name
> Of prophet and of poet was the same:
> Hence British poets, too, the priesthood shar'd,
> And every hallow'd druid was a bard.
> But no prophetic fires to me belong;
> I play with syllables, and sport in song.[10]

Despite Cowper's praise for contemporaries such as Churchill, his language is a reminder that a long line of vatic poets seems to have exhausted itself in the urbanities of the post-Augustan satirist. The disability he describes is meant to be representative not only of the speaker or his age but of an entire history of secular writing:

> Pity religion has so seldom found
> A skilful guide into poetic ground!
> The flowers would spring where'er she deign'd to stray,
> And ev'ry Muse attend her in her way. (716–719)
>
> . . . .
>
> The shelves are full, all other themes are spread;
> Hackney'd and worn to the last flimsy thread,
> Satire has long since done his best; and curst
> And loathsome ribaldry has done his worst[.] (726–729)
>
> . . . .
>
> And 'tis the sad complaint, and almost true,
> Whate'er we write, we bring forth nothing new.(732–733)

Here, Cowper is rousing himself to draw the evangelical mission and the vocabulary of prophecy back together: "'Twere new indeed to see a bard all fire,/Touch'd with a coal from heav'n, assume the lyre[,]" and bring the news "[t]hat He, who died below, and reigns above,/Inspires the song, and that his name is love" (742–743; 750–755). The language is resounding, but *Table Talk* wisely ends on a note of genteel anticlimax, its two speakers wondering what would happen if all base and profane poets, which means almost all poets, were to disappear: "No matter – we could shift when they were not;/And should, no doubt, if they were all forgot" (770–771). Offsetting the spiritual call to arms is a wry reminder that British literary culture, long bereft of prophets, may not be especially relevant anyway.

What I have described as ambivalence may to this point be as fairly be characterized as virtuous humility. The poet will not claim prophetic power for himself, and he will not overvalue his own literary vocation. As suggested in Chapter 4, however, the relationship of evangelicalism to the establishment is complicated by the possibility that reform will become dissolution, that, for Cowper in particular, persuasive poetry might have revolutionary effects. His religious speech has it two ways at once. In *The Task*, after again bewailing the limited ability of "satire" to "reclaim" and "reform," the poet turns to describe the most important force in "virtue's cause":

> The pulpit, therefore (and I name it fill'd
> With solemn awe, that bids me well beware
> With what intent I touch that holy thing) –
> The pulpit (when the sat'rist has at last,
> Strutting and vaporing in an empty school,
> Spent all his force and made no proselyte) –
> I say the pulpit (in the sober use
> Of its legitimate, peculiar pow'rs)
> Must stand acknowleg'd, while the world shall stand,
> The most important and effectual guard,
> Support, and ornament of virtue's cause.
> There stands the messenger of truth; there stands
> The legate of the skies! – His theme divine,
> His office sacred, his credentials clear. (II: 326–339)

On the one hand, he is apologizing for his assumption of moral authority. His emphasis on the importance of preaching gives an edge to his subsequent commentary on the state of the church and may also be construed as praise of local figures such as Moses Browne, a pen-cutter and poet before taking orders, and Browne's curate at Olney, John Newton. As the pulpit shades into the cleric it has represented by synecdoche, religious authority comes to be conceived of as the product of an official commission and also as a matter of having the proper "credentials." Cowper's insistence on the pulpit's legitimacy remains an insistence on some kind of regulated, contextualized speech. Yet despite this, the rhetorical device of the parenthesis insists repeatedly that the authorized "messenger of truth" is an ideal or an abstraction, while the speaker here, both prolix and aphasic, is overwrought and real. "I name it," he says, and "I say," his protestations of solemn awe undercut by the formal demands of a conversational style that suddenly boosts the speaking self up into the diction of the sermonizing it claims to resist.

The Task is a solution to the problem Cowper sets out for himself, which is how to write enthusiastically while nominally respecting institutional boundaries, and it differs from *Night Thoughts* in the nature of its elaborately spontaneous excursiveness. Whatever Young's politics, his appeal to noble patronage distinguishes his gentrified sermonizing from Cowper's associative and descriptive style, a style, as Fulford points out, that would be usable for Wordsworth precisely because it was neither "identifiable with the landowning classes nor with the local peasants."[11] Yet at the conclusion of the poem, the language of patronage signals that the professional problem continues to frame Cowper's thinking about his own work:

> In vain the poet sings, and the world hears,
> If [God] regard not, though divine the theme.
> Tis not in artful measures, in the chime
> And idle tinkling of a minstrel's lyre,
> To charm his ear, whose eye is on the heart;
> Whose frown can disappoint the proudest strain,
> Whose approbation prosper – even mine. (VI: 1020–1024)

Frown, approbation, prosperity: God succeeds where, for Johnson and Beattie, George III had failed, exercising an extra-empirical faculty of evaluation, healing the wounds of professional futility, and choosing among performances not according to technical criteria but according to an internal qualification that perfectly counters the politics of cronyism and technique of which Cowper had run so disastrously afoul. A virtuous order recognizes merit, but Cowper's last word has to be that such virtue is inherently supernatural – as in Savage's *Wanderer*, the institutions of the world have proven unable to measure merit precisely, but unlike Savage, Cowper will balance his prophetic mode against a reluctance to take the evaluative role on himself.

II COWPER AND THE LAKE POETS: THREE EXAMPLES

The influence of Cowper on the Lake poets, as I have mentioned, is well known, and some of the most familiar examples, such as Coleridge's echoes of *The Task* in "Frost at Midnight" and "Kubla Khan," or the explicit pursuit of mission borrowed from *The Task* by *The Prelude*, demand continued notice.[12] In what follows, however, I am particularly interested in a sequence of texts that depend less on direct citations of Cowper than on an association of major themes and concerns. In Wordsworth's *Peter Bell*, Wordsworth revisits the question of persuasive, evangelical speech in a framework that is persistently Cowperian; in *The Rime of the Ancient Mariner*, the story of the helpless itinerant echoes Cowper's first popular poem, "The History of John Gilpin"; and in *Madoc*,

Southey also examines the dynamics of charismatic persuasion in ways that finally offer to subsume church and state to the energies of the hard-working professional poet.

The connections between *Peter Bell* and Cowper are intriguing if indirect. *Peter Bell* is roughly contemporary with "Tintern Abbey" – a reading of an early version of the poem is reported between May and June of 1798, with "Tintern" composed in July – and "Tintern" is closely indebted to *The Task*. Cowper remains on Wordsworth's mind in June of 1802, in the defense of "The Idiot Boy" discussed in Chapter 4. According to the letter to Wilson, Cowper has almost, but only almost, overcome "false notions" regarding natural objects, and this genteel distaste is directly assaulted not only by the "Idiot Boy" but by *Peter Bell's* tale of working-class violence and enthusiastic conversion.[13] Wordsworth's plot is set into motion by cruelty to animals, and Cowper is a significant predecessor on this point. In particular, Cowper's disquisition on the subject (in Book VI of *The Task*) is punctuated by an allusion to the story of Balaam's ass, where the beast of burden, after enduring cruelty, is supernaturally transformed into a prophet's savior. The circumstance is reprised in *Peter Bell*, where an ass's stubbornness triggers Peter Bell's enlightenment. The subject of cruelty ripples outward to Peter Bell's tragic flaw, his lack of "human heartedness." As Cowper notes that "the heart is hard in nature, and unfit for human fellowship ... that is not pleased with sight of animals enjoying life" (VI: 321–325), Wordsworth's narrator laments that "Small change it made in Peter's heart/To see his gentle panniered train/With more than vernal pleasure feeding ... " (220–223).

A yet more suggestive connection is between *Peter Bell's* "pious Methodist" and Cowper's own evangelical reputation. It is unclear to what extent the Lake poets had detailed knowledge of Cowper's religious position until the publication of Hayley's 1803 collected letters, although generic gossip about the poet's "madness" was available much earlier, as at least one exchange between Coleridge and Lamb demonstrates.[14] In addition, the sermon Peter Bell overhears accords poorly with the top-down Calvinism dramatized in the *Olney Hymns* and that is the theological basis for Cowper's intermittent, angst-ridden state of conviction-without-conversion. More broadly, though, "Cowper," "evangelicalism," and "Methodism" are terms that converge on the question of professional identity. "The Gentleman's Muse, wears Methodist shoes," Cowper would imagine a reviewer saying about his first volume, and although he is using the term "Methodist" casually, the very ease of the reference distinguishes close doctrinal and ecclesiological debate from the generic, late-century sense that enthusiastic poetry is always somehow "Methodist."[15] As the story of *Peter Bell* depends on evangelical rebirth narratives, Wordsworth discovers the possibility already encoded in *The Task* that spiritual rebirth can serve as a metaphor for the achievement of other kinds of powers of speech.

Damnation is another one of the subjects that connects and divides *The Task* and *Peter Bell.* Among the most widely noted examples of *The Task's* restraint is the relative absence of threatening religious rhetoric in a poem that is both theologically grounded and fiercely satirical. While *The Task* speaks lightly of "grace," allowing a Calvinist element to manifest itself, its final religious vision is of the broad, perhaps even universal "accomplish'd bliss" of the end of days (VI: 760). Cowper can be ferocious as a social critic, but *The Task's* supernatural vocabulary is generally benign, and its brief scary hints of "unrepealable enduring death" are more than offset by any number of visions of "other heavens than these we behold" (V: 610; 571). Even the "stricken deer" passage, psychologically unprotected as it is, describes the speaker's salvation, not his conviction, which is among the reasons Southey and others would later associate *The Task* not with Cowper's evangelical conversion but with his escape from religious madness. In *Peter Bell*, on the other hand, we have one of the most famous instances of hell-talk in Romantic literature. Gazing into the pool where the ass's master has drowned, Peter, unable at first to discern the master's body, is treated to visions of damnation which include this one:

> Is it some party in a parlour,
> Crammed just as they on earth were cramm'd –
> Some sipping punch, some sipping tea,
> But as you by their faces see
> All silent, and all damn'd?[16]

The passage is radical. First of all, it comes to Peter Bell as a vision which might be psychotic – another form of religious madness – and is granted only rhetorical authority in the actual poem. More importantly, if read literally the stanza becomes an attack on genteel complacency, a highly compressed but recognizably Cowperian

satire on class-bound forms of urban life. But from what consciousness does this portrait emerge? The potter is more at home in
a brawling tavern, as the poem takes pains to point out, so why does
he conceive of damnation in terms of parlors? Wordsworth is
interpreting Cowper, and making the point Cowper almost but
does not make himself, which is that enthusiastic subjectivity may
produce overlapping critiques from multiple status perspectives.

Salvation also comes from outside any particular point-of-view:

> It is a voice just like a voice
> Re-echoed from a naked rock,
> It comes from that low chapel, list,
> It is a pious Methodist
> That's preaching to his pious flock.
>
> "Repent, repent," he cries aloud,
> "God is a God of mercy – strive
> To love him, then, with all your might,
> Do that which lawful is and right,
> And save your souls alive.["] (1191–1200)

Most readers agree that Wordsworth is not endorsing Methodism
here but treating the preacher's voice as part of a natural scene that
is generally educative.[17] Nonetheless, in *Peter Bell* the scene has to be
interpreted for a religious madman who otherwise does not
understand its point. "The heart is hard in nature," Cowper has
said, perhaps with a pun in mind, but Wordsworth opposes to this
the possibly Arminian notion that even a naturally hardened heart
can be softened under the right circumstances. The distance which
the poem's speaker adopts toward the character of the "pious
Methodist," instituted by the poem's framing tale, by the extra-
textual understanding that *Peter Bell* will provide a rational explanation for magical phenomena (made explicit in the 1819 publication of the poem, in its dedication to Southey), and by the
narrative fact that the Methodist remains unseen, suggests that the
efficacy of the Methodist's message has always been controlled by
the narrator's approval. Wordsworth responds to Cowper's
ambivalence about poetic speech by elevating poetry above evangelical speech, as Alan Bewell suggests, but only in such a way that
Cowper's enthusiasm and charisma as well as his skepticism about
certain rhetorical gestures are retained for the narrator's didactic
purposes.[18] The speaker and his evangelical character are mutually

interdependent – as an anonymous voice, the Methodist is freed
from the ambivalence which at times plagues Wordsworth and
Cowper both. Because of its success in triggering Peter Bell's conversion, this voice, as reported speech, justifies the narrator's ministry to the squire and his daughter, the parson and his wife, and the
other community leaders who have demanded "the promised tale"
but are in the end rendered silent by it (123–135).

It is possible to trace Cowper's importance to the Lake poets in
other ways, particularly if we bear in mind the longstanding association of *Peter Bell* with *The Rime of the Ancient Mariner*.[19] Because of
what Bewell notes is the interest in "salvific narratives" that *Peter
Bell* and *Rime* share, it is of some interest to correlate the mariner's
moment of regeneration with the protracted revelation of *The
Task*.[20] I would like to proceed, however, by locating Cowper's
importance to *Rime* differently. *The Task* is Cowper's most
important and most highly regarded work, but his writing was first
brought to prominence by the mock-ballad "John Gilpin," which
details the adventures of a linen-draper who is taken on an
uncontrollable ride, from his home in Cheapside to Ware and
back again, by a disobedient horse. Without denying its humorous
effect, close readers of Cowper have always recognized that "John
Gilpin" is also serious. The poem is "[a]rtistic capital wrung from
darker feelings," one such concludes, and another makes a more
pointed case: "Gilpin's horse *is* Cowper's Pegasus, the exhilarat-
ing inspiration which impels him effortlessly forward, but which
he is afraid he may not be able to control, so that it may overshoot
its mark ... returning him to where he began with a sense of
futility and pain."[21] "Gilpin" shares with *Rime* and *Peter Bell* both
the figure of the author as out-of-control itinerant and an innate
seriousness that is at odds with its generic markers.

Some of the lessons "John Gilpin" teaches about eighteenth-
century authorship are reflected in the details of its production,
distribution, and re-appropriation by Cowper and Joseph Johnson.
Published anonymously in 1781, it circulated widely; its dissemination included a popular performance by the actor John
Henderson (not to be confused with Cottle's tutor) in 1784. As
long as it remained anonymous, the ballad was reprinted, redis-
tributed, illustrated, publicly recited, and occasionally added to by
other writers. During this period of circulation, Cowper's main
authorial project was the composition of *The Task*, and upon

completion of that poem there was some discussion about whether "John Gilpin" should be printed along with it. Johnson was concerned that, because the ballad had already been circulated so widely, the reprint would hold the volume back. Cowper argued that, because "Gilpin" was already popular, its inclusion might bring in readers. Ultimately, *The Task* (1785), a volume which concluded with "Gilpin," was highly successful. Cowper was happy to equate good sales with the effective execution of *The Task's* serious work, but "Gilpin" had also been reclaimed. As an anonymous street-ballad, the poem had faced a certain kind of competition: "You tell me that I am rivaled by Mrs. Bellamy; and [Mr. Unwin], that I have a competitor for fame, not less formidable, in the Learned Pig. Alas! what is an author's popularity worth, in a world that can suffer a prostitute on one side, and a pig on the other, to eclipse his brightest glories?"[22] But Cowper is misrepresenting the case for effect. Anonymously circulating, "John Gilpin" competes with pigs and actresses, but the "author's popularity" would not appear to be an issue. Once signed by "William Cowper, esq. of the Inner Temple," and appended to *The Task*, the poem has been privatized while its utility moves from the private to the public – from the purpose of diverting Cowper alone, to the purpose of drawing extra attention to the not-clerical good news of *The Task*. As Cowper puts it, "Causes in appearance trivial produce often the most beneficial consequences, and perhaps my volumes may now travel to a distance, which if they had not been ushered into the world by that notable horseman, they would never have reached."[23]

A brief reading of "John Gilpin" that concentrates on those aspects which are echoed in *Rime* has the double virtue of displaying Coleridge through Cowper and Cowper through Coleridge. It emerges that a central fact of "John Gilpin'"s plot is its sociable occasion. Gilpin and his wife are celebrating a wedding anniversary, their twentieth, and they have arranged to dine at an Edmonton inn, the "Bell," with their three children, Gilpin's sister-in-law, and her child. That is, John Gilpin is a character who is enmeshed in a number of conventionally authorized social relationships. Alongside his immediate and extended family are his involvement in the military, an enduring tie, and in the community, where business and friendship (in particular, the draper's with the calender) are easily combined. This is in contrast to *The Task*, which, as Andrew Elfenbein argues, underscores

Cowper's specific kind of isolation, dangerously making the sub-
urbs a site of the normative and the subversive at once: "By placing
his solitary in a setting so closely associated with women, marriage,
and the family, he drew attention to his anomalous celibacy."[24]
The anomaly, as Elfenbein explains, would only become threatening in the nineteenth century, but it serves to intensify Cowper's
participation in the "literary commonplace" of the "solitary, con-
templative man" by throwing the cost of such isolation, or alter-
natively the different kind of subjectivity such isolation entails, into
relief. The same contrast pertains in *Rime*, where a wedding celebration underscores the positively Cowperian isolation of the mariner during his supernatural voyage – "So lonely 'twas, that God
himself/Scarce seemed there to be" – and it also presents a version
of sociability which the text, by interrupting and forestalling it,
appears to reject in principle. Cowper offers "John Gilpin" as an
antidote for his own melancholy, and the gesture implies more than
the opposition of what is light and humorous to what is not. The
relief "John Gilpin" offers is in its socially consolidated as well as
perfectly cheerful middle-class milieu.

Yet this analysis under-reads "John Gilpin" at least partially. The
fortunes of social understanding are in "Gilpin" mixed, and in ways
that Coleridge will reiterate. While Gilpin and his social habitat are
mutually familiar in many ways, his wild ride has the effect of
immersing him in a less stable interpretive context. The loss of his
cloak anticipates the entry of the ancient mariner's ship into
unknown seas, not as an effect of direct influence, but because both
poems are producing language under the twin pressures of the
jingling ballad line and an authorial fixation on public perception:

> The wind did blow, the cloak did fly,
> Like streamer loud and gay,
> Till, loop and button failing both,
> At last it flew away. (101–104)

The loss of the "long red cloak, well-brushed and neat" (75)
follows the loss of hat and wig, an event of which Gilpin had "little
dreamt" (99) and which signifies the loss of the outward signs of
Gilpin's "credit and renown" (2). Subsequently, his career from
Cheapside to Ware is witnessed, and is commented on, by observers who do not know who he is or do not understand his actions.
Free to misinterpret the outward signs of his predicament, the

out-of-control horse and the wine bottles which look like weights, they understand these not as symptoms of a desire for reunion but as the props of a violent acquisitiveness. Either Gilpin is in a race for a large financial stake, as some speculate, or he is an escaping thief, as "six gentlemen" later assume (116; 233).

Even his reunion with his family has a component of disappointed display:

> Said John – It is my wedding-day,
> And all the world would stare,
> If wife should dine at Edmonton,
> And I should dine at Ware! (193–196)

As noted, John may be worrying for nothing, or at least to no good effect. "The world" will be staring anyway, and at least some members of it will be persistent in attributing commercial motives to his diverting ride. Like his attempt to manage the calender's horse, his attempt to manage the public perception of his domestic habits will be thwarted by forces outside of his, or anybody's, control. Perhaps only the most neurotic reader is worried that, because "where he had got up/He did again get down," he has not yet reached the inn at Edmonton. One supposes that the post boy who has followed him back to Cheapside will, for the promised guinea, reunite Gilpin with his wife and family. Still, the conclusion holds out the troubling possibility that Gilpin, like the wedding-guest, will miss the communal celebration which he has been promised.

John Gilpin's banter, one of the primary ingredients of the poem's humor, reinforces Cowper's comic vision, but here, too, the price of good cheer is the loss of volition. Gilpin's final words, addressed to the mischievous horse, are quickly designated as "luckless speech, and bootless boast!" (21) (In fact, Gilpin's language is outdone by a "braying ass" whose song startles the horse back into his gallop. [203]) The character has the gift of commenting with sympathy on what has already taken place, but his speech makes nothing happen. He is the obverse of the ancient mariner, in that he makes his auditors happier but no wiser. The poem comes to a particularly apt conclusion:

> Now let us sing – Long live the king,
> And Gilpin long live he;
> And, when he next doth ride abroad,
> May I be there to see! (249–252).

Having run out of commentary, the narrator brings in George III
and raises the possibility that the ride will repeat itself. This kind of
repetition is plainly both impossible and undesirable. Gilpin's
adventure is interesting and funny only because its exact circumstances (the bottles, the runaway horse, the twentieth anniversary)
are unlikely to repeat themselves. The narrator's banter serves the
same function as that of his character's, off-setting the universe of
significant things by failing to influence or participate in it. This is
why "John Gilpin" is a fit companion-piece for *The Task*, wherein
the things of the universe are rescued from insignificance by the
attention of an authorial consciousness whose preparation,
including the preparation entailed by loss, injury, and desolation
as well as conversion, has been perfect.

It is also a reason "John Gilpin" serves as a precursor to *The Rime of
the Ancient Mariner*, the text to which I now turn. My association of
Ancient Mariner with the ballad forerunner "John Gilpin" does not
aim at confusing two very different kinds of poems but at highlighting certain dynamics that they share. In both cases, authorial
stand-ins are subjected to a world of experience that does not appear
to be motivated or coherent, but while in "John Gilpin" this lack of
coherence ultimately means that the author stand-in remains without credentials, unable to and perhaps unwilling to establish himself, in *Rime* the lack signifies what is arbitrary but nonetheless real
about professional development. The mariner and his adventures
do not explain but abstract the way the urgent speaker comes to find
himself within his task, thus finding himself in a position to compete
with the institutions that have preceded him.

Because of the poem's obscurity, recognized from its publication
on, and because of the successive series of glosses and frames that
only foreground the matter of interpretive authority, *Rime* has
inevitably raised the question not only of what the poem means but
what it means to read it. Thus Frances Ferguson recognizes that
the poem "is filled with arbitrary events," but rigorously avoids
the conclusion that it therefore "has no discursively translatable
meaning."[25] Instead, the poem proves to be about the impossibility
of learning what you don't already know, a morally perilous
although humanly inevitable position since, at least for Coleridge,
"original sin [is] interpretation from a limited perspective."[26]
Similarly, recent, historically conscious critics implicitly acknowledge the poem's involvement with interpretation as an after effect

of violent experience. Accounting for its attitudes toward slavery, for example, Debbie Lee argues that *Rime of the Ancient Mariner* becomes a lesson in the work of "the distanced imagination"; stricken by the fever of "European guilt," the by turns compelling and repulsive figure of the mariner tells two stories at once: slavery is a moral disease, not a physical one, and the cure for it is "to relate to what is other than self."[27] As in Ferguson, the mariner becomes the object of his own lesson, and the dynamics of understanding his tale prove to be what the tale is meant to express.

In other words, varied critical perspectives tend toward the observation that while the poem at first appears to be about the mariner's experiences, it is more particularly about how those experiences are the precondition for a relationship between mariner and audience. Further, while "experience" might be expected to reveal or develop character in narrative, the mariner's lack of what Wordsworth called "distinct character" has become central to how we read the poem.[28] Susan Eilenberg has noted that "The 'Rime' [is] one of the most deeply and elaborately anonymous poems ever written"; interestingly, she also joins those readers who consider the poem to be at least partially autobiographical.[29] A consequence of this interpretation is that what is impossible for the nameless mariner is merely a subset of what is impossible for authors. There is no plenum of meaning within which "identity" and "character" are joined, a situation that both recalls and adjusts the narrative of "John Gilpin," where a socially determined set of recognized values is either undermined or darkly mirrored by an audience's failure of understanding and a traveler's failure of expression and control.

As in some other poems of itinerancy, *Rime* seeks to redeem destructive trials by claiming that experience is cumulative. Yet *Rime* is also far too conscious of horror to draw this moral directly. The wisdom- (and sadness-) bringing mariner is both characterless and cruelly embodied. Similarly, his experiences are both illegible and carefully detailed. The great outbreak of randomness in the poem occurs during the dice-game between life and death-in-life, and I take this as my example:

> Her lips were red, her looks were free,
> Her locks were as yellow as gold:
> Her skin was as white as leprosy,

> The Night-Mair Life-in-Death was she,
> Who thicks man's blood with cold.
>
> The naked hulk alongside came,
> And the twain were casting dice;
> "The game is done! I've won, I've won"
> Quoth she, and whistles thrice. (1834: 190–198)

Now deprived of a proper afterlife, the mariner's death-in-life has become, as the result of what was presumably a fifty-fifty chance, the constitutive principle of his ministry. *Rime* thus demonstrates how random and terrifying a process it is to come even to partial knowledge, especially the risk-laden knowledge of life, death, maritime law (or its absence) and sin that the mariner has been exposed to and now must share. What follows is gothic, and it is no wonder the wedding guest recoils from the mariner and his story. The acquisition of expertise, the poem suggests, is not pretty. To put this another way, this wanderer has been convicted and is reborn, but the process is excruciating.

The armature of the poem is the inverted enthusiasm of the mariner's mission, which, like the mission of "Adventures on Salisbury Plain'"s sailor, is profoundly unwilled. A "woeful agony" wrenches the mariner's "frame," compelling him to spread the news:

> I pass, like night, from land to land;
> I have strange power of speech;
> The moment that his face I see,
> I know the man that must hear me:
> To him my tale I teach. (1834: 586–590)

While Graham Davidson has observed that the "kirk" of the poem's conclusion is "sufficiently close to 'church' to share some of its significance, but sufficiently removed from 'The Church' not to disturb Coleridge's Unitarian sympathies," the kirk/church remains notional.[30] As in "Adventures on Salisbury Plain," the scope of this ministry to the guilty is inherently extra-institutional. Like the ending of that poem, the conclusion here is colored by a sense of reprobation which the Unitarian Coleridge may not have formally accepted, but which is one pole in the dialectic that drives a figure like Cowper and which always shadows the workings of enthusiasm. Whereas "The Idiot Boy" is a poem about the necessary distance between the individual poet and the secrets of experience that may empower him or strike him mute, *Rime* is more aggressive in confronting the poet-figure with experience and marking him as directly touched by it. "The Idiot Boy" had insisted on an unexpected beauty where an untrained audience found repulsiveness, but *Rime* enacts the conviction that precedes professional conversion and is inseparable from it. Unlike John Gilpin, finally, the mariner really is able to establish a new if sad regime, one that is both self-reflexive and self-perpetuating. Like Cowper, however, the figure at the center of this regime remains in a state of profound spiritual conflict. William Ulmer has recently and convincingly emphasized that the mariner's experiences make him an apostle who suffers, humanly, from "residual guilt"; "he must be reborn through an emotional reorientation no moral calculus could predict."[31] My claim, that this structure of experience and effect is a professional one, is not meant to eclipse or revise interpretations such as Ulmer's, which demonstrates that Coleridge's Unitarian meditation on guilt and suffering is the product of a human-hearted theology. Rather, I argue that for Cowper, Coleridge, and the mariner, a search for redemption is indivisible from a search for meaningful, enthusiastic work. Further, this search inevitably and productively opposes itself to those actual forms of work with which the poets were most closely, if sometimes disappointingly or violently, engaged.

Southey's *Madoc* has a special place in the articulation of texts I have been examining and in Southey's self-construction as a writer. A running project over the course of the 1790s that Southey finally published, after much revision, in 1805, the poem roams freely over Cowperian subject matter, particularly the role of persuasive religious speech in the foundation and maintenance of social order. At the same time, it is profoundly unlike *The Task* in theme and tone, international where Cowper is domestic, event-driven where Cowper's poem is meditative, unremittingly sonorous and declamatory where Cowper offers a range of often quieter modes and moods. Given their common interest in evangelical speech, however, and given the natural link between the eighteenth-century failed lawyer/author and the Romantic law student (and fellow Westminster student) who would become his biographer, it is profitable to consider the poems as a sequence. Southey's energetic "vulgarity," as Marilyn Butler describes it, is a counter to the Cowperian divine chit-chat that Wordsworth and

Coleridge would temper into an idiom of lyric transcendence, but it is also a counterpart.[32] While *Madoc* is aggressive in depicting charismatic, successful speech, the poem finally diminishes the importance of this speech for the sake of a bureaucratic, and ironized, version of the professional poet.

The aphasia which *Peter Bell* cures and *Rime* transforms is almost entirely absent from *Madoc*, in which characters give rousing speeches, generally to great effect, with some regularity. Many of these speeches have manifest evangelical sources, such as the sermon given by the blind Cynetha, which is drawn directly from the North American adventures of Wesley.[33] (Southey would mock the Guardian Angel's analogous moment in Joseph Cottle's evangelical *Alfred*, but he found his own uses for this kind of set-piece.[34]) The final sermon given by Madoc himself, which results in "The Conversion of the Hoamen," similarly derives force both from its Catholic iconicity and from an evangelical mode of performance:

> ... Before them, raised
> On high, the sacred Images are borne.
> There, in faint semblance, holiest Mary bends
> In virgin beauty o'er her blessed babe, ...
> A sight, that almost to idolatry
> Might win the soul by love ....
> ... Madoc then advanced,
> And raised, as if in act to speak, his hand.
> Thereat was every human sound suppressed;
> And every quicken'd ear and eager eye
> Centered to wait his word. (VIII: 25–30; 43–46.)

Southey's employment of Catholic and evangelical modes is licensed by the historical and geographical context of Madoc's story, but this is in turn a license to reconsider the foundations of institutional order, which, since both sermons follow the military pacification of local populations, depend on a combination of physical bravery, theatricality, and conviction. Madoc is a literalized ancient mariner, and the grip of the mariner's hand on the wedding-guest's arm has been expanded to the control of a mythical Welsh army over the land of the Hoamen. In fact, every kind of national power, religious, ideological, bureaucratic, comes to the hand of the peace-loving Madoc, and the convergence of the mythical prince and real-world mechanisms of dominance makes it possible to argue that *Madoc* is a poem that abandons poetic professionalism in favor of nationalist ideology – Madoc's power is no longer the power of speech but an emblem of British industrial and military force. Caroline Franklin emphasizes that the 1805 version of the poem contains vestiges of a revolution-era "enlightenment cosmopolitanism," represented perhaps by Cynetha's Wesleyan observation that "Our God . . . is the same,/ The Universal Father" and his Wordsworthian intention "to waken up that living sense/That sleeps within ye!", but she argues that these impulses are overcome in favor of raw imperialism (VIII: 151–152; 179–180).[35] Conveniently, from this perspective, Southey's warrior-evangelist sees print just in time to celebrate the establishment of British naval dominance with Nelson's victory off the coast of Trafalgar.

To the extent that this is the case, *Madoc* presents a sophisticated understanding of the monarchical function in an increasingly commercial and industrial nation. Given the centrality of the charismatic warrior-bard to the poem which bears his name, and given the poem's apparent investment in his heroic, evangelical imperialism, it is striking that Prince Madoc, most readers feel, never fully holds the stage. The Wordsworths were not the last to complain of *Madoc*, as they had complained of *Rime*, that "it cannot be said that any of the characters interest you much," but the critique seems as inappropriate for Southey's poem as it did for Coleridge's, although for slightly different reasons.[36] One interpretive possibility is that, over the long duration of history, the organizational skills of the founder become retrospectively de-personalized. Southey had very recently said about Wesley that his power "was actually monarchical or papal while he lived, and yet his death occasioned no more change or difficulty to the society, than would have been produced at Berne by the loss of the national bears."[37] Madoc may be unlovable, or virtually unrepresentable, because he stands in for an abstract historical process. Here, Southey's Napoleon-era conservatism both inverts and confirms Cowper's constitutional patriotism. Describing the British attitude toward the monarchy, Cowper tells an imaginary, possibly French auditor that "We love the man. The paltry pageant you./We the chief patron of the Commonwealth;/You the regardless author of its woes" (V: 348–349). "The man," reduced in the way Beattie would also discover, is lovable only because he exists within a humanly designed and containing social framework that draws charisma out of the office of the monarch. Southey's Madoc, who is not humanized or domesticated, deflects the luxurious suasions of courtly tyranny by remaining abstract.

Madoc's failure to found a lasting civilization is another symptom of the poem's wartime conservatism. Lynda Pratt explains that the radical ideals of the 1790s grow more remote during the composition of *Madoc* as early versions of the poem that depend on a Pantisocratic vision get rewritten, and the 1805 edition only bears the traces of an ideal, pantisocratic community for which Madoc, in other historical guises, might have claimed responsibility.[38] In place of utopia, *Madoc* presents an account of natural and human history that appears to be a brutal reduction of Cowper's providentialism as well as of his admittedly bellicose Country ethic. Finally driven out by a volcano that ironically interrupts a human sacrifice, the Aztecas leave Madoc "sole lord" of Aztlan and migrate to Mexico, where they will "rear a mightier empire" based on

> foul idolatry; till Heaven,
> Making blind Zeal and bloody Avarice
> Its ministers of vengeance, sent among them
> The heroic Spaniard's unrelenting sword. (XXVII: 389–395).

Commenting on a series of late-century natural disasters, Cowper had similarly attributed geological and meteorological violence to human sinfulness, but he exploits a relatively more nuanced vocabulary of crime and punishment to explain the circumstances: "[W]here all/Stand chargeable with guilt ... / ... God may choose his mark" (II: 154–155). Southey's quick, lethal conclusion, another symptom of what has been called *Madoc*'s "hybrid horror," seems by comparison to reveal an impossibly narrow and inhumane worldview.[39]

What I would like to argue, however, is that Southey is taking advantage of a still-available providential shorthand that Cowper had believed it was necessary, and possible, to justify at length. The divine machinations that appear linear and causal in the context of a merely imperial epic are not expected to be taken literally by a sophisticated British audience that can distinguish romance from reality and magic from theology (although, as Elisa E. Beshero-Bondar points out, the poem was usually read straight).[40] As in the relationship of Peter Bell to the narrator, or the ancient mariner to the wedding guest, Southey's approach to his audience is affirmed by a ratio. Here, the schematically drawn prince represents the possibilities and the long-term failures of a primordial institution, while the author, who commands the reader to "LISTEN TO MY LAY!" in his table of contents, has thoroughly ironized just as he has depersonalized the evangelical power of the prehistoric, not-quite-professional leader. Without an adequately supportive civilization, Madoc's heroic efforts fade into myth. Within an advanced institutional ecology, the author Southey is able to depict successful evangelical speech while withholding his full endorsement of it.

One way of defining the difference between the Lake writers and Cowper is by opposing the latter's pre-romantic, explanatory discursiveness to Romantic figurality and suggestion. As Marshall Brown observes, Cowper succeeds in "divorc[ing] consciousness from attention" but does not recognize the dialectical relationship between them – as a corollary, one Romantic claim to authority is based on the poet's possession, and expression, of new dialectical knowledge.[41] It may be argued that for Southey, the claim to know has become too submerged or is not being made at all. Absorbed by the bardic apparatus that "Hymn to the Penates" treats self-consciously, the Southeyan epic remains most easily read in terms of its arguments and its surfaces. Southey's depiction of the hero-bard, however, indicates the limits of the imaginary poetic claim, while the author, happily pushing his material as far as it will go, signals an instrumental distance between author and text, intention and expression. Unlike Cowper, Southey has discovered the professional creed that draws on the eighteenth century and will in many ways shape the ideologies of work in the years to come: produce! produce! Madoc's evangelical power stands as a display of poetic expertise, not (or not only) of religious enthusiasm or imperialist commitment.

Southey repeats *Madoc*'s professional adaptation of the enthusiastic impulse in other places. As the author of important biographies of both Wesley (1820) and Cowper (1835), he is the Lake writer who is most transparently involved with the subjects invoked by this chapter and the previous one. As mentioned in Chapter 4,

Southey's public identity as an establishment spokesman would lead him to resist enthusiastic challenges to Church order. Thus, in the Cowper biography, Southey works to distance the author from professional failure and from his enthusiastic New Birth, an agenda which requires Southey to read the evangelical Cowper against himself. Cowper's *Adelphi* describes the poet's resistance to public speech as the proximate, but it insists that the sinful state of his soul is the ultimate cause of his vocational trouble, and it does so in such a way that the corruption of place-holding is intertwined with Cowper's personal failings. Impatient to get his career under way, Cowper reports, he had wished for the death of the clerk who held the position he wanted, and "[t]hus did I covet what God had commanded me not to covet, and involved myself in still deeper guilt by doing it in the spirit of a murderer. It pleased the Lord to give me my heart's desire and in it, and with it, an immediate punishment of my crime."[42] Southey re-interprets this sense of conviction into a vocabulary of rigorous preparation that comes down to a different kind of personal failure: "The fault Cowper had committed," he informs us, "was that of neglecting those professional studies by which he might not only have maintained himself [until the clerkship became available], but render himself independent of it if any unforeseen event should disappoint his reasonable expectations."[43] Southey denies that the "wish whereof he accuses himself" could have been formulated except retrospectively, once the excessive introspection of the enthusiast has distorted his recollection: "Common nature is not so depraved as to form murderous wishes for such motives."[44] Instead, Southey interprets Cowper's career so that enthusiasm, which leads to the wrong kind of work, must be overcome by a responsible authorship that takes the place of a too-irresponsible legal career.

Southey's Cowper biography further poses itself against its evangelical competition by arguing that Cowper's religiosity is a cause or a symptom, not the cure, for his mental problems, and Southey's recuperation of Cowper's common-sense orthodoxy is part of a broader project to reinterpret the sources of his literary significance. Of the period of the *Olney Hymns*, Southey writes,

His malady in its latter stage had been what is termed religious madness; and if his recovery was not supposed by himself, and Mr. Newton also, to have been directly miraculous, it had been occasioned or accompanied by impressions, which, though favourable in their consequences at that crisis, indicated a frame of mind to which any extraordinary degree of devotional excitement must be dangerous. The ministerial offices in which his friend engaged him were highly so; and in composing the Olney Hymns he was led to brood over his own sensations in a way which rendered him particularly liable to be deluded by them.[45]

The solution for Cowper's melancholy would be a kind of poetry that dispersed "religious madness" instead of honing it to a point. Southey suggests of the eleven-year period between his second breakdown and his renewed poetic career that "Cowper was rarely so miserable as he suggested himself to be when speaking of his own case."[46] Writing the more diffuse (although still fervent) *Task* alleviated Cowper's condition even if it could not cure him, and ultimately, Southey grants Cowper a kind of professional heroism that belies his public diffidence. Identifying Cowper as the figure who breaks Pope's hold on British prosody, Southey cites a great cleric and man of letters on behalf of a figure whose independence would question the entire structure upon which that cleric's style of life depended: "Bishop Hurd said," Southey reports, "'that Pope had shut the door against poetry ... [but] if Pope shut the door, Cowper opened it.'"[47] Yet while Cowper also measured himself against Pope, the full implications of Hurd's liberatory metaphor were difficult for Cowper to embrace.[48] Convict and convert, his own printed exhortations enacted the drama of a new professionalism temporarily immobilized by the claims of the old.

PART IV

The Lake school, professionalism, and the public

CHAPTER 6

Robert Southey and the claims of literature

The talk of ministering to the higher wants and more refined pleasures of the species, being both more dignified and more agreeable than that of supplying their vulgar necessities, multitudes are induced to undertake [literature] without any great preparation; and the substantial business of life is defrauded of much valuable labour, while the elegant arts are injured by a crowd of injudicious pretenders ... Shoemakers and tailors astonish the world with plans for reforming the constitution, and with effusions of relative and social feeling.
– The *Edinburgh Review*, April, 1803[1]

In 1802, Southey engaged in a brief but intense feud with the Reverend Herbert Croft over a group of letters written by Thomas Chatterton. Croft and Chatterton represented two divergent, even opposite, attitudes toward authorship, and the feud gave Southey the opportunity to articulate his most progressive version of poetic professionalism. Croft, an Anglican priest and man-of-letters, combined entrepreneurial literary endeavors with an ongoing (if perpetually frustrated) search for preferment within the Church. In addition to the biography of Young discussed in Chapter 1, his literary projects included a never-completed revision of Samuel Johnson's dictionary, a "tract against treason" sparked by the Gordon Riots, and an epistolary novel, *Love and Madness*, that detailed a widely known love affair which ended in murder.[2] An impoverished baronet as well as a priest and dependent on the support of a genteel readership, he was the type and form of the establishment writer. On the other hand, Chatterton was, for Southey, the writer-without-means, a poor sexton's son who meets his doom when he pins his hopes on the untrammeled workings of the literary marketplace. Croft's attachment to the established powers of his society transcended his commitment to his writerly vocation. Chatterton, striving (and failing) to earn his living as an author in the absence of other resources, represented a literary underclass that opposed itself to Croft's favored network of institutions. Croft, despite the financial difficulties he endured, stood for (and by) the establishment – that is, for the collection of social and economic interests defined by the political supremacy of landed property and the cultural supremacy of the Church and the universities.

In 1778 Croft acquired, published, and profited by letters which Chatterton had written to his mother and his sister, and Southey, seeking in 1799 to get help for Chatterton's poor relatives, publicly touched on the issue of the letters and on Croft's behavior. Twenty-three years younger than the conservative Croft and recently known for his political radicalism, Southey was at that time in the process of defining himself in relation to his own literary practice, and, as my discussion will show, the form of his allegiance to Chatterton's surviving relatives constituted a strong repudiation of Croft's establishment and its system of essentially hereditary affiliations. In his commitment to this entity, Croft represented for Southey an undesirable subsuming of professional integrity as well as an increasingly unsatisfactory vision of social affiliation. On the other hand, Chatterton's death represented an unacceptable outcome and demonstrated the necessity of replacing the reticular relations of establishment patronage, not with a wild marketplace, but with some form of professional protection and control. Southey's own professionalism would attempt, in effect, to split the difference between these two figures. A poet's encounter with the marketplace would, ideally, be profitable, but an ideology of vocational solidarity would also serve as a new source of status and affiliation transcending birth. Further, it would provide grounds for the protection of individual poets and their families from some of the negative decisions of the marketplace without endorsing the exhausted paternalisms of patronage and charity.

When Croft and Southey argued about Croft's treatment of Chatterton's relatives, they were not only involved in a personal dispute. They were also enacting a broader struggle over the nature of status-determining social categories and the means by which public identity was to be constituted and evaluated.[3] As illustrated by this chapter's epigraph, which is taken from the

Edinburgh Review's discussion of Thelwall's first collection of poems, the question of social category is directly related to the literary marketplace and its function, which is itself dependent on the public identity of writers and thus on understandings about the constitution of public identity in general. The *Edinburgh Review*'s conceptual mingling of poetic ministry and political radicalism underlines the fact that establishment discussions about literary labor do not merely present a metaphor for anxieties about labor or about the working classes in general. Rather, in an age marked by the rise of public opinion as a literary phenomenon, the literary marketplace is crucial in the adjudication of questions about status and identity. While the ''astonishment'' the Edinburgh reviewer displays at the imagined spectacle of scribbling shoemakers and radical tailors expresses one real worry – that men organically suited to trade and drawn to the literary marketplace by its gentlemanly pleasantness will overrun it and establish their own categorical supremacy – it is not primarily fear of the working man or of the debasement of public intellectual life that defines the establishment position. Rather, that position is defined by a defense of gentlemanly control over the construction of gentility and by the fear that control of the construction of status might revert to different, radical, hands. When Croft and Southey fight in the literary arena it is not surprising to find them contesting the very grounds of classification which entitle men to enter that arena.

The Croft-Southey feud is thus an exemplary skirmish not only in Southey's personal career but in the battle over categories which the *Edinburgh Review*er so vividly addresses. In the following sections, I first examine the feud in close detail, paying particular attention to the rhetorical strategies of the two men and the ways in which these strategies play off of opposing understandings of affiliation and vocation. I then turn my attention to another statement about literary professionalism, that made by the founder of the Royal Literary Fund in 1802, which recapitulates Southey's position and participates in a related political-cultural conflict. Finally, I address the treatment of Thomas Chatterton and the constructions of gentility and literary professionalism in Croft's *Love and Madness*. In his novel, Croft reveals the acute contradictions that underwrite his own establishment position.

I CROFT VS. SOUTHEY

The Southey-Croft feud erupts in 1799, but it originates nineteen years earlier. In 1780, Croft had published the epistolary novel *Love and Madness*, a fictionalized account of the murder of the singer Martha Ray (the mother of Wordsworth's friend Basil Montagu) by James Hackman, a former army officer turned Anglican clergyman.[4] While the novel is ostensibly about the romance of Hackman and Ray, nearly a third of it is devoted to an account of Thomas Chatterton's life and work – Croft includes his biographical sketch of Chatterton under the conceit that his fictionalized Hackman, an amateur man of letters, is given to incorporating literary biography and criticism into his correspondence with Martha Ray. The Chatterton section features the eight genuine letters from Thomas Chatterton to Chatterton's mother and his sister, Mrs. Newton, which were the immediate point of contention between Southey and Croft.

In 1799 Southey and Joseph Cottle set out to edit and publish a subscription edition of Chatterton's works and remains for the benefit of Mrs. Newton. (Mrs. Chatterton had already died.) In the course of generating publicity for this edition, Southey published a letter in the *Monthly Magazine* detailing the misfortunes of Chatterton's sister which had inspired Southey and Cottle to produce the edition on her behalf. Southey's proposal includes the following account:

When Chatterton was ... particularly the object of public curiosity, a clergyman called upon his sister, presented her with half a guinea, and requested to see whatever letters of her brother she had preserved. She produced them. He then begged permission to take them away for one hour, assigning as a reason, that it would be too painful to his feelings to read them in the presence of that sister, to whom they were addressed. On the same pretext he procured the letters in Mrs. Chatterton's possession, who lived separately from her daughter; these also, he promised to return in an hour, and the present of a guinea, and the language of consolatory friendship prevented all suspicion; indeed, so consolatory and so full of religion was his language to the mother, that she said she almost looked on him as a guardian angel.[5]

The clergyman (who was not, in fact, a clergyman – at least, not yet) would however prove to be no angel. It was not an hour but a fortnight before the gentleman, who had remained anonymous during his visit, communicated with Mrs. Chatterton again, this time in a letter in which he identified himself as Mr. Herbert Croft:

"Be not alarmed, Mrs. Chatterton," [Croft] said; "all the little treasure shall be faithfully returned to you again;" with the originals he promised to send transcripts of all the letters, with which the curiosity of strangers might be gratified, while the handwriting of Chatterton should be preserved. He again consoled Mrs. Chatterton for the fate of her son. "Perhaps," said he, "he now beholds with pleasure the deserved progress his reputation is making every day, and the friends and assistances which his name brings to you and his sister."(100)

After a second letter soliciting "recollections" from the sister, Chatterton's original letters were returned to the family. This was in the fall of 1778. As Southey's account continues,

Nothing further was heard till in the following July, to the astonishment of the family, Mr. C – published the letters, and the information he had obtained from Mrs. Newton, in his *LOVE AND MADNESS*. The mother wrote to him and upbraided him for duplicity; he replied, by sending ten pounds, to be divided between her and her daughter; again professing friendship for them, and saying, "Be assured the family of Thomas Chatterton shall never be forgotten by H – C – ."(100)

After three more letters, promising service and aid and asking for a receipt for the ten pounds,

Mr. C – dropt his correspondence with the family: they heard no more of his future services and the public subscription. His *Love and Madness* had a great and rapid sale, undoubtedly in a considerable degree owing to the letters of Chatterton; and his purpose was served. (100–101)

According to Southey, there followed a pair of letters from Mrs. Newton to Croft requesting further assistance; Croft replied that he had no obligation to the family, as he had paid for Chatterton's letters:

"[Mrs. Newton] is either ill-advised, or she has not told her advisers the money [sic] which I gave her, when I had the copies of the letters, and afterwards. The sort of threatening letter which Mrs. Newton's is will never succeed with me: but if the clergyman of the parish will do me the favour to write me word, through Mrs. Newton, what Chatterton's relations consist of, and what characters they bear, I will try, by every thing in my power, to serve them; yet certainly not, if they any of them pretend to have the smallest claim on me."(101)

The substance of Southey's charge, then, is that the baronet-vicar, operating under false pretenses, swindled Chatterton's family out of the eight letters, published them for his own profit, and then abandoned all pretense of concern for the two women. Croft would not let these charges stand unchallenged.

Croft's reply to Southey's letter begins in the February 1800 issue of the Whig-aristocrat *Gentleman's Magazine*, not in the more liberal *Monthly Magazine* which is Southey's chosen forum. The first part of Croft's defense is political: he accuses Southey of Jacobinism and portrays the attack on himself as an attack on the establishment. The second part of Croft's defense turns away from the realm of party conflict and addresses the issue of the money, which Southey's account represents as a courtesy or a retainer but which Croft represents as an outright purchase of the letters. This second defense, with its invocations of rationality and fairness, contains the purest form of the economic and social contradictions which Southey attempts to reconcile in his own professional positioning. Each man, in this dispute, calls on the rhetorical strategies which his social position makes available to him; but at the same time, the assumption of particular strategies constitutes a willful assumption of particular discursive rights as potentially – and contestably – determined by the larger working frame of eighteenth-century status distinction.

Croft's reply to Southey is vigorously indignant. He first explains that his career has been misrepresented by Southey. Croft had not taken orders until 1785; consequently, he was no clergyman in 1778. Further, as Croft announces in the introductory part of his letter, Southey is "PANTISOCRATIC," and he continues on the basis of this identification to question Southey's motives:

Mr. S[outhey] very well knows his motives for making such a character, as he represents me, a clergyman, before I ever was one. Our country and all countries are in the situation in which we see them, because such lurking attacks upon religion and government have not been openly met and repelled . . . . I appeal to those whose good opinion I value, whether I might not have run a chance at least of being treated a little better by Mr. Southey, had my principles been republican, or had I been a dissenter from the religion of my country, or of no religion at all. (103)

As evidence of Southey's bad and radical motives Croft refers to Southey's widely-known status as a radical and in particular to the famously revolutionary sentiments of *Joan of Arc*. However, Croft has, knowingly or not, misidentified Southey's interests and intentions. By 1799, the definitive and motivating feature of his own public identity is for Southey no longer radicalism but professional standing. Although nominally engaged in the study of law, Southey had recently published second editions of his radical epic and of the *Letters Written During a Short Residence in Spain and Portugal,* as well as a second poetry collection, shorter poems for the *Annual Anthology,* which he was editing, and poetry and criticism for the *Morning Post* and the *Critical Review.*[6] While his patron Charles Wynn expected him to take up the law, and his uncle, Rev. Hill, had only recently given up the idea of Southey entering the Church, it was literature, and poetry in particular, that engaged his energies and generated income. In December of 1799 Southey's medium-term plans at least are clearly tied to the pursuit of literature:

Thalaba is my dependance. Cottle got 150 £ by the second [edition of] Joan of Arc. Thalaba will be 12 books and as many notes, and surely I ought to get as much by it. To-night, if no time assassins drop in, I shall cut the 20 or 30 lines that finish the fifth book. My plan is to print 1000 copies, and sell the impression; four months from this time is sufficient to get this done.[7]

Legal studies or not, and enduring liberal sentiments notwithstanding, Southey is a working writer now, and his concerns are the concerns of a man who has linked his fate to his vocation, the profession of letters. He has essentially renounced other means of making his way in the world, although his continuing good relations with his Uncle Hill illustrate that, despite Croft's accusations, he is not at war with the Anglican Church. Like Wordsworth at Grasmere, Southey is in the process of digging in and cementing the status of both his professional standing and the standing of his profession, and it is in this light that we must understand his attempt to serve Thomas Chatterton's family.

Whereas Southey wishes to derive his status from his commitment to his profession, Croft's defense throughout emphasizes the relative stability of birth status, as distinct from the mutability of professional identity, in the constitution of the public man. Before Croft took orders, he reminds his readers, he studied law, and for this reason attacks on him as a clergyman are rendered moot. However, while he cannot be attacked as a clergyman for actions undertaken as a law student, his behavior, including his indignation at Mrs. Newton's later correspondence, also indicates that he is entitled to deference either as a law student or as a clergyman, because he remains in both cases a gentleman. If anything, according to Croft, his professional status hinders his ability to express his genuine, gentlemanly self:

> In governments purely pantisocratical, i.e. LEVELLING, such a reasoner and such a gentleman [as Southey] would be referred to Johnson's indignant answer to Macpherson, which says, that "he carried a stick to repel insult; after which, the law should do for him, what he could not do for himself." But I am a clergyman; as Mr. S. remembered, when he held such language and published it in such a manner. On my return to England, it is possible I may see whether the law can do for me what it would not become me to do for myself. (103)

This is a familiar conservative accusation: the badly-faithed radical both demands and expects to be physically protected by the very social institutions that he attacks. When Croft emphasizes that he is restrained only by his clerical status and notes Samuel Johnson's good fortune in lacking such restraint, he is also insisting on the gentleman's right to use force in the absence of such particular and even accidental factors as his own clerical collar. His wistful contemplation of honorable violence reminds his audience that he is a gentleman above all, with a gentleman's sense of dignity and a gentleman's martial spirit. When insulted by the likes of Southey, Croft at least has recourse both to the law and to what he assumes is the sympathetic audience of the *Gentleman's Magazine*: that is, he has recourse to the resources of an establishment gentleman, minus the potential violence he has grudgingly given up.

In his brief reply to Croft's reply, Southey concedes the point that Croft had not yet taken orders until five years after the appearance of the Chatterton letters in *Love and Madness*.[8] As Southey notes, this detail would not seem to alter the strongest aspects of his case against Croft's behavior. However, Southey's own misrepresentation of Croft's career is telling because it illustrates the tangle of identities and affiliational categories that both he and Croft have to confront as they attempt to establish (or maintain) their own status. For each man, status is defined by affiliation, but it is not always clear what one's affiliations are or how they are to be evaluated.

Deriving status from profession, that is, is a risky as well as a contentious strategy on Southey's part not least because professional careers, as illustrated by both Southey's fortunes and Croft's, are so unstable in the latter stages of the eighteenth century. One relevant consequence of this instability is that it would not have been at all obvious to an uninformed observer, such as Southey, what a given lawyer or clergyman, such as Croft, might have been doing for a living at some earlier stage of his career. And this sociological fact, itself a product of the grip the establishment maintained on certain forms of professional education and legitimation, can in its turn be represented by men like Croft as a rationale for the identification of birth as a more stable, and hence more reliable, measure of a man's place in society than his job is. Southey's mistaken identification of Croft as a clergyman is thus a double impertinence: it is an implied slur on the Church, as Croft takes it, and at a deeper level it implies an identity of vocation with individual that Croft categorically rejects. Croft's attention to the chronology of his own ordination not only gives him rhetorical leverage on Southey's motives. It also indicates in another way Croft's insistence on the detachment of personal identities from professional ones, implying again that essential identities are separate from work and even from higher callings like the call to the Church. For Croft, as a committed member of the establishment, the essence of one's identity remains to be found within the familiar hierarchies of birth and status.

Membership in the learned professions was flexible in part because a single course of study at the universities went so far to qualify one as an educated gentleman, who might then pursue training in any of them. Under these circumstances, what is striking is not Croft's ambivalent attitude toward the potentially definitive nature of his own calling and his alternative privileging of birth status, but the gravity with which Southey (like Wordsworth) attempts to elevate his own profession. Southey is a product of the same system as Croft, and the practice of moving through different professions is entirely familiar to him. As a potential clergyman and occasional law student himself, Southey would be among the first to realize that the mutability of profession in this social milieu is finally inescapable. There are, for example, two clergymen in this story who are not always clergymen: Croft, and the murderer James Hackman, the protagonist of *Love and Madness*. Hackman begins as a lieutenant and ends as a priest, and I will discuss his shifting professional identities, and their genteel, stable core, below. But at this level of the discussion the most important profession-shifting non-clergyman remains Southey himself. Despite Croft's attempts to make Southey out as a "dissenter" as well as a leveler, his professional and social trajectory bear a strong resemblance to Croft's own. Croft had been born to a baronetcy – a considerably higher birth than Southey's – but his title was no longer attached to what had been the family estates. In 1778, when Croft acquired the Chatterton letters, he was at the end of his training for the law and had not yet taken orders. Croft took orders in 1785, the option which Southey had spent his young manhood avoiding but which was still a live option for him as late as 1796. Because Croft's vicarage was not heavily endowed, however, he also drew income from a series of literary endeavors, including a life of Young that was included with Johnson's *Lives of the Poets*.[9] Both Croft and Southey, finally, are educated men with a facility for composition and without economic independence who attempt to parlay their literary gifts into acceptable incomes. Despite their party differences, therefore, their positions in society are, except for Croft's title and age, very similar, particularly because while both men have claims to gentility, if in varying degrees, they both have to try out different professional options in the attempt to fortify their status. It is true that Southey, whose father was a linen draper, is only on his way up by virtue of his education, and a baronet like Croft would certainly know the difference between himself and a linen draper's son. But Southey, a product of the commercial democracy of Bristol, clearly feels himself to be within social range of the struggling Croft, particularly when compared to the Chatterton family – the object of their mutual attention.

The thrust of Southey's criticism of Croft is not, then, that the establishment should be overthrown. Rather, Southey is attacking Croft from his own assumed if defensible position as a fellow gentleman and a fellow professional. He would remind Croft that the establishment (as defined both by status and by occupation) and its privileged members are obliged by their position to act responsibly. Croft, in his aggressively political interpretation of events, neglects or obscures the resemblance that authorizes Southey's rhetoric; at stake in his conflict with Southey is not only or primarily the treatment of a gentleman cleric (Croft) by a radical (Southey) but the treatment of one gentleman by another, and the further question of what either or both of these men owe to the lower orders as represented by Mrs. Newton.

Privately discussing the exchange with Croft, Southey takes on an appropriately gentlemanly tone:

I have replied to [Croft's letter], solely for the purpose of making another advertisement. My answer is short and calm, without one term of asperity, or one personal allusion. I have merely hinted at the stile of his letter, to request that no party dislike toward me, might hinder the success of the subscription.[10]

Southey here displays a sense of decorum which belies at least the implications of Croft's charge of "radicalism," and Southey's allusion to "party dislike" also implies an essential social likeness between the two men which does not bear on (or derive from) their political views. Southey's sense of a hierarchy of affiliations which is markedly different from Croft's is also indicated. Whereas Croft's nominal concern is to defend his own honor and the honor of the establishment, Southey makes the fate of Mrs. Newton the primary issue: "She is advancing in years," his letter of reply informs the readers of *Gentleman's Magazine*, "and her sight begins to fail. Should the subscription for [Chatterton's] Works be extensive, it will render her old age comfortable, and provide for her child" (226). Croft's party defense has finally put him in a bad rhetorical position, and Southey is able to conflate his own sense of collective well-being for poets with reference to a more generally held and generally recognizable charitable impulse. Southey fully assumes the role of the gentleman, and he uses that role to further his professional project.

If Southey and Croft differ about the nature of one's public identity, as defined by various kinds of affiliations, they also differ on how those affiliations should determine one's economic relationships. For Southey the most important relationships are those of poets to other poets (and their families), and economic relations within this group should thus reflect a collective sense of well-being; for Croft, a rational neutrality is to prevail among equivalent and individual economic actors. This brings us to the second component of Croft's defense, which he most succinctly expresses in the following:

If Mrs. N.'s memory were stronger, she might perhaps recollect that I was at liberty to do what I pleased even with the originals, in return for what I gave her and her mother. Had ten pounds more been demanded for them, or even another guinea, I imagine that I should have refused. (104)

In addition, Croft argues that if his only intention had been to copy the letters fraudulently he could have done so and returned them immediately. (It will be recalled, however, that Croft contacted Mrs. Newton in search of further "recollections." This furnishes a reason for Croft to extend his correspondence with Mrs. Chatterton that is consistent with Southey's unflattering portrait of him.) These are Croft's rational arguments. His exchanges with Chatterton's family, according to this line of thought, are conducted as honest and open pieces of business, and it is dishonest to go back on them at a later date. As he puts it, "It is more possible that Rowley existed, than that ... both the mother and the daughter could be weak enough to be so robbed." (103). According to Croft, to suggest that he took advantage of Chatterton's relations is not only a mistake; it is also condescending to the two women, who are presumed by Southey's politically motivated intervention to be "weak" and unable to take care of themselves.

Croft's defense involves a starkly contradictory overlap. He wishes on the one hand to characterize the relations between the baronet and the impoverished women as a rational, cash-based exchange between free, equal, and responsible agents. However, he also wants to emphasize and attack the "levelling" tendencies of his pantisocratic opponent, opposing those tendencies to the vital national interests of the landed establishment as those interests are made manifest in his own title and ordination. In practical terms, Croft's account ignores the real effect the presence of the imposing young baronet (clergyman or not) would have on the two women, as well as denying the traditions of deference that would necessarily intervene in what Croft portrays as a neutral exchange. The situation, incidentally, offers a penetrating view of the state of conservative ideology at the turn of the century. Because the aristocracy, speaking broadly, continued to control most of the nation's assets and had not yet been challenged in its position by industrial capital, market economics easily could be viewed by Croft as an adjunct to the establishment, and Croft could freely invoke the establishment while simultaneously invoking the kind of economic individualism that would later be construed, in its theoretical form, as antagonistic to landed interests.[11]

In contrast, Southey had come of age in the radical milieu of Bristol, where "trade" often meant "the slave trade" and where free-market economics could be held morally suspect when the occasion demanded. While Bristol was built on commerce, radical intellectuals there were acutely conscious that certain kinds of exchanges might be exploitive and the success of Bristol merchants did not necessarily imply a systematic commitment to laissez-faire economics.[12] Strictly speaking, for Southey there can be no arrangement at all between Croft and Newton that would deprive Newton of the material benefits of the letters. While the letters are property, they are heavily entailed. It is not within Croft's power to purchase them outright or within Mrs. Newton's power to sell them because the letters are directly attached to the family identity which is established by Chatterton and inherited by his sister. The property of the poet, that is, is not land, but it is legitimate and cannot be exchanged outright for cash. It is or should be protected by a professional ethic that determines not only who individuals are but what their relationships should be.

Southey's own views on the relationship of class to professional identity are explicit, and are directly opposed to those held by Croft. Southey assumes that class affiliations obscure professional judgment, as he suggests to Coleridge just at the time of the encounter with Croft:

The Gentlemen of the Literary Fund are about to commence a review I hear – now these Gentlemen write books themselves – and when one Gentleman reviews another Gentlemans poetry – what pretty gentleman-like criticism we shall have! .... – but these Gentleman Critics who will be so civil to one another must vary their reviews by a little severity – and that must fall upon the poor writers who are not Gentlemen.[13]

Although I have argued for Southey's effectively genteel status in 1800, or at least for his right to the rhetorical strategies of a gentleman, it is important not to oversimplify the category. Southey may be a gentleman-in-effect by virtue of his education and perhaps by virtue of his prospects, but his radical politics and the realities of his birth and his financial situation mean that he may well expect to be treated as something other than a gentleman at the hands of the gentleman reviewers. I do not think it is the case that Southey directly identifies himself with the "poor writers" who stand to bear the brunt of gentle wrath, but it is probable that his acid references to "pretty gentlemen" stem in part from an old sensitivity about the station of his family.[14] What is certain is that Southey is sensitive to, and hostile to, the idea that class affiliation should transcend critical judgment. At the same time he assumes that the Gentleman-Critics will necessarily make the error of placing class before critical judgment, because their original sin is precisely that they identify and organize themselves as "gentlemen" and not as writers.

Southey's efforts on behalf of the Chatterton family stem from his sense of professional affiliation. Consequently they differ from Croft's attempts not only in degree but in kind. Croft maintains of Chatterton that "[his] little finger I have ever reverenced, more than Mr. Southey knows how to respect his whole body" (99), but Southey's material efforts on behalf of Chatterton's sister are more useful and ultimately more laudable than Croft's "reverence." Southey's means of aid are nicely appropriate, as the new edition would serve Chatterton's reputation as well as contributing to the financial state of his sister, and would allow Chatterton's professional output to continue to be of use to his family in the absence of a relevant copyright law. Southey is further using his own professional capability, his genuine knack for getting books into print, in the service of a fellow poet. This professionalism is the telling difference between the kinds of aristocratic "assistances" the baronet is at his leisure to offer Mrs. Newton (and then rescind) and Southey's professionally based actions.

It is not hard to choose between Croft's conduct and Southey's, but what I would like to emphasize is not Southey's generous nature but the collective overtones of his actions. In his concern for Chatterton's family, Southey evinces a professional sense of collective identity and mutual aid.[15] At the same time the use of a subscription edition forms a bridge between the faceless marketplace and older kinds of patronage. The edition is not commissioned, but there is a personal, named relationship between the audience for it and its producers, and the appearance of one's name in the subscription lists is a potential source of status for the purchaser that would not be available in anonymous marketplace circumstances. That is, Southey's position has some potential contradictions of its own, drawing as it does on a roughly chivalric code of protection and aid, but these contradictions are tactically resolved because a code of professional conduct allows Southey to behave as a proper gentleman would while elevating the object of his charity to a kind of nominal equality. Southey's position reconciles paternalist ideologies with professional ones by rejecting

Croft's emphasis on the legitimacy of market exchanges (represented by the ten-pound payoff) and the gratuitousness of charity, and by replacing market relations with professional ones.

Southey is not, of course, the first writer to worry about the poverty of other writers or their families, but this enduring concern was also directly relevant to the new and wider contest in which the related issues of authority, affiliation, and the appropriate function of the literary marketplace were being debated. In general, writers who supported the establishment perceived a free market as their ally and organized support of writers, when construed as anything but charity, as a radical enemy. On the other hand, radical intellectuals had an affinity for the kind of self-determining professionalism pursued by Southey. Two years after the Southey-Croft exchange, for example, David Williams would reiterate his 1773 proposal for the Royal Literary Fund in the pages of that organization's *Claims of Literature*.[16] Part of his argument runs as follows:

The basis of our obligation to relieve the misery of genius and literature is of a nature more extensive [than the obligation to other poor]; it is as extensive as that of our moral duties, for it is formed by actual services rendered to us in every relation of life, and to the whole community of which we are members .... Authors who have formed our understandings, taught us the art of reasoning and directed us in the best modes of profiting by our bodily exertions, have the strongest claim on our justice and gratitude.[17]

By attempting to organize financial assistance for writers, Williams comes close to invoking older writer-audience relations, but he is at pains finally to reject these; two chapters of *Claims of Literature* are devoted to describing the shortcomings of Charity and Patronage. At the same time, and more significantly, Williams introduces the notion of "service." It is not merely charity to support authors, but a moral duty implied in the relationship of professional and client which the marketplace has not yet been able to account for:

Presuming therefore that the distress of an useful writer [sic] affixes on the public an imputation of ingratitude of the worst definition, because it suffers a benefactor to be punished by the benefit he has conferred ... it is proposed to establish a fund on which writers of real utility may rely for assistance in proportion to its produce.[18]

Because of the imperfections of the literary marketplace, the service rendered by authors tends not to be immediately repaid, and those who would undertake the service of authorship therefore give up those benefits to which their service actually entitles them. Williams would correct the pernicious blindness of the marketplace with an organized attempt to reward authors for the "real utility" of their services:

The remunerations of genius would not then be left to PATRONAGE, the most capricious and unjust of all judges; they would be adjusted by some reasonable scale of equivalents, in the jurisdiction of a competent court. A LIBERAL JUDICATURE is imperiously demanded, by the injuries of genius, and particularly by the dreadful evils of its resentment and revenge.[19]

Although the Royal Literary Fund was made up in a large degree by Southey's "pretty gentlemen," the Napoleonic fury of Williams' imaginary "spurned geniuses" amply illustrates the revolutionary charge of this brand of professionalism, and it underlines the substantial difference between the genteel patronage society the Fund actually became (and that Southey complained about) and Williams' own original conception of it.

Williams, himself a famous radical, describes the political resistance to his contribution to *Claims of Literature*:

At the first meeting of [the Royal Literary] society, without the usual notice on the introduction of peculiar business, Sir James Bland Burges ... appeared, and abruptly attacked [Williams' contribution to Claims of Literature] .... He undertook to prove the book contained principles subversive of religion, government, and morality.[20]

Although Williams does not elaborate on Burges' charges, it is clear that the idea of support for writers poses a challenge to enlightened conservative self-interest for at least two reasons. The first reason is that such subsidies might move workers out of trade and into literature – the trouble identified by the *Edinburgh Review*, as described at the beginning of my discussion. Considered in this way, the resistance to organized aid for writers is an attempt by gentleman writers to perpetuate their own individual and collective monopoly over the production of literature. Clerical livings, legal practices, and various sinecures and inheritances provide the subsidies that support gentlemanly literary practice and that shoemakers and tailors must do without. The literary market is thus the domain of men whose identities are already indemnified by their birth (Burges is another baronet, and a lawyer-litterateur) and must not be open to those who would first go about the business of establishing their identities by entering it. The larger challenge to the establishment is implicit in this formulation, for the men who enter the marketplace in order to earn their legitimacy there are also and consequently those who would establish their identities in relation to each other and their chosen work, and not in relation to established status systems.[21]

Like Sir James Bland Burges, Croft and the *Anti-Jacobin Review* line up against Williams' imperious "demands" of literature. The *Anti-Jacobin Review*, discussing *Claims of Literature*, predictably takes a more severe view of the issue of remuneration for writers than Williams does. For the *Anti-Jacobin Review*, as for Croft, the open market is the place to make or break poets as it is the place to prove other kinds of virtues. The reviewer wonders: "How a man can be said to be born to make a book any more than it can be said that he was born to make a writing desk, we cannot conceive."[22] For this reviewer, the idea of the inspired and far-seeing poet is intimately involved with the idea that poets should be protected from the marketplace, and in his conflation of the bookmaker with the desk maker he disposes of both notions. The reviewer's emphasis on the inherent justice of the market, softened perhaps by gentlemanly charity, is consonant with Croft's rational defense of his treatment of Mrs. Newton: because she gave up the letters freely and accepted payment for them (as Croft's version has it) the deal is done, and no more should be said about the matter. Even writers must take responsibility for their own financial decision-making, and consequently for their own material circumstances:

Here let me pause a moment to rescue the world from blame it does not merit [for the poverty of Chatterton]. The world is not accountable for every man of abilities who has perished, however miserably, in an alehouse or a prison. Profligacy and Genius, Ability and Prodigality are not, as many imagine, the same thing.[23]

In their eagerness to echo Johnson's observations about Savage, Croft and the *Anti-Jacobin Review* are attacking a position that none of their immediate opponents actually hold. Neither Williams nor Southey believe that anyone who calls himself a poet is entitled to a government subsidy for it. Williams specifically identifies "useful"

writers as the objects of his concern.[24] On the larger point,
however, the disagreement is real. According to Southey and
Williams a good writers' service deserves to be rewarded, and these
rewards are not, generally, fairly meted out by the market. Instead,
fairness demands some kind of managed, secondary sphere of
literary/monetary adjudication. Williams states outright what
Southey and Cottle obviously assume: that the families of "great
and useful" writers should profit by the public veneration of
departed "men of genius."[25] It is in this context that Chatterton's
letters become an example of professional property, a con-
cretization of the writer's legacy of which the family, and not
speculators like Croft, should have the advantage, and which
should be protected by Chatterton's fellows.

III *LOVE AND MADNESS*

Croft attempts to distinguish between good, establishment writers
and bad, "pantisocratic" ones, but as discussed earlier, another
running distinction is between writers who are "gentlemen" and
everybody else. I have argued that Southey's reproach of Croft is
not cast as a reproach from a radical to a conservative but as one
from a responsible member of the upper reaches of the writerly
community to an irresponsible one. It is now necessary to return to
the point that within the broad category "gentleman" professional identities are meaningful but also extremely slippery. This
slipperiness indicates the cultural recognition of an individual
identity that is transportable and that functions independently of
occupation but not of status. Occupation, as vocation or profession, finally does enter into the constitution of the individual and
his social identity, but only as an inflection. From the establishment perspective it is status that fits one for a profession and not
the other way around. Consequently, profession can only have a
limited effect on one's store of cultural capital. I have discussed
this point in reference to Croft's reply to Southey, but the
surprising consequences of Croft's position, which takes an
emphasis on the immitigable value of status over profession to its
extreme, are most vivid in his novel *Love and Madness.*
   The real James Hackman, the protagonist of *Love and Madness,*
had been in the army and had advanced as far as lieutenant, but in
1776 he resigned his commission and prepared to enter the

church. In 1779 he was ordained deacon and later priest, and presented to a living in Norfolk. Since his days in the army, however, Hackman had been in love with Martha Ray, the mistress of John Montagu, the fourth Earl of Sandwich. A month after he was presented to his living Reverend Hackman shot Martha Ray dead in front of Covent Garden, in an apparent fit of jealousy, and was put to death less than two weeks later.[26] *Love and Madness* is a fictionalized, epistolary account of their relationship. In the novel, Croft briefly acknowledges Hackman's clerical status at the time of the murder but he makes very little of it. Hackman's profession must have been a large part of the public's fascination with the tale, but Croft treats the murder of Martha Ray as the generic consequence of uncontrolled passion – as indicated by the title – which ultimately provides a vaguely cautionary message about abstaining from extreme behavior. Hackman's own vocational peregrinations recall Southey's as well as Croft's, and the real moral of the tale might be that in ages when the taking of orders comes to be conceived of as a financial decision, all kinds of moral chaos can be expected. But that conclusion is too congenial to the radical thought of the day, and Croft settles for the broader one, which allows him to cast a lurid and sentimental tale as a conventional fable.

However, although Hackman's status as a gentleman-soldier-priest is virtually unremarked, it is crucial to the thematic work of the novel because it allows Croft to make an elevating tragedy out of Hackman's murderous fall from the social graces. Had Hackman been a crofter, for instance, his crime might be notorious but would lack the horror and pity Croft hopes the reader will find in it. Reflecting on Hackman's refusal to commit suicide in prison, Croft (or his narrator) cries out: "Worthy soul! While we abhor, we pity and respect: and so will posterity. That justice which condemned thee to death cannot refuse a sigh, a tear to thy virtues. Rest, rest, perturbed spirit!" (331) Hackman has rejected suicide because, as he explains, should he kill himself he "may be considered by Despair, or by Folly, as another precedent in favour of the propriety of suicide." (331) A gentleman may be a soldier, a priest, or a murderer, but he must in any case consider the kind of example his conduct will provide to those who look up to him. Hackman thus emerges, in Croft's terms, as more honorable than Othello, whose final speech provides the introduction to this fictional correspondence. He also proves in this way to be more honorable than the poor sexton's son, Thomas Chatterton, whose life takes up nearly a third of the novel, and whose own suicide makes him the thematic foil to the "virtuous" Hackman. The issue of suicide is the single link between the life of Chatterton and the life of Hackman, and so the novel finally leads us to understand that the poetic genius is less "upstanding" than the killer, precisely because the poet is less of a gentleman than the gentleman. As Croft's Hackman declares after his discussion of the death of Chatterton, "Let the reader learn, and remember too, that suicide is always holden up to shame" (221).

Croft is not only concerned with Hackman's identity and the surprising moral authority that, as a gentleman, Hackman possesses even as he awaits his execution. Croft is also interested in establishing his own authority, and here his treatment of professional identity, and particularly of the authority of the writer, veers close to David Williams' position. To insure that his studied message-making does not go unnoticed Croft inserts, under the guise of a discussion of Defoe, a theoretical justification of his true life novel:

I can easily conceive of a writer making use of a known fact, and filling up the outlines which have been sketched by the bold and hasty hand of fate. A moral may be added, by such means, to a particular incident; characters may be placed in their proper lights; mankind may be amused (and amusements sometimes prevent crimes); or, if the story be criminal, mankind may be bettered, through the channel of their curiosity. (38)

This notion of authority is compatible with Williams' comments on the same topic. The author serves society by superadding moral meaning where the "bold and hasty hand of fate" has neglected to. The hand of fate is not only a visible hand but an inefficient one, and while the moral of a story might not be apparent in events themselves, it can be found by shifting around or enhancing the facts. This necessary regulation of the linguistic marketplace establishes by administrative fiat the price of a particular incident in units of social utility and simultaneously both prices and creates the moral wealth that is always absent from a given sequence of events until its "outlines" have been filled up by the author. The author potentially serves given, understood social values, but he also establishes values and produces "value" from raw materials in a way that the visible hand of fate cannot. Croft's homiletics are, as Williams suggests of writers in general, both at the service of society and constitutive of it.

Croft is sensitive to the potentially radical character of some of these musings, and to the proto-revolutionary connotations that the figure of the martyred poet-prophet has already acquired, and he makes certain that he cannot be misunderstood. The figure of Chatterton again serves as Croft's lamentably negative example, while a gentlemanly pragmatism in the face of a too-radical literary theoretics is presented as his own ideal, and Hackman's:

> But, after all, the world is only indebted to Chatterton for a few inimitable poems. If Barbarity and Fanaticism be suffered to destroy mankind, Genius will write in vain, where there is none to read. To preserve our fellow-creatures is still a greater praise than to instruct and amuse them. (274)[27]

Further, while Croft's position toward the malleability of facts comes dangerously close to French "theory" in its emphasis on the regulatory and constitutional powers of the intellectual, it should also be strongly distinguished from "poet-prophet" theories (and related celebrations of the enlightened *philosophe*) because Croft clearly holds that morality exists outside of the writer's tinkering and is ultimately the provenance of the establishment in general and the Established Church in particular.[28]

It is in Southey's ongoing attempt to institute a gentlemanly professionalism based on the vocational affiliations of writers, rather than on a prior gentlemanly identity that qualifies one for the job of writer, that this brief feud illustrates both a key moment in the cultural struggle to reconceive of status and affiliation as well as a formative moment in the larger movement that we now understand as British Romanticism. Both Croft and Southey, in their theoretical positioning, display a certain lack of historical prescience. For Croft, as for Burke, individualistic capitalism and aristocratic authority were complementary, but the coming century would show that their coexistence could not be sustained in its eighteenth-century form. Southey's thought would eventually divide against itself; the radical and paternal aspects of his professional instincts would not prove to be as compatible in 1830, in the face of a real self-consciousness on the part of the working classes, as they were at the turn of the century, when the actual vagaries of class distinction were easier for Southey to ignore.[29] The argument with Croft is thus a kind of zenith in Southey's self-construction. Chivalry and artisanship, gentility and profession-alism, are combined in his defense of Chatterton's relations. Yet, as *Madoc* is not alone among Southey's epics in demonstrating, it is not really possible to maintain this blend of principles indefinitely.

CHAPTER 7

"Ministry more palpable": William Wordsworth's romantic professionalism

Despite moments of high argument which insist that the inspired poet transcends normal economic and cultural arrangements, Wordsworth's vocational theorizing, publicly articulated in the Preface to *Lyrical Ballads*, aligns the poet with the new model of professionalism described in the introductory section of this book. In this chapter, I will first reconsider the vocational trajectory that leads Wordsworth to the full-time pursuit of poetry and also underwrites his insistence that poetry be treated as new, progressive professional labor. Aware of the growing possibilities of specialization, Wordsworth is also aware of its potential burdens, and he finds it necessary to describe a course of training that is particular to the poet while also being natural and spontaneous. In turn, this democratic ethic poses difficulty for the specificity of poetic practice that Wordsworth also wants to maintain. In the Preface, he makes his strongest statement about the special identity of the poet, an identity that he bases on the relationship between the poet and his informed but lay "client" audience. In the end, he cannot propose a new professionalism without taking into account the perseverance of traditional, landed values, and so he attempts to figure professional expertise in terms that will allow it to serve the same authorizing and status-generating function as landed property.

In 1805, retrospectively considering the attractions of the French Revolution, Wordsworth remarks that chief among these was the resemblance of certain revolutionary ideals to the dominant criteria of social advancement that he remembered from his own childhood:

> It was my fortune scarcely to have seen
> Through the whole tenor of my schoolday time
> The face of one, who, whether boy or man,

> Was vested with attention or respect
> Through claims of wealth or blood.[1]

These potentially egalitarian values had been repeated in Cambridge,

> Where all stood thus far
> Upon equal ground, that they were brothers all
> In honour, as of one community –
> Scholars and gentlemen – where, furthermore,
> Distinction lay open to all that came,
> And wealth and titles were in less esteem
> Than talents and successful industry. (IX 230–236)

However, there is no easy equivalence between the "attention and respect" that a Cumberland farmer may earn from his peers and the scholarly, genteel "distinction" available to the talented and industrious members of Cambridge's republic of letters. The sequence of Wordsworth's observations may imply a likeness of values between the Lake Region and the University, but he is more importantly narrating a transition in his own career, from the agricultural milieu that he observed as a child, to the intellectual one that he participated in as an adult and from which he expected to draw his own livelihood. His own chances in the Church were typically, and uncomfortably, dependent on the favor of close relations. Even as he was announcing his plans to "take orders in the approaching winter or spring," Wordsworth's involvement with Annette Vallon, in addition to his lack of academic success at Cambridge, had already complicated his access to the fellowship that his Uncle Cookson was supposed to offer him.[2] Under the circumstances, the idea of a world in which "wealth and titles were in less esteem/Than talents and successful industry" has a particular, local poignancy.

Wordsworth's active vocational consideration takes place over the long term. He always wanted to write, and particularly to write poetry, but it was not originally his intention to take up that pursuit as his sole source of income. While he is already, in 1792, on the verge of giving up the Church, writing for pay is not his only or even his main alternative. He had traveled to France, for example, to learn the language, in order to fit himself for the job of a tutor.[3] Although he continued to write when he returned to England, he did not publish anything between the 1793 *An Evening Walk* and *Descriptive Sketches* and the 1798 edition of *Lyrical Ballads*.[4] Nor can we take the first edition of *Lyrical Ballads* as the signal that Wordsworth had come to think of himself as professional, full-time poet, despite its achievements. This volume was itself arranged during 1797–98 to finance a trip to Germany which, like the earlier one to France, was motivated by the chance of getting a non-poetic job out of it. Dorothy and William intended to learn German in order to become translators.[5]

In the end, they did not learn the language well enough to execute this plan, and the failure both indicates and exacerbates Wordsworth's decision to abandon the alternatives to authorship. Prior to the Germany trip, poetry was one kind of writing for Wordsworth, if a favored one, and writing was one vocational option out of several. After Germany, Wordsworth considers no other form of remunerative labor, literary or otherwise.[6] It is important to note that family funds, the patronage of friends such as the Pinneys and the Calverts, and the expectation of the settlement of the Lowther debt all allowed Wordsworth to defer his vocational decision-making.[7] However, even considering these other sources of income, it is not going too far to say that the need to earn was central to most of the decisions that Wordsworth made before the settlement of the debt in 1802, and that poetry held a special place in his thinking. It was always a potential path to remuneration, but its status as a gentlemanly pursuit was also always preserved.[8]

As I have argued, early-century versions of the patriot and the flying wanderer adumbrate the kind of specialist preparation that must occur over time for the enthusiast as well as for the poet and the professional. The contours of this transformation are recapitulated in Lake school writing as seen, for example, in Coleridge and Southey's youthful collaboration on *Joan of Arc*. In the 1795 version of this poem, lines written by Coleridge dwell on the possibility that the result of error and pain may be a kind of wisdom or success:

> If there be beings of a higher class than Man,
> I deem no nobler province they possess
> Than by disposal of apt circumstance
> To rear some realm with patient discipline,
> Aye bidding PAIN, dark ERROR'S uncouth child,
> Blameless Parenticide! his snakey scourge
> Lift fierce against his Mother! Thus they make

> Of transient evil ever-enduring Good
> Themselves probationary, and denied
> Confess'd to view by preternatural deed
> To o'erwhelm the will, save on some fated day
> Headstrong, or with petitioned might from God. (ii.120–131)[9]

The sentiment is readily adapted to the French situation after 1792. For the British sympathizer, the "transient evil" of massacres, Regicide, and the Terror offers to "discipline" the realm in order to prepare it for a state of "ever-enduring Good." (As a prediction of Napoleonic order, the lines are incidentally and vaguely prophetic.) The difficult language that follows expresses bewilderment, and some revulsion, in the face of "PAIN" and "ERROR." Coleridge's syntax breaks down as he tries to explain exactly how it is that the dark angels of his vision are allowed to work such mischief. "Themselves probationary," Coleridge uneasily concludes, they must act only on the fated day, or, in what is likely an appositive idea, act with strength from God.

When Coleridge borrows back these lines for his own "Destiny of Nations," he is even more explicit that the birth of nations requires a crossing of status and class, since the lines now refer not to the abstract complexities of history but, specifically, to the threat Joan's non-aristocratic leadership poses to a recognizable establishment of corrupt monarchs and complicit minstrels:

> If there be beings of a higher class than Man,
> I deem no nobler province they possess,
> Than by disposal of apt circumstance
> To rear up Kingdoms: and the deeds they prompt,
> Distinguishing from mortal agency,
> They chuse their human ministers from such states
> As still the Epic Song half fears to name,
> Repelled from all the Minstrelsies that strike
> The Palace-Roof and sooth the Monarch's pride. (121–129)

As Ann W. Astell has written, Joan of Arc, an inspired wanderer who embodies "Jacobin equality," is easily understood as a figure for the Jacobin poet.[10] In these revised lines, the "beings of a higher class" have been transformed into the instigators of an apocalyptic class mobility, their "human ministers" drawn from such sublimely terrifying, because downscale, "states/As still the Epic Song half fears to name." This class-terror refurbishes literature, as well, since mere court poets, beholden to the tastes of the patron, prove unable to sing the song of the future. Astell emphasizes the Spenserian and Miltonic resonances in *Joan of Arc*, but given the criticism of dependent, soothing minstrels and *The Minstrel*'s generic assaults on "tyranny," the precedent of Beattie is more than an accident or an analogy. The structures of patronage come under explicit attack as soon as the heaven-chosen minister is opposed to the bad poet, even as the magic of inspiration ("the deeds they prompt") serves to separate the chosen figure from the kingdom she is intended to save.

Lynda Pratt has identified at least one echo of Southey's *Joan* in Wordsworth and Coleridge's correspondence, and there is another, and important, Wordsworthian reference to Coleridge's Joan-of-Arc lines.[11] While failing to become an adept translator in 1799, Wordsworth had had an extremely productive winter writing poetry, including the first draft of the "Poem to Coleridge" that would eventually become *The Prelude*, and when he returned to England he approached *Lyrical Ballads* with a new sense of professional entitlement. In his consideration of his own perceived hardships and of the pressures not only of money but of status that consistently bore on him – his brothers had already gained responsible positions in the law, in the church, and at sea – Wordsworth, explicitly adopting the position both of Coleridge's Joan and Coleridge's France, concludes that his protracted consideration of vocation amounts to a credential of its own:

> I believe
> That there are spirits which, would they form
> A favored being, from his very dawn
> Of infancy do open out the clouds
> As at the touch of lightning, seeking him
> With gentle visitation – quiet powers,
> Retired, and seldom recognized, yet kind,
> And to the very meanest not unknown –
> With me, though rarely, in my boyish days
> They communed. Others too there are, who use,
> Yet haply aiming at the self-same end,
> Severer interventions, ministry
> More palpable – and of their school was I. (I 68–80)

The Wordsworthian school of hard knocks (Coleridge: "[T]he Maid/Learnt more than Schools could teach" [146–147]) is emphatically not the school in which visionary light touches the bard in his youth and provides an effortless way for him for ever after. Rather, the "severe" and "palpable" "ministrations" of these powers (by the 1805 version of *The Prelude* the "spirits" are redefined as "Nature") will be manifested in the gothic, frightening, or distressing spots of time as well as, in the 1805 version and after, in the "impairment" of mass revolutionary slaughter. Intellectual and moral giftedness are presumed on the part of the poet (in the 1802 Preface Wordsworth names the "endow[ments]" of "sensibility," "enthusiasm," "tenderness," "knowledge of human nature," and a "comprehensive soul") but what is essential to Wordsworth's account is that these gifts have to be trained before a poet is ready to do his job. The nation-forming and radical content of the Joan sequence have here been rewritten. Wordsworth neither directly equates his own growth with national rebirth nor associates the ministry more palpable with an attack on status boundaries, but this content, absorbed into the experiential formation of the poet, is latent in the progressive features of the professional project.

Although various versions of *The Prelude* wrestle inconclusively with the question of how active the human mind has to be during this phenomenological training (thus holding the question of "labor" as a path to knowledge and value in strategic abeyance while saving a place for "inheritance"), the cluster of ideas which guides Wordsworth's account is at least this clear: the growth of a poet's mind is a process in which credentials are earned – the poet is made, and perhaps self-made, as well as he is born, and he is to be honored for his efforts and for the use he will make of them. For Wordsworth, who is not quite financially independent, not quite genteel, and, by 1799, no longer willing to throw himself into the "mighty gulf" of full-time journalism, this is not just talk: it is essential that poetry and poetic practice be defined in ways that give the poet respectable status, while rejecting the institutional bases for authority – Church and University in particular – which have become, to Wordsworth's way of thinking, corrupt or inadequate.[12]

In poems like "Expostulation and Reply," "The Tables Turned," and "The Nightingale," Wordsworth and Coleridge had appeared to act as the arbiters of spontaneous feeling, not institution or system. Coleridge takes to task the "Poet, who hath been building up the rhyme/When he had better far have stretched his limbs/Beside a brook," and Wordsworth utters his famous complaint against reason, book-learning, and "murder[ing] to dissect." Mainly, however, Wordsworth and Coleridge resisted the sterilities of a University education, and the career boredom that seems to the poets so often to follow such an education. They did not denounce the systematic training and use of the intellect, and when they consider questions of methodology both endorsed accumulated knowledge and emphasize the value of specific, relevant experience. The generalization of this empirical and utilitarian impulse leads, finally, to the institutionalized and credit-based nature of the modern professions, but as Larson suggests in her account of the rise of professionalism, this nascent rationalization was not directly available to Wordsworth and Coleridge as a generalized structure of legitimation: "In the nineteenth century . . . . Scientific legitimation still appealed only to small enlightened minorities, even within the professions themselves."[13] Letting nature be your teacher is, in a rough sense, an empiricist's creed, but an empirical method was not enough, in 1800, to establish professional credibility. Thus, while Wordsworth claims to have what is in effect special expertise earned through a specialized training process, he also tries to mitigate the kind of "rationalization," or specialized division of labor, that Larson associates with later professional projects. Instead, he takes on the identity of a "man speaking to men" (or ministering to men). This allows him to cite his encounters with Nature as a qualifying process, but a process that is not yet held as a monopoly by its practitioners and which does not obviously depend on the still-tenuous authority of the man of science.

Particularly between 1799 and 1802, Wordsworth's rhetorical stance that he is a "chosen son," selected by Nature for some undefined task, is essential, but his sense of his own giftedness is tempered by the contention that his experiences and the use he has made of them are at least theoretically reproducible by anybody. Yet this position is unstable. The democratic nature of poetic professionalism as Wordsworth construes it, standing only on the strength of his rhetoric and lacking any formal institutional structure, always has a tense relationship to the specific authority that he wishes to claim for the poet and his professional function. Wordsworth is determined to establish "poet" as a valid vocational category, with its own rules and its own, restricted, criteria of entrance, but given the breadth of concerns potentially encompassed by the training of Nature and its palpable ministrations, it is a continuing question how the professional poet can be differentiated from any native of the Lake region who reads and thinks with some concentration.

Wordsworth's attempt to formulate this distinction emerges publicly in the Preface to *Lyrical Ballads*. The poetically fruitful Goslar winter and the satisfactory sale of the first edition of *Lyrical Ballads* justified Wordsworth's new vocational confidence, and his failure to learn German, which underlined the fact that poetry was going to be his only remunerative literary labor, made it all the more important that subsequent volumes be argued for. Despite his protests, Wordsworth really is trying to talk reviewers into accepting his work and prospective buyers into buying it. More generally, in 1800 Wordsworth begins working systematically to establish a regular, domestic life, and one that promises finally to answer family expectations: the move to Grasmere is an embodiment of the willful nature of his project at this time, and he is also busy settling the debts he had accrued in Germany and getting the second edition of *Lyrical Ballads* ready for the press.[14] Until his marriage to Mary Hutchinson and the settlement of the Lowther debt, Wordsworth had few financial resources,[15] but Wordsworth at Grasmere is determined to establish his social standing and to behave like the professional gentleman he conceives himself to be. The grounds of this professional gentility, in the absence of such accoutrements as a conventional profession or a steady income, needed to built, in some ways, from the ground up.

In the Preface, Wordsworth attempts to attach the nature of the poet and good poetry to the needs of a client audience by identifying the radical, structural identity of poet and reader. Immediately, however, this structural identity is altered by the facts of the poet's preparation. Wordsworth begins setting up this identity/distinction by describing the mind of the poet in broadly familiar psychological terms:

All good poetry is the spontaneous overflow of powerful feelings; but though this be true, Poems to which any value can be attached, were never produced on any variety of subjects, but by a man who being possessed of more than usual organic sensibility, had also thought long and deeply.[16]

Contemplation of the object of study, undertaken by the man of aptitude (that is, a man with "organic sensibility") is the path to right poetic practice. Right practice also provides the link to the reader, whose own healthy aptitude enables him to benefit from the poet's work on his behalf:

By the repetition and continuance of this act [of contemplation], feelings connected with important subjects will be nourished, till at length, if we be originally of much organic sensibility, such habits of mind will be produced that by obeying blindly and mechanically the impulses of those habits we shall describe objects and utter sentiments of such a nature and in such connection with each other, that the understanding of the being to whom we address ourselves, if he be in a healthful state of association, must necessarily be in some degree enlightened, his taste exalted, and his affections ameliorated. (126)

Wordsworth presumes a reader who is sensitive enough to respond to poetic treatment but is at the same time in need of at least a degree of enlightenment, exaltation, and amelioration. Therefore, the crucial margin of difference between poet and client must not be in the sensibility of the poet, which the reader must to some degree share, but in the work of the poet, that is, in the poet's specifically literary/professional function.

David Simpson, identifying some of Wordsworth's anxiety about his poetic labor, describes in particular "the predicament of the bourgeois experience of authorship: radical uncertainties about readership, affiliation, and determination."[17] Simpson's thesis acutely analyzes the "patterns of deconstruction and reconstruction" that mark Wordsworth's self-fashioning, but as a nascent professional Wordsworth also has active and specific remedies for the predicament of the bourgeois author.[18] Theorizing a professional/client relationship is one way for Wordsworth to (theoretically) control readership and affiliation, and to enter into productive social relations with an anonymous literary marketplace while maintaining the gentlemanly integrity he also craves. In turn, as Siskin has noted, this relationship does, finally, reproduce hierarchical differences:

[The collapsing of kind into degree] functions to naturalize the transformation of hierarchy from a structure based on inherited, unchanging distinctions to one that posits an initial equality subject to psychological and developmental difference. The latter, of course, is the democracy of the modern subject – an order in which inequities are rationalized as the inevitable product of the realization of the individual.[19]

If the poet is to maintain his position of sympathetic authority over his client audience, he must continue to posit a larger social structure within which reader and writer can identify a set of common interests. Otherwise, the poet runs the risk of being rejected by an audience that feels imposed upon by poetry it does not fully understand. Further, as he draws on (and helps institute) an emerging "democratic" vocabulary, Wordsworth also preserves the sense of hierarchical order which is necessary to the very concept of gentility, professional or otherwise, that motivates him.

The emerging vocabulary of democratization and rationalization also helps to explain Wordsworth's disturbingly mechanistic account of the poetic imagination, which works away "blindly and mechanically" and "emits" descriptions of ameliorating and elevating form.[20] In this account of poetic creation, which is very nearly an inversion or a parody of the "wise passiveness" of "Expostulation and Reply," Wordsworth insists that by obeying the laws relevant to his profession the poet can always and predictably achieve the desired results of his practice. Behind the personal and spontaneous poet of feeling stands the empiricist professional, who operates according to impersonal and fixed laws which also apply to the reader. Even when the sympathetic reader cannot attain the full body of skills required to make him a poet in his own right, he can rest assured that he is not being practiced upon by someone of a different party. For Wordsworth's professionalism, following its eighteenth-century roots, aspires in its structure to the status of representative democracy without party.

The Preface to *Lyrical Ballads* not only insists on the specialized nature of the poet and the structural nature of his relationship to his client audience. It also makes specific claims for the control a poet should have over the evaluation of his own labor, and here too Wordsworth pursues his professional agenda. The 1802 version of the Preface is usually distinguished from the 1800 version because the section on what a poet is has been added, but we might also say that the earlier version is distinct because questions of the poet's identity have been left out. In fact, the rhetorical burden of the 1800 version is to depersonalize the relationship between the poet and his audience and to reduce the object in question, the poem, to an "experiment," the "metrical arrangement" of the "real language of men," in order to discover "what quantity of pleasure may be imparted, which a Poet may rationally endeavour to impart" (118). The forensic distance between the poet and what he has done establishes that the poet's service and its value are not directly related to the poet's personality or the taste of the reader, but can be judged, as experiments, according to empirical or rational criteria. In the 1799 *Prelude* Wordsworth had reviewed his own credentials, but in the Preface, the question of credentials is subsumed by the question of how readers should identify the poet's task and judge his success in fulfilling that task.

While he would not be "suspected of having been influenced by the selfish and foolish hope of reasoning [the reader] into an approbriation of these particular poems" (120) he has and demands the right to set his own tasks for himself as a poet:

It is supposed, that by an act of writing in verse an Author makes a formal engagement that he will gratify certain known habits of association .... I am certain that it will appear to many persons that I have not fulfilled the terms of an engagement thus voluntarily contracted. I hope therefore the Reader will not censure me, if I attempt to state what I have proposed to myself to perform ... that I may myself be protected from the most dishonourable accusation which can be brought against an Author, namely, that of an indolence which prevents him from endeavouring to ascertain what is his duty, or, when his duty is ascertained prevents him from performing it (122).

The terms of the relationship between writer and reader may be voluntary and contractual, but it is still the role of the poet to "ascertain what is his duty," not to seek out and provide what will answer the demands of the marketplace by answering the unprofessional "expectations" of readers. Wordsworth demands that poetic work be treated as educated, cultured work, that is, as professional work which is allowed to establish its own standards and which confers status on its practitioners. The value of that work is to be judged objectively, according to the standards which it (or its practitioners) provides for themselves. "Indolence," according to Wordsworth, is "the most dishonourable accusation that can be brought against an author." Because the responsible and hard-working poet has the automatic right to pursue his own experiments and declare them poems, he can proceed without the need for any "species of courtesy" on the part of the reader.

This does not mean that the poet is self-sufficient and self-serving. His status is justified not only by his training but because he is in the position to provide a necessary service: he is in charge of the appropriate "excitement" of the human mind, and of preparing others to experience and appreciate that excitement at a time when "a multitude of causes" are working to blunt the mind's powers (128). His training enables him to train others in the art of feeling poetically, and, conversely, readers require this training: "an accurate taste in Poetry ... is an acquired talent" (156). While readers are to "decide by [their] own feelings genuinely," they should also work hard to appreciate all the work of the poet who has "by any single composition ... impressed us with respect for his talents" (154). Wordsworth acknowledges the existence of the impersonal marketplace and claims for himself and his peers the expert knowledge which allows him (or should allow him) to control it and establish its standards. The poem is finally figured not as a commodity but as the embodiment of a professional service.[21]

As we have seen, Wordsworth qualifies his familiar praise of spontaneity by insisting on both "sensibility" and long, deep thought on the part of the poet. He carefully preserves the authority of professional, trained poets over readers and sporadically inspired dilettantes. However, the generic and democratic language that Wordsworth uses, which identifies "men" who possess sensibility and intellect but does not distinguish such men from poets, is finally inadequate for Wordsworth's professional construction, even with its implied and essential "difference in kind." In the 1802 additions to the Preface, Wordsworth thus takes care to pose the more specific question, "What is a Poet?" He answers that

He is a man speaking to men: a man, it is true, endowed with more lively sensibility, more enthusiasm and tenderness, who has a greater knowledge of human nature, and a more comprehensive soul, than are supposed to be common among mankind; a man pleased with his own passions and volitions .... To these qualities he has added a disposition to be affected more than other men by absent things as if they were present. (138)

Although the phrase "a man speaking to men" is a famous example of Wordsworthian egalitarianism, the idea of "endowment" makes professional talent both essential and inalienable. The burden of this passage is to distinguish the poetic "man" from other men, and it does so by taking up a language not only of sensible refinement but also of economic priority.[22]

In the rhetorical and conceptual maneuvers I have so far described, Wordsworth emerges as the genuine prophet of the ascendancy of the professional middle classes, but he is also writing in advance of a historical moment that poses its own historiographical problem. Professional ascendancy, when it arrives after the middle of the nineteenth century, is neither simple nor total. The status categories of eighteenth-century society remain strong, and professional gentility, despite its purportedly utilitarian and rational basis, retains the hierarchical structures of traditional status society.[23] Wordsworth takes the opportunity of the successive editions of *Lyrical Ballads* to make his strongest public claims for the social necessity of the poetic professional, but however brilliant he might be, in private, on the subject of his own mind and its growth, he cannot create the taste by which he is to be enjoyed out of thin air. Thomas Pfau has suggested that Wordsworth seeks "to achieve community ... as the effect of interpretive participation elicited by a complex array of rhetorical forms, rather than being postulated conceptually," distinguishing between the Wordsworth of the Preface, a "writer ... so troubled by the conflict between his democratic convictions and his professional ambition" and a later "public author" who is less troubled and more prepared to assert his own prior, that is, conceptual, authority.[24] But as I have argued, Wordsworth's rhetoric in the Preface alludes throughout to a coherent, specific, and conceptual source of authority: the poet's own aptitude and training. The real conflict is not that the professional and the democrat are at theoretical odds, but that the professional democrat, or the democratic Wordsworthian professional, continues, despite Wordsworth's wishes, to require extra-rhetorical grounds in order to authorize his own project. Gentility is finally the source of Wordsworth's professionalism while also being its object.

Wordsworth's understanding of newly emerging means of professional self-authorization is matched by an equally intense appreciation of the enduring strength of landed values. His professional rhetoric is genuinely dialectical in its use of the idea of inheritance and, particularly, in his deft treatment of the value and function of landed property as a possible structural counterpart to professional expertise. In his efforts to preserve the structural differentiations of a status-society by construing his own status as "inherited" (as a gift of Nature, and in his own organic sensibility) while also claiming that that status is "earned" (through the rigors of his training), he also preserves and reconfigures the emphasis on property that is the single most important tenet of traditional British society. Wordsworth seeks to discover how far his professional expertise can be treated as property, and landed property in particular. As he argues that professional poets of his type will become more necessary than ever in a rationalized and industrialized age, he links this position to his treatment of property – "expertise" must stand in for "property," which is losing its ability to generate virtue – and it is in this linkage that the 1802 version of Wordsworthian professionalism logically culminates.

On 14 January 1801, shortly after completing the first version of the Preface, Wordsworth writes a now-famous letter to Charles James Fox:

> [There] is a class of men who are now almost confined to the North of England. They are small independent proprietors of land here called statesmen, men of respectable education who daily labour on their own little properties .... Their little tract of land serves as a kind of permanent rallying point for their domestic feelings, as a tablet upon which they are written which makes them objects of memory in a thousand instances when they would otherwise be forgotten. It is a fountain fitted to the nature of social man from which supplies of affection, as pure as his heart was intended for, are daily drawn.[25]

In this passage, Wordsworth conjures with the kind of materialist metonymy that has in the past enabled him to figure his own work as both private property, which can properly be sold for profit, and collective service, which can command deference from a client audience. In 1792 it was the metaphorical Field of Letters (as commons) that yielded up material necessities to the tiller. Now, in a significant reversal, it is land itself that yields up the less tangible but, in Wordsworth's current view, more important "domestic feelings" that hold families and communities together. But this property is endangered, and inextricably bound up with the plight of the statesman is the emerging need for poet-specialists. Independent proprietors perform the same service for themselves that Wordsworth's poets might provide for them, because it is their property, instead of poetry, that acts as the "permanent rallying point" which sharpens their appreciation of social life and domestic affection. Whereas the poet has "a disposition to be affected more than other men by absent things as if they were present" (138), the proprietor already has access to the things that are present, in the form of his property. For this reason statesmen do not need poets, and while Wordsworth bemoans their passing, it is that passing, itself the type and sign both of

industrialization and of the reconfiguration of agricultural relations, that will make the service of the poet ever more necessary in
years to come.

It must be remembered that in this context "property" can only
mean "land," so, according to Wordsworth, it has been private,
landed property that has had the power to circulate the stable
meanings constituting the communities of domestic affection
which have been "weakened, and in innumerable instances entirely
destroyed" by "the spreading of manufactures through every part
of the country, by the heavy taxes on postage [a perennial Wordsworthian concern], by workhouses, Houses of Industry, and the
invention of Soup-shops &c.&c."[26] Wordsworth's conceptual
structures come full circle here. If the nation is to be deprived of its
small, virtue-bearing land-holders, their place must be taken by
the professional poet, whose own expertise is transformed into a
new kind of property which bears "virtue" and status for the poet
and consequently for the nation. (The virtue-function of land
underwrites both "Michael" and "The Brothers," two poems
Wordsworth particularly recommends to Fox.)[27] The emphasis on
property does not only provide a source of status for the poet which
refers to and offers to replace traditional, familiar kinds of status. It
also fixes the basis of poetic value in an idealized, professional
ground – an imaginary and unnamed institution that can nonetheless be expressed in the idea of property and community, land
and circulation, tablet and fountain.

Finally, in the 1802 Preface, the professional Romantic poet
retains the rights of the professional who owns and controls his
own intellectual property while taking on the wings of the flying
visionary:

The knowledge both of the Poet and of the Man of science is pleasure;
but the knowledge of one cleaves to us as a necessary part of our existence, our natural and unalienable inheritance; the other is a personal
and individual acquisition, slow to come to us, and by no habitual and
direct sympathy connecting us with our fellow beings (141).

Here Wordsworth speaks the language of the Whig aristocracy
which, after the death of Sir James Lonsdale in May, would indeed
yield up an inheritance – the £8,000 settlement of the family debt.
The knowledge of the poet is homologous to the property of the
aristocrat. It "cleaves" to him necessarily and naturally, and

theoretically links him to larger social configurations. It is explicitly contrasted to the knowledge of the scientist, which, precisely because it is earned "slow[ly]" and "individual[ly]" is, while in general an asset, neither natural nor necessary. The Wordsworthian professional may be a trained specialist, but he does not thereby abdicate his "powers of sympathy" or his special role in collective life.

There is a final, surprising turn. In order to retain his organic link with a national community (and a national readership) while also preserving the abstract and uninstitutionalized form of his professionalism, Wordsworth finds that he must "unland" the professional property that has all along taken the place of land and its attendant legitimacy. Knowledge must exist in some humanizing context, as Wordsworth recognizes, and he allows that context quickly to expand beyond the borders of church and culture:

In spite of difference of soil and climate, of language and manners, of laws and customs: in spite of things silently gone out of mind, and things violently destroyed; the Poet binds together by passion and knowledge the vast empire of human society, as it is spread over the whole earth, and over all time. The objects of the poet's thoughts are everywhere ... he will follow wheresoever he can find an atmosphere of sensation in which to move his wings (141).

At first glance this is the visionary language of Coleridge or of Shelley. It also reflects the language of Bolingbroke's patriot king and the ideals of Richard Savage's wanderer, airborne over a magic kingdom that will sustain, reward, and punish a figure whose self-election is, at its most enthusiastic, presented as the miracle of human flight.

The rhetorical balancing act Wordsworth performs as he attempts to derive authority and conventionally gentlemanly status from the wide-ranging flights of the poet finally stands as an attempt to have one thing two ways, and poets in the reign of Victoria would find Wordsworth's Anglican claim to catholic efficacy insupportable. (The ranks of these disappointed Victorians would include Wordsworth himself). Poets would re-learn what physicians, lawyers and priests also find out: it is important for any vocational group to limit its claims of efficacy to those it can systematically defend. Wordsworth would come to seek his own authority not in a tactically limited definition of poetry, but in the renewed legitimacy of the British establishment. Here, however, he participates in a social drama of long standing. While determined to define his own work in his own way, Wordsworth, like Coleridge and Southey, discovers he must look in two different directions: toward the institutions that frame social action, including work, and toward the necessary, imaginative impulses that change and improve them.

Notes

INTRODUCTION: PROFESSIONALISM AND THE LAKE
SCHOOL OF POETRY

1 For the distinction between "technique" and "character," see Andrew
  Abbott, *The System of Professions: An Essay on the Division of Expert Labor*
  (Chicago: University of Chicago Press, 1988), pp. 190–191.
2 Immanuel Kant, *Critique of the Power of Judgment*, ed. Paul Guyer,
  trans. Paul Guyer and Eric Matthews (Cambridge: Cambridge
  University Press, 2000), p. 198; Isaac Disraeli, *An Essay on the
  Character and Manners of the Literary Genius* (London: T. Cadell, 1795;
  repr. Garland Publishing, 1970), p. 4.
3 A. S. Collins, *Authorship in the Days of Johnson: Being a Study of the
  Relation Between Author, Patron, Publisher, and Public, 1726–1780*
  (London: Robert Holden, 1927), p. 212.
4 Roger Chartier, *The Order of Books: Readers, Authors, and Libraries in
  Europe between the Fourteenth and Eighteenth Centuries*, trans. Lydia
  G. Cochrane (Stanford: Stanford University Press, 1994), p. 37.
5 Martha Woodmansee, *The Author, Art, and the Market: Rereading the
  History of Aesthetics* (New York: Columbia University Press, 1994),
  p. 32.
6 To William Sotheby, 10 September, 1802, *Collected Letters of Samuel
  Taylor Coleridge, Volume II: 1801–1806*, ed. Earl Leslie Griggs
  (Oxford: Clarendon Press, 1956), p. 863.
7 William Wordsworth to Joseph Cottle, Summer 1799, *The Letters of
  William and Dorothy Wordsworth: The Early Years, 1787–1805*, ed.
  Ernest de Selincourt, rev. Chester L. Shaver (Oxford: Clarendon,
  1967), pp. 267–268.
8 Southey to Grosvenor Charles Bedford, 11 November 1796, *New
  Letters of Robert Southey Volume I: 1792–1810*, ed. Kenneth Curry (New
  York, Columbia University Press, 1979), p. 117.
9 *Ibid.*
10 Coleridge to Isaac Wood, 19 January 1798, *Coleridge Letters* I, p. 375.
11 On Coleridge and medicine, for example, see Jennifer Ford,
  Coleridge on Dreaming: Romanticism, Dreams, and the Medical Imagination

(Cambridge: Cambridge University Press, 1998) and Neil Vickers, *Coleridge and the Doctors, 1795–1806* (Oxford: Clarendon Press, 2004); a study that discusses the intersection of Romantic and medical discourses of "health" is Martin Wallen, *City of Health, Fields of Disease: Revolutions in the Poetry, Medicine, and Philosophy of Romanticism* (Burlington: Ashgate, 2004); for Wordsworth and the law, see Mark Schoenfield, *The Professional Wordsworth* (Athens: University of Georgia Press, 1996).

12 Mark Rose, for example, argues that the new legal standing of the writer's "mental" activity is central to modern concepts of authorship; what is new for Rose is the combination of the traditional "mystification" of authorship with the production of commodities. *Authors and Owners: The Invention of Copyright* (Cambridge: Harvard University Press, 1993), p. 74.

13 Alan Liu, *Wordsworth: The Sense of History* (Stanford: Stanford University Press, 1989), p. 332; Abbott, *Professions*, p. 33.

14 Abbott, *Professions*, p. 134.

15 The phrase is attributable to Max Weber. For example, Weberian "class" is determined when "a number of people have in common a specific causal component of their life chances, insofar as … this component is represented exclusively by economic interests." (Max Weber, *Economy and Society: An Outline of Interpretive Sociology*, Volume II, Guenther Roth and Claus Wittich, eds. [Berkeley: University of California Press, 1978], 927. As Ralf Dahrendorf has observed, over the course of *Economy and Society* Weber offers a "salad" of meanings of the word "chance" (which for Dahrendorf includes those places translators have represented the German *Chance* as "probability"). Dahrendorf's summary is tactically broad enough to allow him to put "life chance" at the center of a disquisition on "the central areas of sociological analysis, the theories of norms and laws, of power and authority"; Weber "describes chance as the crystallized probability of finding satisfaction for interests, wants, and needs, thus the probability of the occurrence of events which bring about such satisfaction." *Life Chances: Approaches to Social and Political Theory* (Chicago: The University of Chicago Press, 1979), 72–73, 63.

16 To William Mathews, 17 February 1794, *Early Years*, p. 112.

17 To Robert Southey, 13 November 1795, *Coleridge Letters I*, p. 170.

18 *Ibid.*, p. 171.

19 To William Mathews, 8 June 1794, *Early Years*, p. 123.

20 *Ibid.*, p. 124.

21 To William Mathews, 19 May 1792, *Early Years*, p. 76.

22 Michael Burrage, "Beyond a Sub-set: The Professional Aspirations of Manual Workers in France, the United States, and Britain," in *Professions in Theory and History*, ed. Michael Burrage and Rolf Torstendahl (London: Sage, 1990), p. 165.

23 See Rosemary O'Day, *The Professions in Early Modern England, 1450–
1800: Servants of the Commonweal* (Harlow: Longman, 2000), p. 261.
As the title of her study indicates, O'Day looks back to the
Reformation to frame the chronological development of the
professions, but she accepts the broad view that a developing
monopoly of specialized knowledge defines the professions, with
local variations, after the seventeenth century.

24 *Ibid.*, p. 43.

25 Roy Porter, *Disease, Medicine and Society in England, 1550–1860*,
second edition (Cambridge: Cambridge University Press, 1995),
p. 44.

26 Geoffrey Holmes, *Augustan England: Professions, State and Society,
1680–1730* (London: George Allen and Unwin, 1983), p. 18;
p. 211.

27 Michael Hawkins, "Ambiguity and contradiction in 'the rise of
professionalism': the English clergy, 1570–1730," in A. L. Beier, David
Cannadine, and James M. Rosenheim (eds.), *The First Modern Society:
Essays in English History in Honour of Lawrence Stone* (Cambridge:
Cambridge University Press, 1989), pp. 266, 269.

28 Magali Sarfatti Larson, *The Rise of Professionalism: A Sociological
Analysis* (Berkeley: University of California Press, 1977), p. 5. The
association of a fully formed professionalism with late-nineteenth-
century capitalism has led several critics to define aesthetic
"modernism" in terms of the rise of the professions, in particular
because modernism's supposed inherent difficulty aligns it with the
"inaccessibility" of the expert's "esoteric knowledge." See Thomas
Strychacz, *Modernism, Mass Culture, and Professionalism* (Cambridge:
Cambridge University Press, 1993), p. 24.

29 Clifford Siskin, *The Work of Writing: Literature and Social Change in
Britain, 1700–1830* (Baltimore: The Johns Hopkins University Press,
1998), p. 108.

30 For a typical example of the "disciplinary" approach, see the facile
"history" of the "disciplines" offered in David R. Shumway and
Ellen Messer – Davidow, "Disciplinarity: An Introduction," *Poetics
Today* Volume 12, Number 12 (Summer, 1991), 201–225. The
difficulty of reconciling Foucauldian accounts based on French
institutional models with Anglo-American circumstances has often
been noted. See, for example, Jan Goldstein, "Foucault among the
Sociologists: 'The Disciplines' and the History of the Professions,"
History and Theory Volume 23, Number 2 (May, 1984), 192. For a
recent recuperation of Foucauldian models for British studies,
emphasizing "governmentality" over "disciplinarity," see Lauren
M. E. Goodlad, *Victorian Literature and the Victorian State: Character
and Governance in a Liberal Society* (Baltimore: Johns Hopkins
University Press, 2003), pp. 1–31.

31 James Chandler, *England in 1819: The Politics of Literary Culture and the Case of Romantic Historicism* (Chicago: University of Chicago Press, 1998), p. 185. The challenge is not to identify "examples" that define the period but to examine "cases" that pose specific events ("exemplary anomal[ies]") against a "normative frame of reference" (p. 299).

32 Of course, other versions of this divide have been proposed in Romantic studies. Colin Jager argues that the Romantic period has been misread along a historical/philosophical divide because accounts of modernity accept secularism's division of the interior self from the state and the world; in fact, Jager argues, for the Romantics, design theory unites the person and the object. "Natural Designs: Romanticism, Secularization, Theory," *European Romantic Review* 12 (1), Winter 2001, 54–55.

33 Forerunners of this criticism are the classic Freudian or Hegelian treatments by Abrams and Bloom, while its most influential new exponents have been inclined to treat romantic consciousness, not as an inevitable and universal fact of human existence, but, as Marjorie Levinson puts it in a still-influential treatment, as a historically contingent "white elephant." *Wordsworth's Great Period Poems: Four Essays* (Cambridge: Cambridge University Press, 1986), p. 57.

34 I borrow the term from a recent collection of essays: Gillian Russell and Clara Tuite, eds., *Romantic Sociability: Social Networks and Literary Culture in Britain, 1770–1840* (Cambridge: Cambridge University Press, 2002). Russell and Tuite's introductory claim, that "the solitary self has stood for Romanticism for far too long" (p. 4), may be overstated, but it does identify a central critical crux. Three books that explicitly complicate the identification of "Romanticism" with an untroubled (or ideologically sutured) "interiority" are David Simpson, *Wordsworth's Historical Imagination: The Poetry of Displacement* (New York: Methuen, 1987), Don H. Bialostosky, *Wordsworth, Dialogics, and the Practice of Criticism* (Cambridge: Cambridge University Press, 1992), and Sarah Zimmerman, *Romanticism, Lyricism, and History* (Albany: SUNY Press, 1999).

35 The most widely cited formulation of the imperative to resist "an uncritical absorption in Romanticism's own self-representations" belongs to Jerome McGann. See *The Romantic Ideology: A Critical Investigation* (Chicago: University of Chicago Press, 1983), p. 137.

36 Forest Pyle, *The Ideology of Imagination: Subject and Society in the Discourse of Romanticism* (Stanford: Stanford University Press, 1995), p. 93.

37 Individual subtleties will naturally pose a challenge to the very broad distinction I am offering, as in Sonia Hofkosh, *Sexual Politics and the Romantic Author* (Cambridge: Cambridge University Press, 1998). Hofkosh offers a series of closely argued case-studies which examine the way authorship in the Romantic period is constructed

according to gender difference; of particular interest in this context is her critique of Byron's attempt to both suppress and exploit the "feminization" an author is subjected to at the hands of readers and rivals: "The male writer also dreads, even as he desires, being read by others – a reading that rewrites him and thus challenges the powers of self-creation that seem a peculiarly masculine inheritance" (p. 38). Another sociable challenge to the distinction between the sociable and the isolate is Anne Janowitz, *Lyric and Labour in the Romantic Tradition* (Cambridge: University of Cambridge Press, 1998). Janowitz argues that "We should consider romanticism to be the literary form of a struggle taking place on many levels of society between the claims of *individualism* and the claims of *communitarianism*; that is, those claims that respond to identity as an always already existing voluntaristic self, and those that figure identity as emerging from a fabric of social narratives, with their attendant goals and expectations" (p. 13).

38 Another powerful example of context-building and authorship-situating is Paul Keen, *The Crisis of Literature in the 1790s: Print Culture and the Public Sphere* (Cambridge: Cambridge University Press, 1999). Chapter Two, "Men of Letters," provides a highly "sociable" and highly persuasive view of Romanticism and the professional gentleman: "Professional authors" took advantage of their essentially middle-class status "by insisting on the need to earn a living as a positive social characteristic rather than a necessary evil, and by highlighting the fact that they did so by means of an intellectual rather than manual vocation" (p. 91). Also, see Keen's "'The Most Useful of Citizens: Towards a Romantic Literary Professionalism," *Studies in Romanticism* 41 (Winter 2002). "Professional" has been a key term in several recent treatments, but as I will discuss, it is important for my purposes not to equate "the professions" with "the middle class" or "professional ideology" with "modernity," as such studies tend to. Schoenfield is a major exception. His thesis, that Wordsworth defined himself in relation to the discourse of the law, is in general consonant with my own discussion, which shares its largely biographical basis and also its commitment to the tactical, "non-foundational" nature of Romantic interventions in professional questions. Specifically, Schoenfield is interested in the ways that law, history, and new forms of property interact in Wordsworth's poetry, and his analyses are powerfully supported. I will return to his commentary in the course of the following pages. However, my own emphasis on an amorphous professionalism, and on the surprising lack of clear-cut delineations among the professions at this time (a lack to which these poets addressed themselves) distinguishes this discussion from Schoenfield's systematic concentration on the law.

39 Regina Hewitt, *The Possibilities of Society: Wordsworth, Coleridge, and the Sociological Viewpoint of English Romanticism* (Albany: SUNY University Press, 1997). Hewitt finds in Romantic poetry a habit of abstracting and studying an object, "society," that anticipates the work of Weber, Durkheim, and the institutions of society more generally, a possibility that emerges, I would argue, in conjunction with their own developing sense of authority and status in professional terms.

40 I am referring to the definition of reflexive action developed by Anthony Giddens in *The Constitution of Society: Outline of a Theory of Structuration* (Berkeley: University of California Press, 1984).

41 Goffman's theory of "stigma" provides a useful counterpoint to theories of ideological or cultural production that presume harmony between the actor and his world. The closing pages of Goffman's argument suggest the extent to which stigma may distributed across a range of roles and situations: "The general identity-values of a society may be fully entrenched nowhere, and yet they can cast some kind of shadow on the encounters encountered everywhere in daily living." *Stigma: Notes on the Management of Spoiled Identity* (1963) (New York: Simon and Schuster, 1986), pp. 128–129.

42 J. W. Saunders, *The Profession of English Letters* (London: Routledge and Kegan Paul, 1964), p. 147; A. S. Collins, *The Profession of Letters: A Study of the Relation of Author to Patron, Publisher, and Public, 1780–1832* (New York: E. P. Dutton and Co., 1929).

43 Harold Perkin, for example, points out that while "the professional class" is a class in straightforward Marxist (and, it might be added, Weberian) terms – its members are united by the source of their income – "what characterized ... professional men as a class was their comparative aloofness from the struggle for income," an aloofness which allowed for a disinterested "freedom to choose" in various social contests (*The Origins of Modern English Society: Second Edition* (London: Routledge, 2002), pp. 252–257.

44 Herbert Marcuse, "The Affirmative Character of Culture," in *Negations: Essays in Critical Theory*, trans. Jeremy Shapiro (London: Allen Lane, 1968).

45 Siskin, *The Work of Writing*, p. 124.

46 Clifford Siskin, *The Historicity of Romantic Discourse* (New York: Oxford University Press, 1988), p. 95.

47 Thomas Pfau, *Wordsworth's Profession: Form, Class, and the Logic of Early Romantic Cultural Production* (Stanford: Stanford University Press, 1997), p. 10.

48 Sigmund Freud, *The Interpretation of Dreams* (1900) ed. and trans. James Strachey (New York: Avon Books, 1965), p. 355.

49 As Erik Erikson observes, "the limited usefulness of the *mechanism of identification* becomes at once obvious if we consider the fact that none of the identifications of childhood (which in our patients

stand out in such morbid elaboration and mutual contradiction) could, if merely added up, result in a functioning personality ... The final identity ... is superordinated to any single identification with individuals of the past: it includes all significant identifications, but it also alters them in order to make a unique and reasonably coherent whole of them." "The Problem of Ego Identity" (1959), in *Pivotal Papers in Identification*, George H. Pollock, ed. (Madison: International Universities Press, 1993), 269.

50 David Chandler, "The Early Development of the 'Lake School' Idea," *Notes and Queries* 52 (25), no. 1 (March 2005), 35.

51 William St. Clair, *The Reading Nation in the Romantic Period* (Cambridge: Cambridge University Press, 2004), p. 210.

52 Notably, Jeffrey does not use the term "Lake School" in this essay, nor is he the first to use it. On the precise development of the nomenclature, see Peter A. Cook, "Chronology of the Lake School Argument: Some Revisions," *Review of English Studies* (n.s.) Vol. 28, No. 110 (May, 1977), 175–181. Cook notes that although these three poets were associated with each other throughout their careers, "the term 'Lake Poets' was not established among reviewers even in 1813," although "it may have been in use in conversation at this time" and would come into currency a year later (179).

An essay that also begins with Jeffrey's review in order to explore the dynamic literary relationships of these poets is Alison Hickey, "Coleridge, Southey 'and Co.': Collaboration and Authority," *Studies in Romanticism* 37 (Fall 1998). Hickey is particularly interested in the threat the idea of the "school" poses to the supposed integrity of the individual literary intelligence, and argues in part that "Jeffrey's review of *Thalaba* shows that a critic's charges of collaboration may serve as a means to establish his own authority as a voice allied with standards, taste, integrity, and 'independence' " (326). I hope to show that these standards can themselves be understood in collective, professional terms.

Since the interactions of Wordsworth and Coleridge, both before and after the *Lyrical Ballads*, have been studied so carefully, it is important to remember how closely Southey was identified with each of them. While Hickey concentrates on the intense relationship of Coleridge and Southey, a necessary point of focus for any consideration of the "Jacobin" years, work by David Chandler reminds us that Southey and Wordsworth are also intertwined; on Southey as the possible source of the Arab dream, see David Chandler, "Robert Southey and *The Prelude*'s 'Arab Dream,' " *The Review of English Studies* (n.s.) 54: 214 (April 2003); for the argument that Southey's largely self-willed association with Wordsworth "eclipsed the international perspectives of most of his own work," perspectives which have been central to the recent re-consideration of Southey and his career, see "Wordsworthian Southey: The Fashioning of a Reputation," *Wordsworth Circle* Winter 2003 (34:1), 18.

53 For example, see Jonathan Wordsworth, "Introduction" to *On the Lake Poets*: "Wordsworth was the 'individual delinquent' whom [Jeffrey] wished to chastise, but ... as luck would have it, it was Southey who came into print" in 1802 (n.p.). All three authors would resist the identification at various times. The most significant attempt at differentiation is in the *Biographia* (I: 50–52).

54 Marilyn Butler, *Romantics, Rebels and Reactionaries: English Literature and its Background, 1760–1830* (Oxford: Oxford University Press, 1981), p. 70. Butler argues that the "man of letters" is "a man representative of the educated 'professional' class in everything but his eloquence" (p. 72).

55 Philip Flynn, *Francis Jeffrey* (Newark: University of Delaware Press, 1978), 31–40.

56 John Hayden, *The Romantic Reviewers: 1802–1824* (Chicago: University of Chicago Press, 1968), 17.

57 Review of *Thalaba* 66.

58 The conflict between Jeffrey and the Lake poets is often accounted for in party terms, a point that Jeffrey's review obviously substantiates. Alternative readings of the situation have been proposed. In addition to Hickey, above, Keen argues that in distinction to Cowper, the Lake poets "contravened the code of sociability which (at the level of self-representation, at least) characterized the learned community's relations with one another" (pp. 251–252).

59 Siskin, *Work of Writing*, p. 103.

60 Schoenfield, *Professional Wordsworth*, p. 208. Tellingly, Schoenfield indicates that while the major dispute is between the lawyer/critic and the poet, both proceed according to the language of medicine.

61 Perkin, *Modern English Society*, p. 257.

62 Robert Southey, *Letters Written During a Short Residence in Spain and Portugal*, 2nd edn. (Bristol: Biggs and Cottle, 1799), pp. 225–226.

63 William Haller, *The Early Life of Robert Southey: 1774–1803* (New York: Columbia University Press, 1917), pp. 168–174.

64 Southey, *Letters from Portugal*, pp. 218–219.

65 *Ibid.*, p. 219.

66 *Ibid.*

67 On Wordsworth's continuous awareness of Southey at this time, see Christopher Smith, "Robert Southey and the Emergence of *Lyrical Ballads*," *Romanticism on the Net* 9 (February 1998).

68 Robert J. Griffin, *Wordsworth's Pope* (New York: Cambridge University Press, 1996), pp. 102–107. On a range of eighteenth-century "heroic and mock heroic" associations for the phrase, including the precedents of *Orlando Furioso* and *Samson Agonistes*, see Howard

Erskine-Hill, *The Poetry of Opposition and Revolution: Dryden to Wordsworth* (Oxford: Clarendon, 1996), p. 183.

1 CURSING DOCTOR YOUNG, AND AFTER

1 Coleridge to Poole, March, 1797, *Coleridge Letters I*, pp. 310–312.
2 Eliot Freidson, *Professional Powers: A Study of the Institutionalization of Formal Knowledge* (Chicago: University of Chicago Press, 1986), pp. 22–23.
3 See, for example, W. J. Reader, *Professional Men: The Rise of the Professional Classes in Nineteenth-Century England* (London: Weidenfeld and Nicolson, 1966), pp. 32–40.
4 Or at least relatively more respectable; as Reader reports, the 1841 census listed "Other Educated Persons" alongside the traditional professions of clergy, lawyers, and medical men and included "authors, editors, journalists" in the description, but "the *Contemporary Review* in 1859 remarked severely that [journalism] was 'not within the list of professions which give the conventional standing of gentlemen to their members'" (pp. 147–148).
5 *Power and the Professions in Britain, 1700–1850* (New York: Routledge, 1995), p. 140.
6 See Norman Gash, "The Crisis of the Anglican Establishment in the Early Nineteenth Century," in *Pillars of Government* (London: Edward Arnold, 1986).
7 In the history of the professions, a paradigmatic conflict is between the provincial apothecary-surgeon, generally trained as an apprentice, and the London physician, whose institutional preparation, whatever its actual pertinence, would have been certified by fellow gentlemen without examination. On the apothecary-surgeon, see Irvine Loudon, *Medical Care and the General Practitioner, 1750–1850* (Oxford: Clarendon Press, 1986), pp. 34–39; for the Royal College of Physicians, see Reader, *Men*, pp. 17–19.
8 Philip Elliot, *Sociology of the Professions* (New York: Herder and Herder, 1972), pp. 14–16.
9 In medicine, the shift from one model to the other has been tracked in relation to a variety of legal decisions, such as the 1815 Apothecaries' Act, which established the dispensing of medicines as a monopoly. However, historians such as S.W. F. Holloway have argued that the act was a step backward in the professionalization of medicine insofar as it "was a reassertion of the theory of 'orders' at the very moment that this theory was crumbling in the face of the new social structure"; that is, it was an attempt to keep the underclass of the apothecaries separate from the genteel practitioners of the Royal College of Physicians. "The Apothecaries' Act, 1815: A Reinterpretation. Part I: The Origins of the Act," *Medical History* 10 (2), April, 1966, 129.

10 In Larson, *The Rise of Professionalism.*

11 Larson, "Experts and Professionals," p. 25. In addition see Larson, "The Production of Expertise and the Constitution of Professional Power," in *The Authority of Experts and the Constitution of Expert Power*, ed. Thomas L. Haskell (Bloomington: Indiana University Press, 1984).

12 Abbott, *Professions*, p. 323.

13 The experiments involved inhaling nitrous oxide, "the most interesting of the gases" from a medical point of view. For an account that emphasizes the co-existence of rigorous experiment and recreational drug use at the institute, see Dorothy A. Stansfield, *Thomas Beddoes M.D., 1760–1808: Chemist, Physician, Democrat* (Dordrecht: D. Reidel Publishing, 1984), pp. 162–171. Stansfield notes the participation in the experiments of Southey, Coleridge, Josiah and Thomas Wedgwood, John Rickman, Poole, and Anna Letitia Barbauld (pp. 166–167). Everybody seems to have enjoyed the nitrous, but when Humphry Davy became ill, Coleridge quickly assumed that his "chemical researches might have exposed him to unwholesome influences" (Trevor H. Levere, *Poetry Realized in Nature: Samuel Taylor Coleridge and Early Nineteenth-Century Science* [Cambridge: Cambridge University Press, 1981], p. 25).

The other side of this is that the risks taken on behalf of society are aimed at producing safety for the culture at large, and a recent essay describes the ways poets and scientists competed, at least rhetorically, to appear to fulfill this function. Catherine E. Ross, " 'Twin Labourers and Heirs of the Same Hopes': The Professional Rivalry of Humphry Davy and William Wordsworth," in *Romantic Science: The Literary Forms of Natural History*, ed. Noah Heringman (Albany: SUNY University Press, 2003), p. 38. Ross points out that while Davy and Wordsworth each pursue professionalism in the terms set out by writers such as Larson, Davy is successful and Wordsworth is not; ironically, as Ross demonstrates, Davy is better at swaying his audience than Wordsworth at least partially because "he ousted the pain usually associated with gain by representing scientific improvements as familiar, exciting, and requiring no real change in human behavior or English social structures" (p. 43); to put this in the terms of the present argument, Davy is less honest than Wordsworth about the risk-sharing that modernity increasingly entails.

14 A theoretical interest in "risk" has been prominent in the work of both Ulrich Beck and Anthony Giddens. I draw the term from the title of Ulrich Beck, *Risk Society: Toward a New Modernity*, trans. Mark Ritter (London: Sage Publications, 1992).

15 Thus Giddens points out that, "because the specialization inherent expertise means that all experts are themselves lay people most of

the time, the advent of abstract systems sets up modes of social influence which no one directly controls." *Modernity and Self-Identity: Self and Society in the Late Modern Age* (Stanford: Stanford University Press, 1991), p. 138.

16 This is Beck's main conclusion. See, for example, *Risk Society*, pp. 183–187 on the "unbinding" of politics. As Giddens argues, the "modern subject" is uncomfortably aware that "no expert system can be wholly expert in terms of the consequences of the adoption of expert principles." *The Consequences of Modernity* (Stanford: Stanford University Press, 1990), p. 125.

17 *The Collected Works of Samuel Taylor Coleridge: The Watchman* ed. Lewis Patton (London: Routledge and Kegan Paul, 1970), p. 6.

18 On this definition of "class," see Beck, *Risk*, pp. 39–40.

19 To Josiah Wedgwood, 5 January 1798, *Coleridge Letters I*, p. 366.

20 Two important and sympathetic essays about Cottle are Timothy Whelan, "Joseph Cottle the Baptist," *The Charles Lamb Bulletin* July 2000 (n.s. 111), and Alan Boehm, "Was Joseph Cottle a Liberal Bookseller?" *ELN* 32:3 (March 1995). Together, Whalen and Boehm provide a portrait of Cottle which is also a portrait of one segment of Bristovian literary culture – politically progressive, but theologically cautious.

21 For basic biographical information on Henderson, see "John Henderson," *The Dictionary of National Biography* 9, ed. Leslie Stephen and Sidney Lee (1890), reprinted Oxford University Press, 1921.

22 See Kathleen Coburn in *The Notebooks of Samuel Taylor Coleridge, Volume I 1794–1804: Notes*, ed. Kathleen Coburn (New York: Bollingen, 1957), p. 174.

23 *Ibid.*

24 John Wesley, quoted in *DNB*, "Henderson" (p. 402).

25 *DNB*, "Henderson" (p. 401).

26 [C.C.], "Anecdotes of Mr. Henderson," *Gentleman's Magazine*, April, 1789, 296; for Pembroke College, see Stansfield, *Beddoes*, pp. 14–15.

27 See Mary E. Fissell, *Patients, Power, and the Poor in Eighteenth-Century Bristol* (Cambridge: Cambridge University Press, 1991), Chapter 3, "The Marketplace in Medicine."

28 Joseph Cottle, "Sketches of the Character of John Henderson," in *Poems* (1795), reprinted in *Poems, Containing John the Baptist; Malvern Hills; An Expostulary Epistle to Lord Byron; Dartmoor, and Other Poems* (New York: Garland Publishing, 1978), pp. 117–118. Except where noted, subsequent citations of Cottle's writing refer to this edition, and will be given by page or line number.

29 Richard G. Swartz, " 'Their terrors came upon me tenfold': Literacy and Ghosts in John Clare's *Autobiography*," in *Lessons of Romanticism: A Critical Companion* ed. Thomas Pfau and Robert F Gleckner (Durham: Duke University Press, 1998). Swartz writes that Clare's

"ghosts begin to take on a ... disruptive, disturbing character. They become psychological tropes capable of shattering the logic of symbolic identification and therefore of exposing the difficulties in his relationship to official culture" (p. 339).

30 R. C. Finucane, *Appearances of the Dead: A Cultural History of Ghosts* (Buffalo: Prometheus Books, 1984), p. 169.

31 Colleen McDannell and Bernhard Lang, *Heaven: A History* (New Haven: Yale University Press, 1988), pp. 210–211. As Michael Wheeler writes, "The two most important models of heaven in the nineteenth century – heaven as worship and heaven as community – were difficult to reconcile .... Negotiations between past, present, and future revelations are transacted in Protestant and Catholic liturgies of the eucharist, and in Victorian hymns." *Death and the Future Life in Victorian Literature and Theology* (Cambridge: Cambridge University Press, 1990), pp. 126–127.

32 Neil Vickers, "Coleridge, Thomas Beddoes, and Brunonian Medicine," *European Romantic Review* Winter, 1997 (8:1), 67.

33 On this point, Vickers cites Michael Barfoot, "Brunonianism Under the Bed: An Alternative to University Medicine in Edinburgh in the 1780s," in W. F. Bynum and Roy Porter, eds., *Brunonianism in Britain and Europe* (London: Wellcome Institute, 1988). Barfoot argues that "Brunonian ideology" "involved a republican attitude to medical free-thinking, which related developments in medicine to the history of human understanding within political society" (39).

34 Anya Taylor, "Ghosts, Spirits, and Force: Samuel Taylor Coleridge" in *The Occult in Language and Literature: New York Literary Forum 4* ed. Hermine Riffaterre (New York, 1980), 76.

35 To Thelwall, 17 December 1796, *Coleridge Letters I*, p. 278.

36 The Rev. William Agutter, "A Sermon Occasioned by the Death of the Celebrated Mr. J. Henderson, BA of Pembroke College, Oxford: Preached at St. George's, Kingswood, Nov. 23, and at Temple Church, Bristol, Nov. 30, 1788" (Bristol: Bulgin and Rosser, 1788), pp. 1, 5, 25. Thirteen years earlier, Agutter had preached on Samuel Johnson's death at St. Mary's Church, Oxford; comparing Johnson's death to Hume's, Agutter was led to "suggest several reasons for the apprehensions of the good, and the indifference of the infidel in their last hours." James Boswell, *Life of Johnson* (1791), ed. R. W. Chapman (Oxford: Oxford University Press, 1989), p. 1396.

37 "Original Letters from Mr. Henderson to Dr. Priestley," *Gentleman's Magazine* April, 1789, 288.

38 *Ibid.*, 289.

39 John Henderson, "Postscript: Dissertation on Everlasting Punishment," in William Matthews, *The Miscellaneous Companions, Volume*

III, Containing Dissertations on Particular Subjects and Occasions; and Dialogues in the World of Spirits (Bath: R. Crutwell, 1786), p. 111.

40 In addition to the "experiment solitary" pertaining to "spirits" in Bacon's *Sylva Sylvarum*, to which it seems likely that Henderson is directly alluding, see Stuart Clark's more general observation that in considering Bacon's speculations on witchcraft and "prodigies," "we are faced with the artificiality of bringing the modern notion that there is a difference of kind between the 'scientific' and the 'occult' to the investigation of what were simply differences of degree between varying concepts of nature." Francis Bacon, "Experiment Solitary Touching the Secret Processes of Nature," in *Sylva Sylvarum: or, A Natural History* (1627) in *The Works of Francis Bacon (Volume IV)*, ed. James Spedding, Robert Leslie Ellis, and Douglas Denon Heath (Boston: Brown and Taggard, 1872), p. 219; Stuart Clark, "The Scientific Status of Demonology," in *Occult and Scientific Mentalities in the Renaissance*, ed. Brian Vickers (Cambridge: Cambridge University Press, 1984), p. 356.

41 Agutter, *Sermon*, p. 4.

42 *Ibid.*, p. 7.

43 Anthony Giddens, *Modernity and Self-Identity* (Stanford: Stanford University Press, 1991), p. 146.

44 "Monody on the Death of John Henderson, A.B. of Pembroke College, Oxford," in *Poems: Second Edition. With Additions* (Bristol: Bulgin and Rosser, 1796), p. 107.

45 "Epistle IV. To the Author of Poems Published Anonymously At Bristol, in September, 1795," in *Poems on Various Subjects* (1796), ed. Jonathan Wordsworth (Oxford: Woodstock Books, 1990), p. 125. Further citations will be given in the text, by page number.

46 Although his concern is more broadly with the psycholinguistic dynamics of "loss and figuration" inherent in the elegiac form, Peter M. Sacks notes in passing that when, pursued by Apollo, Daphne is transformed into the laurel tree, she "is thus eventually transformed into something like a consolation prize – a prize that becomes *the* prize and sign of poethood ... a consoling sign that carries in itself the reminder of loss on which it has been founded." *The English Elegy: Studies in the Genre from Spenser to Yeats* (Baltimore: The Johns Hopkins University Press, 1985), p. 5.

47 See, for example, *ibid.*, pp. 91–92.

48 W. David Shaw, *Elegy and Paradox: Testing the Conventions* (Baltimore: The Johns Hopkins University Press, 1994), p. 6. Shaw warns against a kind of "weak elegy" in which the work of mourning is too effectively performed – "though we value elegies that have more tragic catharsis than lyric angst, we recognize that melancholia has its own power and that grief therapy is a dangerous basis for a theory of art" (p. 180). This is a good way of accounting for our resistance,

and I argue Coleridge's resistance, to the "Monody"'s too-happy ending.

49 Schoenfield, *Professional Wordsworth*, p. 254.

50 *Ibid.*, p. 263.

51 *Ibid.*, p. 265.

52 *Ibid.*, p. 260.

53 Richard Matlak treats "Tintern Abbey" as an act of persuasion, and in particular as an act of classical oratory, in *The Poetry of Relationship: The Wordsworths and Coleridge, 1797–1800* (New York: St. Martin's Press, 1997), pp. 119–137.

54 Edward Young, *Night Thoughts*, ed. Stephen Cornford (Cambridge: Cambridge University Press, 1989), IX 768–769. Further citations appear in the text.

55 "Lines Written a Few Miles Above Tintern Abbey," in *Lyrical Ballads and Other Poems, 1797–1800*, ed. James Butler and Karen Green (Ithaca: Cornell University Press, 1992), lines 103–112, and footnote. Subsequent citations will be given in the text, by line number.

56 Herbert Croft, "Young," in *Lives of the English Poets by Samuel Johnson, LL.D.*, ed. George Birckbeck Hill, D.C.L. (Oxford: Clarendon Press, 1905), p. 391.

57 On Croft and Young's nineteenth-century reputation, which culminates in George Eliot's portrait of him as a "servile hypocrite," see Harold Foster, *Edward Young: The Poet of the Night Thoughts, 1683–1785* (Alburgh: The Erskine Press, 1986), pp. 381–387.

58 Isabel St. John Bliss, "Young's *Night Thoughts* in Relation to Contemporary Christian Apologetics," *PMLA* XLIX, 1934, 37–70. Also see John E. Sitter, "Theology at Mid-Century: Young, Akenside, and Hume," *Eighteenth-Century Studies* 12:1 (Fall, 1978), 90–106.

59 Bliss, "Night Thoughts," p. 64.

60 Edward Young, "A Vindication of Providence; or, a True Estimate of Human Life," in *Edward Young: The Complete Works, Poetry and Prose* Volume II, ed. James Nichol (1854) (reprint Germany: Georg Olms, 1968), p. 377.

61 Carey McIntosh, *The Evolution of English Prose, 1700–1800: Style, Politeness, and Print Culture* (Cambridge: Cambridge University Press, 1998), p. 23.

62 Marshall Brown, *Preromanticism* (Stanford: Stanford University Press, 1991), p. 35. My own reading of the poem finds in it something a little more jarring than "consolation."

63 Edward Young, "Conjectures on Original Composition," in *Edward Young: The Complete Works, Poetry and Prose II*, p. 580.

64 On "Tintern Abbey" as a "radical examination of Lockean influx," see Keith G. Thomas, *Wordsworth and Philosophy: Empiricism and*

Transcendentalism in the Poetry (Ann Arbor: UMI Research Press, 1989), p. 66.

65 William H. Galperin, *Revision and Authority in Wordsworth: The Interpretation of a Career* (Philadelphia: University of Pennsylvania Press, 1989), p. 81; Susan Eilenberg, *Strange Power of Speech: Wordsworth, Coleridge, and Literary Possession* (New York: Oxford University Press, 1992), p. 24.

66 Judith W. Page, *Wordsworth and the Cultivation of Women* (Berkeley: University of California Press, 1994), pp. 46–47.

67 *Ibid.*, p. 47.

68 Mary Jacobus, *Tradition and Experiment in Wordsworth's* Lyrical Ballads (*1798*) (Oxford: Clarendon Press, 1976), pp. 107–108.

69 Larson, *Professionalism*, pp. 211–212.

70 C-Stage Reading Text, in *The Prelude, 1798–1799*, ed. Stephen Parrish (Ithaca: Cornell University Press, 1977), 539–563.

71 He was in good company; Henry Pettit's bibliography of *Night Thoughts* reports that John Wesley appropriates lines from it, as well. See "A Bibliography of Young's *Night-Thoughts,*" *University of Colorado Studies: Series in Language and Literature No. 5* (Boulder: University of Colorado Press, 1954), p. 9.

72 William Hazlitt, "On the Living Poets," in *The Selected Writings of William Hazlitt, Volume II: The Round Table, Lectures on the English Poets*, ed. Duncan Wu (London: Pickering and Chatto, 1998), pp. 314–316.

2 MERIT AND REWARD IN 1729

1 A. M. Carr-Saunders and P. A. Wilson, *The Professions* (Oxford: Clarendon Press, 1933), 300.

2 Dustin Griffin, *Literary Patronage in England, 1650–1800* (Cambridge: Cambridge University Press, 1996), p. 258.

3 Wordsworth, *Prelude*, XIII: 360–367.

4 Kenneth R. Johnston, *The Hidden Wordsworth: Poet, Lover, Rebel, Spy* (New York: Norton, 1998), p. 423.

5 Kenneth R. Johnston, *Wordsworth and the Recluse* (Yale: Yale University Press, 1984), pp. 213–214.

6 Nigel Cross, *The Common Writer: Life in Nineteenth-Century Grub Street* (Cambridge: Cambridge University Press, 1985), p. 12.

7 Clarence Tracy, *The Artificial Bastard: a Biography of Richard Savage* (Cambridge: Harvard University Press, 1953), p. 4.

8 W. H. Ireland, "Invocation to Genius," in *Neglected Genius: a Poem Illustrating the Untimely and Unfortunate Fates of Many British Poets From the Period of Henry VIII to the Time of the Unfortunate Chatterton* (London: George Cowie and Co., 1812), n.p.

9 Linda Zionkowski, *Men's Work: Gender, Class, and the Professionaliza-tion of Poetry, 1660–1784* (New York: Palgrave, 2001), p. 187.
10 Griffin, *Patronage*, p. 170.
11 Hal Gladfelder, "The Hard Work of Doing Nothing: Richard Savage's Parallel Lives," *MLQ* 64:4 (December 2003), 457.
12 *Ibid.*, 472.
13 *Ibid.*, 446.
14 Richard Savage, *The Wanderer*, in *The Poetical Works of Richard Savage*, ed. Clarence Tracy (Cambridge: Cambridge University Press, 1962), V. 276. Further references to Savage's poetry are to this edition, and will be given in the text.
15 For the characterization of his exchange with Dyer, see Tracy's headnote to the poem (p. 56).
16 Nicholas Amhurst, *Protestant Popery, or, The Convocation (1718)* in *English Poetry Database* <http://ets.umdl.umich.edu>.
17 On the other hand, Samuel Croxall's "The Vision," written on the accession of George I, is unabashed in attributing merit, virtue and worth to the monarch – although "virtue" is by far Croxall's favorite term of approbation. See *The Vision (1715)* in *English Poetry Database*.
18 On "engrafting" as an oppositional figure for spiritual transforma-tion via scripture, see Rebecca Krug, *Reading Families: Women's Literate Practice in Late Medieval England* (Ithaca, Cornell University Press, 2002), p. 146.
19 The poem's preface and its first line state that it was begun in "Gayer hours," (1), and in his notes to the collected works Clarence Tracy points out that the first, "liberated" part of the poem must have been written before Savage was chastened by the experience of his murder trial, conviction, and pardon (87).
20 J. C. D. Clark, *English Society, 1660–1832: Religion, Ideology, and Politics During the Ancien Regime* (Cambridge: Cambridge University Press, 2000), p. 45.
21 The language belongs to David Armitage, who in fact questions this identification and argues for several practical, progressive con-sequences of the scheme laid out in *Patriot King*. "A Patriot for Whom? The Afterlives of Bolingbroke's Patriot King," *Journal of British Studies* 36 (October 1997), 399. Armitage's argument that Bolingbroke's "Country" patriotism is a forerunner of several strains of British radical thought is a direct counter to the "nostalgic" reading, whose main proponent is Isaac Kramnick: "By the middle of the eighteenth century it is even doubtful whether political action could have restored the past; but there is no doubt that the old order could not have been recaptured by humanist methods and aesthetic performance." *Bolingbroke and his Circle: The Politics of Nostalgia in the Age of Walpole* (Cambridge: Harvard

University Press, 1968), p. 169. On Savage and Bolingbroke, see Tracy, *Artificial Bastard*, p. 104.

22 For a detailed account of Bolingbroke's rhetoric in the 1730s and of the ways in which Bolingbroke's supporters and Walpole's constructed a falsely polar version of contemporary politics, see Alexander Pettit, *Illusory Consensus: Bolingbroke and the Polemical Response to Walpole, 1730–1737* (Newark: University of Delaware Press, 1997).

23 Christine Gerrard, *The Patriot Opposition to Walpole: Politics, Poetry, and Myth, 1725–1742* (Oxford: Clarendon, 1994), p. 209.

24 While Gerrard's treatment of *The Wanderer* detects a strong strain of Jacobite iconography in that poem, I believe her different insight regarding Bolingbroke is equally applicable to Savage, and probably to Johnson as well: "Charismatic monarchs are as much a part of the Whig tradition as they are of the Tory"; although it draws heavily on Jacobite iconography, "The *Patriot King* [joins] a series of other Patriot King works as the product ... of a more widespread cult of Hanoverian princely myth-making" (pp. 208; 211). Gerrard's primary interest is in distinguishing strains of opposition other than the traditionally recognized "Country" one, which is partially why her argument is served by putting Bolingbroke into a Whig-patriot context. On the other hand, I am less interested in what the immediate political ramifications are of these texts than in the ways certain patterns of image and thought become poetic currency, and Gerrard's sense that Jacobite iconography might be appropriated for Hanoverian uses is particularly pertinent. On the Hill circle, see *Aaron Hill: The Muses' Projector, 1685–1750* (Oxford: Oxford University Press, 2003), p. 153.

25 *The Idea of a Patriot King*, in Henry St. John, Viscount Bolingbroke, *Political Writings*, ed. David Armitage (New York: Cambridge University Press, 1997), p. 251. Further references will appear parenthetically in the text.

26 Bolingbroke, "Spirit of Patriotism," in *Political Writings*, p. 195.

27 Michael McKeon, *The Origins of the English Novel, 1600–1740* (Baltimore: Johns Hopkins University Press, 1987), p. 167.

28 *Ibid.*, p. 211.

29 On Byronism, see Andrew Elfenbein, *Byron and the Victorians* (Cambridge: Cambridge University Press, 1995), pp. 51; 91. On Scott, see Dino Franco Felluga, *The Perversity of Poetry: Romantic Ideology and the Popular Male Poet of Genius* (Albany: SUNY University Press, 2005), p. 49.

30 The swain "Receives his easy food from Nature's hand/And just returns of cultivated land!" *Georgics* II. 641–642 (Dryden, *Works of Virgil*).

31 Samuel Johnson, *Life of Savage*, ed. Clarence Tracy (Oxford: Clarendon Press, 1971), p. 59.

32 Griffin, *Patronage* p. 182.
33 William H. Epstein, "Patronizing the Biographical Subject: Johnson's *Savage* and Pastoral Power," in Paul J. Korshin, ed. *Johnson After Two Hundred Years* (Philadelphia: University of Pennsylvania Press, 1986), p. 154.
34 James Sutherland, "Introduction," in Richard Savage, *An Author To Be Lett* (1729), *The Augustan Reprint Society* Publication Number 84 (Los Angeles: William Andrews Clark Memorial Library, 1960), p. i. Quotations from Savage's text will be from this edition, by page number.
35 Richard Holmes, *Dr. Johnson and Mr. Savage* (London: Hodder and Stoughton, 1993), p. 153.
36 *Ibid.*, p. 156.
37 Johnson, *Life of Savage*, p. 135.
38 Tim Milnes, *Knowledge and Indifference in English Romantic Prose* (Cambridge: Cambridge University Press, 2003), p. 68.
39 Jerome Christensen, *Lord Byron's Strength: Romantic Writing and Commercial Society* (Baltimore: The Johns Hopkins University Press, 1993), p. 30.
40 David Hume, "Of the Independency of Parliament," in *Essays Moral, Political, and Literary, In Two Volumes.* T. H. Green and T. H. Grose, eds. (London: Longmans, 1907), I: 120–121.
41 David Hume, *An Inquiry Concerning Human Understanding*, ed. Tom L. Beauchamp (Oxford: Oxford University Press, 1999), p. 122.
42 Hume's examples of "experience" are inherently bookish. Despite the advanced nature of professional training in Edinburgh, Hume seems unable to conceive of professional training in other than classical terms.
43 Jerome Christensen argues that this effect, which depends on an ongoing self-correction, is characteristic of Hume's style in his philosophical writing, and signals a broader project of establishing the man of letters at the heart of an always-changing social order: "We trust that ... although we may be reading a writing to the moment, that writing is nonetheless already a composition." *Practicing Enlightenment: Hume and the Formation of a Literary Career* (Madison: University of Wisconsin Press, 1987), p. 25.
44 Hume, *Inquiry*, p. 122.
45 John W. Yolton, for example, notes that Hume, "like everyone else, recognizes the physiological foundations of all psychological processes," although Yolton finds that Hume's object of analysis is ultimately psychological, which complicates the possibility of reading human difference back onto the body – "it is the *mind*, not the *brain*, on which perception strikes." *Perceptual Acquaintance from Descartes to Reid* (Minneapolis: University of Minnesota Press, 1984), pp. 184; 185.
46 Tracing the use of the concept in eighteenth-century Germany, Anthony J. La Vopa gives a forceful account of its role in the

"confrontation of bourgeois and aristocratic norms": [Talent]'s strength as a criterion for social ranking lay in its status as an elemental force, anterior to social conditioning; as such talent negated, from within nature itself, the mystique of pedigree – of biological inheritance and the superior qualities it supposedly transmitted – in aristocratic ideology." *Grace, Talent, and Merit: Poor Students, Clerical Careers, and Professional Ideology in Eighteenth-Century Germany* (Cambridge: Cambridge University Press, 1988), p. 173. In the context of Humean epistemology, I am arguing, the anteriority presumed by the word also presents a challenge to "bourgeois norms" of training and experience, a challenge expressed in Hume's shift between reason and talent.

47 A well-known exception is Addison's praise of Milton's "talent for the sublime," but when poets of the period are praised for their "talent," it is more often than not a talent for description or "painting." That is, the word remains redolent of manual labor.

48 Thus Kant, addressing the same issue, conflates genius with talent in such a way that it appears to be both universally and subjectively exercised: "Genius is the talent (natural gift) that gives the rule to art. Since the talent, as an inborn productive faculty of the artist, itself belongs to nature, this could also be expressed thus: Genius is the inborn predisposition of the mind ... through which nature gives the rule to art." *Critique of the Power of Judgment*, ed. Paul Guyer, trans. Paul Guyer and Eric Matthews (Cambridge: Cambridge University Press, 2000), p. 186.

49 David Hume, "Of the Middling Station of Life," in *Essays Moral, Political, and Literary* Volume II, ed. T. H. Green and T. H. Grose (London: Longmans, Green, and Co., 1898), p. 378. On Hume's treatment of the succession in *The History of England*, in which "balance" regarding the Stuart dynasty comes to look to some critics like "Toryism," see Duncan Forbes, *Hume's Philosophical Politics* (Cambridge: Cambridge University Press, 1975), pp. 290–296.

50 Hume, "Station," 378.

51 David Hume, *A Treatise of Human Nature* ed. David Fate Norton and Mary J. Norton (Oxford: Oxford University Press, 2000), 85.

52 On Hume's regard for the clergy as agents of social order, see Forbes, *Hume's Politics*, pp. 213–216.

53 For this characterization of the essay see Ernest Campbell Mossner, *The Life of David Hume*, second edition (Oxford: Oxford University Press, 1980), p. 141.

54 Holmes, *Augustan England*, p. 17.

55 Alvin Kernan, *Printing Technology, Letters, and Samuel Johnson* (Princeton: Princeton University Press, 1987), p. 36.

56 *Ibid.*, pp. 38–39.

57 *Ibid.*, p. 47.

58 James Boswell, *Life of Johnson* ed. R. W. Chapman, intro. Pat Rogers (Oxford: Oxford University Press, 1980), pp. 382–383.

59 Beattie was from a poor farming family, not the more affluent background shared by most of his colleagues, and his health and his wife's health were always on the decline. See "Introduction," *James Beattie's London Diary, 1773*, ed. Ralph S. Walker, Aberdeen University Studies 122 (Aberdeen: The University Press, 1946), pp. 8–9.

60 On Dr. Majendie, see *Beattie's Diary*, pp. 124–125.

61 *Ibid.*, p. 86.

62 *Ibid.*, p. 88.

63 *Ibid.*, p. 86.

64 Marjorie Hope Nicolson, *Mountain Gloom and Mountain Glory: The Development of the Aesthetics of the Infinite* (1959) (Seattle: University of Washington Press, 1997), p. 333; Margaret Anne Doody, *The Daring Muse: Augustan Poetry Reconsidered* (Cambridge: Cambridge University Press, 1985), p. 62.

3 JAMES BEATTIE AND *THE MINSTREL*

1 Dorothy Wordsworth to Jane Pollard, 10 and 12 July, 1793, *Early Years*, pp. 100–101.

2 An important exception is Keith Hanley, who recognizes both that *The Minstrel* is formed around a dynamics of identification, and that Wordsworth repeats this identification in his response to the poem: "Wordsworth could recognize the self-reflexivity of both a critical paternal identification [of Edwin with the hermit] *and* the presentation of congenial poetic registers that would enable him to assume a professional discourse." I will argue, however, that Edwin's identification with the minstrel constitutes an interruption of the formation of the poetic, professional self. *Wordsworth: A Poet's History* (London: Palgrave, 2001), p. 81.

3 *Early Years*, p. 101.

4 Thomas Reid, *An Inquiry into the Human Mind on the Principles of Common Sense: A Critical Edition*, ed. Derek R. Brookes (University Park: Pennsylvania State University Press, 1997), pp. 23; 212.

5 *Ibid.*, p. 57.

6 James Beattie, *An Essay on the Nature and Immutability of Truth, in Opposition to Sophistry and Scepticism (new edition, 1776)* in *Essays* (New York: Garland Publishing, 1971), p. 102. Further references will be given parenthetically, in the text.

7 David Hume, *A Treatise of Human Nature*, ed. David Fate Norton and Mary J. Norton (Oxford: Oxford University Press, 2000), p. 42.

8 *Ibid.*, p. 43.

9 *Ibid.*, p. 49. Hume is also attempting to correct Locke, whose faith in the senses extends at least to immediate perception. Locke is an advocate of the idea-of-the-vacuum, and while the *Essay* doesn't juxtapose this material the way the *Treatise* and Reid's *Inquiry* do, Locke's consistent defense of the vacuum idea and of the trustworthiness of the senses depend on commonsense notions of verifiability, communication, and providential order on which Reid would also draw.

10 Various critics have noted that while Hume does not emphasize the synthetic powers of the "imagination" in the *Treatise*, a consequence of his argument is that the imagination becomes "all pervading," in the words of James Engell, *The Creative Imagination: Enlightenment to Romanticism* (Cambridge: Harvard University Press, 1981), 55.

11 Hume, *Treatise*, p. 160.

12 *Ibid.*, p. 162.

13 Marina Frasca-Spada, *Space and the Self in Hume's* Treatise (Cambridge: Cambridge University Press, 1998), p. 193.

14 Hume, *Inquiry*, p. 88.

15 *Ibid.*, p. 95.

16 In other places, Hume is clearer that there is a discernible line between the discursive world that is organized around abstruse musing and the world that is not: "There are in *England*, in particular, many honest gentlemen, who being always employ'd in their domestic affairs, or amusing themselves in common recreations, have carry'd their thoughts very little beyond those objects, which are every day expos'd to their senses. And indeed, of such as these I pretend not to make philosophers, nor do I expect them either to be associates in these researches or auditors of these discoveries" (*Treatise*, p. 177). While the rhetorical aims of the *Enquiry* justify its re-emphasis on the union of borders, I do not think its stance towards its audience is inherently different from the position taken up by the *Treatise*; rather, this is a re-statement of the famous comment on philosophy and difficulty that is taken up below.

17 Heidegger retains the Cartesian *extensio* as "the basic determination of 'the world,'" but insists that space is a phenomenological and not an ontological category; "de-distancing means making distance disappear, bringing it near." *Being and Time: A Translation of* Sein und Zeit. Joan Stambaugh, trans. (Albany: SUNY Press, 1996), pp. 94, 97. Although Heidegger is primarily concerned here with the relationship of human perception to objects, and while it is important to note that Heidegger's approach distinguishes itself from the Cartesian line through its recognition of the persistence of the object, Hume's account of space has the similar effect of becoming relational, albeit in profoundly unintended ways.

18 Reid, *Inquiry*, pp. 57–59.

19 As Reid argues, "a being endued with sight only" would be able to reason geometrically but would have no sense of a third dimension, so that "visible appearance" would not serve as a "sign" for something else (*Inquiry*, p. 106). Only the providential concert of sight and touch teaches us to interpret visual data in terms of physical objects.

20 Reid, *Inquiry*, p. 98. Reid's defense of "visible figure" (what Hume calls "the visible disposition of parts") might with equal justice be applied to Hume's description of a vacuum, which is neither an impression nor an idea although we think it is. As it happens, Reid has Hume wrong here; as Lorne Falkenstein points out, "Hume took our compound tangible impressions and ideas to consist of spatially disposed parts," which means, incidentally, that on Falkenstein's analysis Hume's perceptions really can be "hard," insofar as they can be made of "parts that resist being displaced." "Hume and Reid on the Perception of Hardness," *Hume Studies* 28:1 (April 2002), 34.

21 Reid, *Inquiry*, p. 22.

22 On Reid and the "primordiality of interpretation," see Joel C. Weinsheimer, *Eighteenth-Century Hermeneutics: Philosophy of Interpretation in England from Locke to Burke* (New Haven: Yale University Press, 1993), p. 150.

23 Reid, *Inquiry*, p. 56.

24 This is another shot in the battle over professional authority, since Reid the parson is also a professor, while Hume is a mere man of letters. The full comment is as follows: "I wish the parsons wou'd [...] confine themselves to their old Occupation of worrying one another; & leave Philosophers to argue with Temper, Moderation & good Manners[.]" Letter to Hugh Blair, 4 July 1762, in Reid, *Inquiry* (257). On the likelihood that this is good-natured joking, and itself part of an impersonal technique of "ridicule" that made up philosophical discourse, see James Somerville, *The Enigmatic Parting Shot: What was Hume's 'Compleat Answer to Dr Reid and to that Bigotted Silly Fellow, Beattie'?* (Brookfield: Aldershot, 1995), 101–102.

25 Paul Hamilton, *Coleridge's Poetics* (Stanford: Stanford University Press, 1983), p. 25.

26 *Ibid.*, p. 40.

27 Noel B. Jackson, "Critical Conditions: Coleridge, 'Common Sense,' and the Literature of Self-Experiment," *ELH* 70 (2003) 129. Also, see Weinsheimer, n. 14 above.

28 Giddens, *Constitution*, p. 142.

29 So, Reid to Hume, 18 March 1763: "Your Friendly Adversaries Drs Campbel and Gerard as well as Dr Gregory return their Compliments to you respectfully. A little Philosophical Society [here] of

which all three are members, is much indebted to you for its Entertainment . . . . And since we cannot have you upon the bench [i.e. present at meetings], you are brought oftener than any other man, to the bar, accused and defended with great Zeal but without bitterness. If you write no more in morals politicks or metaphysicks, I am affraid we shall be at a loss for Subjects" (*Inquiry*, 264–265).

30 Beattie, *Truth*, pp. 322–323.

31 John J. Richetti, *Philosophical Writing: Locke, Berkeley, Hume* (Cambridge: Harvard University Press, 1983), p. 202.

32 Thus, Clifford Siskin is able to argue that Literature takes over the work of Scottish Philosophy, in *The Work of Writing*, p. 94.

33 Timothy Dykstal provides an extended discussion of Berkeley that illustrates a train of thought to which Beattie and Reid directly respond. Working from Berkeley's premise that "[W]e ought to *think with the learned, and speak with the vulgar*," Dykstal argues that, for Berkeley, "freethinkers invert" the principle: "Instead of speaking with the vulgar, they attempt to *think* with them, just as they think with one another in their clubs and coffeehouses, and this is why . . . the vulgar are susceptible to being corrupted by them" (*The Luxury of Skepticism: Politics, Philosophy, and Dialogue in the English Public Sphere, 1660–1740* [Charlottesville: University of Virginia Press, 2001], 144–145). An unsystematic method of reasoning, absent useful and ultimately defensible religious "prejudices," leads to sloppy and immature modes of thought for elite and vulgar reasoners alike. Reid would later adjust Berkeley's maxim: "If it is a good rule, to think with philosophers, and speak with the vulgar, it must be right to speak with the vulgar when we think with them, and not to shock them by philosophical paradoxes, which, when put in common language, only express the common sense of mankind" (*Inquiry*, 88).

34 On this function of Humean sympathy, see for instance the *Treatise*, p. 206.

35 David Hume, "Of the Standard of Taste," in *Essays*, p. 281.

36 John Sitter, *Literary Loneliness in Mid-Eighteenth-Century England* (Ithaca: Cornell University Press, 1982), p. 107.

37 Paul J. Korshin, "Types of Eighteenth-Century Literary Patronage," *Eighteenth-Century Studies* Vol. 7, No. 4 (Summer 1974), 453.

38 Gay to Beattie, 2 October 1765, *Correspondence of Thomas Gray, in Three Volumes. Volume II, 1756–1765*, ed. Paget Toynbee and Leonard Whilby (Oxford: Clarendon Press, 1935), p. 896.

39 Suvir Kaul, *Thomas Gray and Literary Authority: A Study in Ideology and Poetics* (Stanford: Stanford University Press, 1992), p. 42.

40 John Guillory, *Cultural Capital: the Problem of Literary Canon Formation* (Chicago: University of Chicago Press, 1993), pp. 114–124.

41 As Scott Hess has argued, Beattie was also "embedded . . . within elite networks of society and patronage," and never claimed a

professional autonomy based only on market-share. *Authoring the Self: Self-Representation, Authorship, and the Print Market in British Poetry from Pope through Wordsworth* (New York: Routledge, 2005), p. 138.

42 I am using the edition provided by Everard H. King in *James Beattie's The Minstrel and the Origins of Romantic Autobiography* (Lewiston: The Edwin Mellen Press, 1992).

43 Conrad Brunstrom, "James Beattie and the Great Outdoors: Common Sense Philosophy and the Pious Imagination," *Romanticism* 1 (1997), 23; Forbes, *Beattie and His Friends*, p. 29. Brunstrom describes the basic affinities between Edwin's life in nature and Beattie's philosophical response to Hume's dark metaphysics: "Beattie and Wordsworth share a need for a philosophy of the great outdoors, a philosophy that imposes itself gradually on the senses and claims a holistic rather than a merely intellectual authority" (21). My argument is that Beattie, no less than Wordsworth, discovers the shortcomings of "holistic authority" in the course of his attempt to describe it.

44 King, *Minstrel*, p. 18.

45 On this function of autobiography see John Sturrock, "Theory vs. Autobiography," in *The Culture of Autobiography: Constructions of Self-Representation* ed. Robert Folkenflik (Stanford: Stanford University Press, 1993), p. 27.

46 Margaret Forbes, *Beattie and his Friends* (Westminster: Archibald Constable and Co., Ltd., 1904), p. 48.

47 In light of various anti-Gallic and anti-"Popery" comments in *The Essay on Truth*, it is possible to read the generic denunciation of tyranny in *The Minstrel* as an expression of patriotism aimed at the despotic religious and political orders that prevailed on the continent and especially across the channel. The *Essay* also contains significant moments of anti-slavery rhetoric (pp. 309–313), and as Suvir Kaul has indicated, and as Beattie's language bears out, anti-slavery writing often has a nationalist component: "These poems are for the most part marked by a certainty of tone, one that derives from ethical and religious convictions, but also from the fact that these poems are committed to a vision of Britain stronger and even more powerful globally once it successfully spearheads the abolition of the slave trade and slavery." *Poems of Nation, Anthems of Empire: English Verse in the Long Eighteenth Century* (Charlottesville: University Press of Virginia, 2000), pp. 231–232.

48 For example, Edwin's dislike of blood sports is described thus: "He wish'd to be the guardian, not the king,/Tyrant far less, or traitor of the field" (160–161). Later lines referring to "conquering kings,/Hands drenched in blood, and breasts begirt with steel" (II. 309–310) are unleavened by reference to other-than-conquering kings, and the polemic here would have an overt radical charge if it came thirty years sooner or twenty years later. In fact, as suggested above,

Beattie's primary mental image of despotism is probably French; but in the context of *The Minstrel,* the concern remains local or generic.

49 Paul Langford, *A Polite and Commercial People: England, 1727–1783* (Oxford: Clarendon Press, 1989), p. 369. According to Vincent Carretta, the figure of the "patriot king" was regularly applied to George III on his accession in 1760, although it could retain a satirical component in this context. See *George III and the Satirists from Hogarth to Byron* (Athens: University of Georgia Press, 1990), p. 46. Charles Churchill's *Gotham,* which provides Carretta with evidence for the satiric uses of the figure, in fact executes a three-way linkage among the monarch, the patriot, and the poet in making Churchill himself the patriot king of Gotham.

50 This distinction, between "the true space" debated in the abstract by philosophers and the "truth of space," which "ties space on the one hand to social practice, and on the other hand to concepts which, though worked out and linked theoretically by philosophy, in fact transcend philosophy as such precisely by virtue of their connection with practice," is drawn from Henri Lefebvre, *The Production of Space* trans. Donald Nicholson-Smith (Oxford: Blackwell, 1991), pp. 398–399.

51 Sir William Forbes, *An Account of the Life and Writings of James Beattie, LL.D. . . . Including Many of His Original Letters, in Three Volumes* 2nd Edition (Edinburgh: Arch. Constable and Co, 1807), I:262.

52 Deborah Heller, "Bluestocking Salons and the Public Sphere," *Eighteenth-Century Life* 99 (May 1998), 70. Heller's argument is that these ideals, of "unity amidst diversity" and "freedom and equality of participation" are reflected in the physical arrangement of Montagu's salon, but that the arrangement, and the ideal, would ultimately fail. As Beattie is tragically aware, the "discourse of disembodied reason" could not long suppress the real interests in class, gender, viewpoint, and experience that divided as well as united the members of the conversation.

53 Radcliffe, 535.

54 Ann Yearsley, "On Mrs. Montagu," 67–76, in *Eighteenth-Century Poetry: An Annotated Anthology, Second Edition,* ed. David Fairer and Christine Gerrard (Malden: Blackwell, 2004), p. 483.

55 Greg Kucich, *Keats, Shelley, and Romantic Spenserianism* (University Park: The Pennsylvania State University Press, 1991), p. 73.

56 Sir William Forbes, *An Account of the Life and Writings of James Beattie, LL.D. . . . Including Many of His Original Letters, in Three Volumes 2nd Edition* (Edinburgh: Arch. Constable and Co., 1807), p. 61.

57 See "Introduction," *Bluestocking Feminism: Writings of the Bluestocking Circle, 1738–1785. Volume I: Elizabeth Montagu,* ed. Elizabeth Eger (London: Pickering and Chatto, 1999), pp. lxii–lxiii.

58 John Gregory, "Observations on the Duties and Offices of a Physician and on the Method of Prosecuting Enquiries in Philosophy" (1770), in *John Gregory's Writings Writings on Medical Ethics and Philosophy of Medicine* (Dordrecht: Kluwer Academic Publishers, 1998), p. 107.

59 For a general account of Gregory's career, and the argument that his version of "sympathy" is directly informed by a Baconian version of Hume, see Laurence B. McCullough, "Introduction," in *John Gregory's Writings*, pp. 33–36.

60 Aberdeen, for example, and its University, were both in a boom period during Beattie's time there. See Fiona J. Stafford, *The Sublime Savage: A Study of James Macpherson and the Poems of Ossian* (Edinburgh: Edinburgh University Press, 1988), p. 26.

61 Richard B. Sher, *Church and University in the Scottish Enlightenment: The Moderate Literati of Edinburgh* (Princeton: Princeton University Press, 1985), pp. 66–68.

62 *Ibid.*, p. 47.

63 Dugald Steward, "Account of the Life and Writings of Thomas Reid ... ," in Thomas Reid, *Philosophical Works* I, ed. and notes Sir William Hamilton, introduction Harry Bracken (Hildesheim: Georg Olms, 1967), p. 5.

64 *Friends*, p. 114.

65 *Ibid.*

66 One of the reasons it is only "imminent" is that Reid's professional work, philosophy, is subsidized by but not directly related to his actual profession in the Scotch Presbyterian Church.

67 Geoffrey Hartman, *Wordsworth's Poetry, 1787–1814* (Cambridge: Harvard University Press, 1987), p. 15.

4 AUTHORITY AND THE ITINERANT CLERIC

1 Emphasizing the tradition that passes through Beattie and others, Harrison argues that "In Wordsworth's oft-noted identification between the poet and the vagrants and rustics that inhabit ... his poetry, he presents a conflicted sign of poetic authenticity that threatens to unmask, even deconstruct, the appropriation of poverty as a sign of poetic value." *Wordsworth's Vagrant Muse: Poetry, Poverty, and Power* (Detroit: Wayne State University Press, 1994), p. 125. A related argument, focusing more prominently on the status of vagrancy but also evincing an awareness of the poet/vagrant identification, is developed in Toby R. Benis, *Romanticism on the Road: The Marginal Gains of Wordsworth's Homeless* (Houndmills: Macmillan, 2000).

2 Anne D. Wallace, *Walking, Literature, and English Culture: The Origins and Uses of Peripatetic in the Nineteenth Century* (Oxford: Clarendon

Press, 1993), p. 166. For walking or wandering as empowering, and as signs of an empowered class position, also see Robin Jarvis, *Romantic Writing and Pedestrian Travel* (Houndmills: Macmillan, 1997), and Celeste Langan, *Romantic Vagrancy: Wordsworth and the Simulation of Freedom* (Cambridge: Cambridge University Press, 1995). For Langan the privilege here is ironic, and is based on a false account of human freedom, as will be discussed below.

3 *The Prelude*, 1805. XIII: 444–445.

4 Richard Brantley has shown how widely evangelical ideas were circulated and how inevitably the poets would be exposed to them, and he also argues for direct affinities between British evangelicalism, particularly insofar as it could be reconciled with church order, and the thinking of Wordsworth and Coleridge. See *Wordsworth's Natural Methodism* (New Haven: Yale University Press, 1975) and *Locke, Wesley, and the Method of English Romanticism* (Gainesville: University of Florida Press, 1984).

5 Jon Mee, *Romanticism, Enthusiasm, and Regulation: Poetics and the Policing of Culture in the Romantic Period* (Oxford: Oxford University Press, 2003), p. 132.

6 Abbott, *Professions*, pp. 186–187; Corfield, *Power*, p. 112.

7 Deryck W. Lovegrove, *Established Church, Sectarian People: Itinerancy and the Transformation of English Dissent, 1780–1832* (Cambridge: Cambridge University Press, 1988), p. 27.

8 The well-educated and well-intentioned "Dr. Green," for example, takes up the "strange course" of an itinerant circuit in order to drive "quacks" out of the eighteenth-century medical market. *The Doctor, Second Edition, Volume I* (London: Longman, 1835), pp. 228–229.

9 *The Collected Works of Samuel Taylor Coleridge: Lectures 1795 on Politics and Religion* ed. Lewis Patton and Peter Mann (Cambridge: Routledge, 1971), p. 35.

10 *Ibid.*, p. 43.

11 Lovegrove, *Itinerancy*, p. 28.

12 Hartman, *Wordsworth's Poetry*, p. 57.

13 Wilfred Prest, *Albion Ascendant: English History 1660–1815* (Oxford: Oxford University Press, 1998), p. 207.

14 James Lackington, *Memoirs of James Lackington, Who from the humble station of a Journeyman Shoemaker, by great industry, amassed a large fortune, and now lives in a splendid stile, in London* (Newburgh, New York, 1796), p. 163.

15 As Robert Hole explains, in the face of Methodist expansion in the late 1790s, "The Church of England felt threatened, especially by the means the Methodists employed – notably that of itinerancy … [although] the major phase of the debate came after 1804." *Pulpits, Politics, and Public Order in England, 1760–1832* (Cambridge: Cambridge University Press, 1989), p. 108.

16 "Review," *Observations on the Political Conduct of the Protestant Dissenters; including a retrospective View of their History from the Time of Queen Elizabeth. In Five Letters to a Friend*, by the Rev. David Rivers, *Anti-Jacobin Review* (Dec. 1798), 633. The *Anti-Jacobin Review* was particularly alarmed by the establishment of dissenting meeting-houses among the village poor, presumably because the poor and ignorant are the most likely targets of revolutionary suasion.

17 John Wesley, *A Farther Appeal to Men of Reason and Religion, Part III* (1745), in Gerald R. Cragg (ed.), *The Works of John Wesley, Volume II: The Appeals to Men of Reason and Religion, and Certain Related Open Letters* (Oxford: Clarendon Press, 1975), p. 294.

18 *Ibid.*

19 *Ibid.*, p. 295.

20 *Ibid.*, pp. 296–297.

21 See, for example, John Wesley, "A Letter to a Clergyman" (1748), in Rupert E. Davies (ed.), *The Works of John Wesley, Volume Nine: The Methodist Societies: History, Nature, and Design* (Nashville: Abingdon Press, 1989), p. 250.

22 See Alan C. Clifford, *Atonement and Justification: English Evangelical Theology 1640–1790: An Evaluation* (Oxford: Clarendon Press, 1990), pp. 190–191.

23 Michael R. Watts, *The Dissenters: From the Reformation to the French Revolution* (Oxford: Oxford University Press, 1978), p. 449.

24 W. R. Ward, *Religion and Society in England, 1790–1850* (London: B. T. Batsford Ltd., 1972), p. 49.

25 Lovegrove, *Established Church*, 142.

26 To Josiah Wade, 27 January 1796, *Coleridge Letters I*, p. 176.

27 To Joseph Cottle, 22 February 1796, *Coleridge Letters I*, p. 185.

28 To Joseph Cottle, 22 February 1796, *Coleridge Letters I*, p. 185.

29 To William Wordsworth, 23 January 1798, *Coleridge Letters I*, p. 378.

30 For example, see Abbott: High-status professionals work behind the scenes with other professionals, but the public "admires practitioners who work with clients" (p. 119).

31 Daniel E. White, " 'Properer for a Sermon': Particularities of Dissent and Coleridge's Conversational Mode," *Studies in Romanticism* Summer 2003 (40,2), 192. Especially helpful is White's recognition of the extent to which "the mainstream of English romantic poetry ... emerges ... from the 'real language' of sermons and religious lectures" (189).

32 For example, see Leonore Davidoff and Catherine Hall, *Family Fortunes: Men and Women of the English Middle Class, 1780–1850* (Chicago: University of Chicago Press, 1987), p. 263.

33 Roger H. Martin, "Evangelical Dissenters and Wesleyan-Style Itinerant Ministries at the End of the Eighteenth Century," *Methodist History* 16(3), April, 1978, 82.

34 Joseph Priestley, "The Use of Christianity, especially in Difficult Times; A SERMON delivered at the Gravel Pit Meeting House in Hackney, March 30 1794. Being the Author's Farewell Discourse to his Congregation," in *Two Sermons* (Philadelphia, 1794), p. 73.

35 Nicholas Roe suggests that Coleridge's radical activities were in some ways an attempt to compensate for the vacuum of radical leadership following Priestley's departure. *Wordsworth and Coleridge: The Radical Years* (Oxford: Clarendon Press, 1988), p. 98.

36 To Grosvenor Charles Bedford, 1 June 1793, *New Letters*, p. 23.

37 To Grosvenor Charles Bedford, 8 February 1793, *New Letters*, p. 17.

38 Nicholas Roe, "Pantisocracy and the Myth of the Poet," in Tim Fulford (ed.), *Romanticism and Millenarianism* (New York: Palgrave, 2002), p. 89.

39 *To May*, July 23, 1798, p. 34.

40 *To May*, September 2, 1798, p. 36.

41 *Ibid.*

42 *Ibid.*

43 See J. G. A. Pocock, "The Mobility of Property and the Rise of Eighteenth-Century Sociology," in *Virtue, Commerce, and History: Essays on Political Thought and History, Chiefly in the Eighteenth Century* (Cambridge: Cambridge University Press, 1985).

44 Jurgen Habermas, *The Structural Transformation of the Public Sphere: An Inquiry into a Category of Bourgeois Society*, trans. Thomas Burger and Frederick Lawrence (Cambridge: MIT Press, 1990), p. 15.

45 Oskar Negt and Alexander Kluge, *Public Sphere and Experience: Toward an Analysis of the Bourgeois and Proletarian Public Sphere*, foreword by Miriam Hansen, trans. Peter Labanyi, Jamie Owen Daniel, and Assenka Oksiloff (Minneapolis: University of Minnesota Press, 1993), pp. 11–12. Negt and Kluge explicitly and fruitfully disregard the walking metaphor, because freedom to walk, "material freedom," is a marker of absolute good for the "proletariat" (p. 58).

46 Celeste Langan, *Romantic Vagrancy: Wordsworth and the Simulation of Freedom* (Cambridge: Cambridge University Press, 1995), pp. 19–21.

47 Mee, *Enthusiasm*, p. 72.

48 Paul Magnuson, "Coleridge's Discursive 'Monody on the Death of Chatterton'." *Romanticism on the Net* 17 (February, 2000).

49 Thomas Percy, *Reliques of Ancient English Poetry, Consisting of Old Heroic Ballads, Songs, and Other Pieces of Our Earlier Poets; Together With Some Few of Later Date*, ed. Charles Cowden Clarke. In three volumes. (Edinburgh: Nimmo, n.d.), I: lviii.

50 On Chatterton's "pro-liberty and anti-government sentiments," see Robert W. Jones, "'We Proclaim Our Darling Son': The Politics of Chatterton's Memory During the War for America," *Review of English Studies* n.s. 53:211, August 2002, 384.

51 See *Coleridge: Poetical Works*, "Monody on Chatterton," n. 41–48, and "Lines on the 'Man of Ross'" and head note, p. 121.
52 "Monody on Chatterton," *Coleridge: Poetical Works: Variorum* 37.1.6–37.1.10; 176.
53 Magnuson, " 'Monody' " (n.p.).
54 Jarvis, *Romantic Writing*, p. 139.
55 *Ibid.*, p. 126.
56 "Hymn to the Penates," in Lynda Pratt (ed.), *Robert Southey: Poetical Works 1793–1810. Volume 5: Selected Shorter Poems c. 1793–1810* (London: Pickering and Chatto, 2004), lines 1–5. Subsequent citations will be parenthetical, by line number.
57 To Grosvenor Charles Bedford, 11 and 17 November, 1796, *New Letters*, p. 116.
58 Roe, "Pantisocracy," p. 100.
59 To Grosvenor Charles Bedford, 2 February 1793, *New Letters*, p. 13.
60 To Grosvenor Charles Bedford, 4 August 1793, *New Letters*, p. 35.
61 Clement Hawes, *Mania and Literary Style: The Rhetoric of Enthusiasm from the Ranters to Christopher Smart* (Cambridge: Cambridge University Press, 1996), p. 132.
62 Mee, *Enthusiasm*, p. 158.
63 Jonathan Ramsey, "Seeing and Perceiving in Wordsworth's *An Evening Walk*," *MLQ* September 1976 (vol. 37 issue 3), p. 386.
64 Pfau, *Wordsworth's Profession*, p. 106; p. 114.
65 William Wordsworth, *Descriptive Sketches*, ed. Eric Birdsall, with the assistance of P. M. Zall (Ithaca: Cornell University Press, 1984), 1793 Reading Text, 810–813.
66 James Thomson, The Seasons *and* The Castle of Indolence, ed. James Sambrook (Oxford: Clarendon, 1972), *Winter*, lines 326–328.
67 David Collings, *Wordsworthian Errancies*, pp. 38–39.
68 Kurt Fosso, *Buried Communities: Wordsworth and the Bonds of Mourning* (Albany: SUNY Press, 2004), p. 71.
69 John Williams, *Wordsworth: Romantic Poetry and Revolutionary Politics* (Manchester: Manchester University Press, 1989), pp. 67–68.
70 John Rieder, *Wordsworth's Counterrevolutionary Turn: Community, Virtue, and Vision in the 1790s* (Newark: University of Delaware Press, 1997), p. 107.
71 William Wordsworth, "The Idiot Boy," in Lyrical Ballads, *and Other Poems, 1797–1800*, ed. James Butler and Karen Green (Ithaca: Cornell University Press, 1992), 441. Subsequent references will be to this text, by line number.
72 Qtd. in Brett and Jones, *Lyrical Ballads*, p. 338.
73 Coleridge, *Biographia* II, p. 48.
74 To John Wilson, 7 June 1802, *Early Years* p. 357.
75 *Ibid.*
76 *Ibid.*, p. 355.

77 *Ibid.*, p. 355.
78 *Ibid.*
79 *Ibid.*, p. 357.
80 Duncan Wu, "Looking for Johnny: Wordsworth's 'The Idiot Boy,'" *Charles Lamb Bulletin* 88 (October, 1994), 172.
81 *Ibid.*, 171.
82 Jacobus, *Wordsworth and Tradition*, p. 261; Ross Woodman, "The Idiot Boy as Healer," in James Holt McGavran, Jr. (ed.), *Romanticism and Children's Literature in Nineteenth-Century England* (Athens: The University of Georgia Press, 1991), p. 73.
83 Coleridge, *Biographia* I, p. 226.
84 *Ibid.*, p. 227.
85 Jon P. Klancher, *The Making of English Reading Audiences, 1790–1832* (Madison: University of Wisconsin Press, 1987), p. 166.
86 Robert Southey, "On the Means of Improving the People" [1818], in *Essays, Moral and Political, Volume I* (London: John Murray, 1832), p. 129.
87 William Wordsworth, *The Excursion*, in John O. Hayden (ed.), *William Wordsworth: The Poems, Volume II* (New York: Penguin, 1977), V: 453–461.
88 Everett C. Hughes, "Institutional Office and the Person," in *The Sociological Eye: Selected Papers* (Chicago: Aldine, 1971), p. 133.

5 WILLIAM COWPER AND THE ITINERANT LAKE POET

1 William James, *The Varieties of Religious Experience: A Study of Human Nature,* (New York: Mentor Books, 1958), p. 191.
2 Shaun Irlam, *Elations: The Poetics of Enthusiasm in Eighteenth-Century Britain* (Stanford: Stanford University Press, 1999), p. 207.
3 Charles Ryskamp, *William Cowper of the Inner Temple, Esq.: A Study of his Life and Works to the Year 1768* (Cambridge: Cambridge University Press, 1959), p. 149.
4 William Cowper, *Adelphi*, in *The Letters and Prose Writings of William Cowper: Volume I*, Adelphi *and Letters 1750–1781*, James King and Charles Ryskamp, eds., (Oxford: Clarendon Press, 1979), pp. 34–40.
5 Cowper, *Adelphi*, p. 41.
6 Julie Ellison, "News, Blues, and Cowper's Busy World," *MLQ* 62:3 (September 2001), 224; Conrad Brunstrom, *William Cowper: Religion, Satire, Society* (Lewisburg, Bucknell University Press, 2004), p. 107.
7 Ryskamp, *William Cowper*, p. 153.
8 Tim Fulford, *Landscape, Liberty, and Authority: Poetry, Criticism and Politics from Thomson to Wordsworth* (Cambridge: Cambridge University Press, 1996), p. 53.

9 Cowper, *Letters II*, p. 322.
10 William Cowper, *Table Talk*, in *Cowper: Poetical Works* ed. H. S. Milford, with corrections and additions by Norma Russell (London: Oxford University Press, 1971), *Table Talk*, 500–505. Further citations of Cowper's poetry will be to this edition, by line number.
11 Fulford, *Landscape, Liberty, and Authority*, p. 178.
12 For example see Ann Matheson, "The Influence of Cowper's *The Task* on Coleridge's Conversation Poems," in *New Approaches to Coleridge: Biographical and Critical Essays*, ed. Donald Sultana (London, Vision Press, 1981).
13 William Wordsworth to John Wilson, 7 June 1802, *EY* 355–356.
14 Charles Lamb to Coleridge, 6 July 1796, in *The Letters of Charles and Mary Lamb, Volume I: Letters of Charles Lamb, 1796–1801* Edwin W. Marrs, Jr. (ed.) (Cambridge: Cambridge University Press, 1975), p. 41.
15 To John Newton, 12 July 1781, *Letters I*, p. 497.
16 William Wordsworth, *Peter Bell*, ed. John E. Jordan (Ithaca: Cornell University Press, 1985), MSS. 2 and 3, lines 541–545. Further references are also to MSS. 2 and 3, by line number.
17 Alan Bewell finds an "anthropological" and Humean story in *Peter Bell*; the potter lives through the history of religion in that he is first driven by primitive and superstitious fear, but he is reclaimed and disciplined by an experience that is originally "biblical," but is to be superseded by a "poetry grounded in nature." *Wordsworth and the Enlightenment: Nature, Man, and Society in the Experimental Poetry* (New Haven: Yale University Press, 1989), p. 141.
18 *Ibid.*, p. 119.
19 For example, see John E. Jordan, "Introduction," *Peter Bell*, p. 23.
20 *Ibid.*, p. 137.
21 Vincent Newey, *Cowper's Poetry: A Critical Study and Reassesment* (Totowa: Barnes and Noble, 1982), p. 229; Martin Priestman, *Cowper's Task: Structure and Influence* (Cambridge: Cambridge University Press, 1983), p. 43.
22 *The Letters and Prose Writings of William Cowper, Volume II: Letters 1782–1786*, ed. James King and Charles Ryskamp (Oxford: Clarendon Press, 1981), "To John Newton," Friday, 22 April 1785, p. 343.
23 *Ibid.*, p. 343.
24 Andrew Elfenbein, *Romantic Genius: The Prehistory of a Homosexual Role*, (New York: Columbia University Press, 1999), p. 80.
25 Frances Ferguson, "Coleridge and the Deluded Reader: 'The Rime of the Ancient Mariner,'" in Samuel Taylor Coleridge, *The Rime of the Ancient Mariner*, ed. Paul H. Fry (Boston: Bedford, 1999), pp. 123, 115.
26 *Ibid.*, p. 129.

27 Debbie Lee, *Slavery and the Romantic Imagination* (Philadelphia: University of Penn Press, 2002), pp. 54; 65.

28 "Note to the Ancient Mariner," from the 1800 edition of *Lyrical Ballads*, in *Wordsworth and Coleridge: Lyrical Ballads*, second edition, ed. R. L. Brett and R. A. Jones (London: Routledge, 1991), p. 276.

29 Susan Eilenberg, *Strange Power of Speech: Wordsworth, Coleridge, and Literary Possession* (New York: Oxford University Press, 1992), p. 31.

30 Graham Davidson, *Coleridge's Career* (New York: St. Martin's Press, 1990), p. 73.

31 William Ulmer, "Necessary Evils: Unitarian Theodicy in 'The Rime of the Ancient Mariner.'" *Studies in Romanticism* 43 (Fall 2004), 355; 354.

32 Marilyn Butler, *Literature as Heritage: or, Reading Other Ways* (Cambridge: Cambridge University Press, 1987), p. 10.

33 Robert Southey, *"Madoc 1805,"* in Lynda Pratt ed., with the assistance of Carol Bolton and Paul Jarman, *Robert Southey: Poetical Works 1793–1810, Volume 2: Madoc* (London: Pickering and Chatto, 2004), Southey's note, pp. 293–295.

34 To John Rickman, January, 1802, *Southey Letters* I, p. 267.

35 Caroline Franklin, "The Welsh American Dream: Iolo Morganwg, Robert Southey and the Madoc Legend," in *English Romanticism and the Celtic World*, eds. Gerard Carruthers and Alan Rawes (Cambridge: Cambridge University Press, 2003), p. 82.

36 To Sir George Beaumont, 3 June 1805, *Early Years*, p. 595.

37 [Robert Southey], "Review," *A Chronological History of the People Called Methodists, of the Connexion of the Late Rev. John Wesley; from their Rise in the Year 1729, to their last Conference in 1802*, by William Myles. *The Annual Review and History of Literature, for 1803 (Volume II)* (London: Longman and Rees, 1804), p. 208; attributed in Geoffrey Carnall, *Robert Southey and His Age: The Growth of a Conservative Mind* (Oxford: Clarendon Press, 1960), p. 74.

38 Lynda Pratt, "Revising the National Epic: Coleridge, Southey, and *Madoc*," *Romanticism* 2:2 (1996), 160–161.

39 Elisa E. Beshero-Bondar, "British Conquistadors and Aztec Priests: The Horror of Southey's Madoc," *Philological Quarterly* Winter 2003 (82:1), 107. Beshero-Bondar argues that, because Madoc's Catholicism never wins the Hoamen to a non-superstitious form of religion, he is a "horrible" and "hybrid" representation of the British evangelical mission.

40 *Ibid.*, 89.

41 Brown, *Preromanticism*, p. 69.

42 Cowper, *Adelphi*, p. 13.

43 *The Works of William Cowper, Comprising His Poems, Correspondence, and Translations. With a Life of the Author By the Editor, Robert Southey, LL.D. In Eight Volumes*, Volume I (London: H.G. Bohn, 1854), p. 76.

44 *Ibid.*

45 *Ibid.*, p. 171.
46 *Ibid.*, p. 265.
47 *Ibid.*, p. 314.
48 See, for example, Ryskamp, *William Cowper*, pp. 58–59.

6 ROBERT SOUTHEY AND THE CLAIMS OF LITERATURE

1 "Review," Poems Written Chiefly in Retirement – Effusions of Relative and Social Feeling, &c. &c. – With a Prefatory Memoir of the Life of the Author, &c., by John Thelwall, *The Edinburgh Review* (April 1803), 197.
2 For biographical information on Croft, see *Dictionary of National Biography*, s.v. "Croft, Sir Herbert, bart."
3 On the transition from a "status" society to a "class" society, and the ways in which this transition can be conceived of as a literary or a discursive struggle, see Klancher, *English Reading Audiences*, esp. ch. 1, "Cultural Conflict, Ideology, and the Reading Habit in the 1790s."
4 In fact, John Brewer speculates that Wordsworth's adoption of Martha Ray's name in "The Thorn" is meant to generate a response both "apposite and jarring" in readers familiar with the actual case; such experiments are undertaken in opposition to the excessive sentimentality of Croft's novel. *A Sentimental Murder: Love and Madness in the Eighteenth Century* (New York: Farrar, Straus and Giroux, 2004), p. 200.
5 "A Letter from Denmark, to Mr. NICHOLS, Printer of the *Gentleman's Magazine*, by the Rev. Sir HERBERT CROFT, Bart. respecting an unprovoked Attack made upon him during his Absence from England," *Gentleman's Magazine* (February 1800), 100. Croft's letter continues in the March and April editions, the pages of which are numbered as a single volume. Further references will appear in the text.
6 William Haller, *The Early Life of Robert Southey, 1774–1803* (1917; reprint, New York: Octagon Books, 1966), p. 195.
7 To Coleridge, *Southey Letters I*, 23 December 1799, pp. 209–210.
8 "Mr. Southey's Reply to Sir Herbert Croft," *Gentleman's Magazine* (March 1800), 226.
9 *DNB* s.v. "Croft, Herbert."
10 *To May*, 12 March 1800, p. 53.
11 This is not a simple or a clean point. Isaac Kramnick, for example, draws a familiar distinction between "bourgeois radicalism," with its emphasis on free market relations and the inviolability of private property, and paternalistic, landed ideologies (Issac Kramnick, *The Rage of Edmund Burke: Portrait of an Ambivalent Conservative* [New York: Basic Books, 1977], 15–16). However, this distinction does not account for all the facts of the case: "That paternalists believed in self-regulating laws [of free-market economics] may surprise

some [but in Burke's *Thoughts on Economic Scarcity*] he in no way hides his laissez-faire economics. 'Labour,' he bluntly asserts, 'is a commodity'; 'the monopoly of capital .... a great benefit'; and the pursuit of profit .... a salutary practice" (David Roberts, *Paternalism in Early Victorian England* [New Brunswick: Rutgers University Press, 1979] 41).

12 On this milieu, see "Introduction," *The Collected Works of Samuel Taylor Coleridge: Lectures 1795 on Politics and Religion* ed. Lewis Patton and Peter Mann (Princeton: Princeton University Press, 1971), esp. xxv–lii.

13 To Coleridge, *Southey Letters I,* January 1800, pp. 213–214.

14 Haller, *Southey,* pp. 7–8.

15 This vocational solidarity has essentially artisan roots, and Southey's freedom in drawing on it in order to further his professional project may be one aspect of his radical legacy. See John Rule, "The Property of Skill in the Period of Manufacture," in *The Historical Meanings of Work,* ed. Patrick Joyce (Cambridge: Cambridge University Press, 1987).

16 The story of the Royal Literary Fund, which held its first official meeting in 1790, is told by Nigel Cross in *The Common Writer.* See especially Chapter One, "Literature and Charity: The Royal Literary Fund from David Williams to Charles Dickens."

17 David Williams, *Incidents in My Own Life Which Have Been Thought of Some Importance* (1802), ed. Peter France (Sussex: University of Sussex Library, 1980), pp. 39–40. Williams had developed the core of his argument in 1773, but it did not take on a wider interest until the later date. As noted by this editor, the 1773 version of the proposal, which Williams reports in his autobiography and which I draw on here, is essentially the same as his later argument (Williams, *Incidents,* p. 124), with the slight difference in emphasis noted below.

18 *Ibid.,* p. 42. Emphasis added.

19 David Williams, in Williams et al. *Claims of Literature: The Origins, Motives, Objects, and Transactions, of the Society for the Establishment of a Literary Fund* (London: William Miller, Bookseller to the Society, 1802), pp. 99–100.

20 Williams, *Incidents,* p. 49.

21 Williams' radicalism and aristocratic patronage were an uneasy mix throughout the founding years of the Fund: "It was against [a] background of growing professionalism and competition undermined by considerable misery that Williams began to contemplate a literary fund, though the concept owed as much to the emancipation of political thought as to commercial change. The growth of radicalism favoured fraternal, rather than paternal, effort ... But as far as the literary fund was concerned, [Williams] was also practical

and recognized the value of ruling-class support" (Cross, *Common Writer*, p. 12). Although the Royal Literary Fund was paid for and run by aristocrats, we can distinguish between the nascently professional and explicitly radical aims of Williams and the gentlemanly patronage of his partners.

22 "Review," *Claims of Literature, Anti-Jacobin Review and Magazine* (January–June 1802), 169–170. The Anti-Jacobin's resistance is not to charity or the support of writers, but to Williams' distinction between charity, which preserves a benevolent hierarchy, and professional obligation, which, as my discussion shows, implies a different kind of status system.

23 Herbert Croft, *Love and Madness: In a Series of Letters, One of Which Contains the Original Account of Chatterton. A New Edition, Corrected* (London: G. Kearsley, 1786), p. 255. Further references will appear in the text.

24 Peter France notes that this qualification actually marks a more conservative position than Williams' earlier one and suggests that it might be a tactical concession to Williams' gentlemanly partners (*Incidents*, p. 125).

25 *Ibid.*

26 *Dictionary of National Biography*, s.v. "Hackman, James."

27 Croft's comment refers at least generally to the events of 1779–80. His reaction to these events (including possible revolution in Ireland and the rising strength of parliamentary reformers and extra-parliamentary opinion) is relevant to his later confrontation with Southey. "The crisis of 1779–80 formed a final and important link between the radicalism of the American and that of the French revolutionary period" (Albert Goodwin, *The Friends of Liberty: The English Democratic Movement in the Age of the French Revolution* [Cambridge: Harvard University Press, 1979], p. 60). These continuities are manifest in Croft's own reactionary biography: in 1794 Croft apparently gained a government pension as a reward for his own anti-Burke (that is, anti-revolution) writings of the American revolutionary period (see *DNB* s. v. "Croft, Herbert").

28 For a discussion of French "theory" as "system" (as opposed to British "common sense") see David Simpson, *Romanticism, Nationalism, and the Revolt Against Theory* (Chicago: University of Chicago Press, 1993), esp. Chapter Two, "The Culture of British Common Sense" and Chapter Three, "The Myth of French Excess."

29 In a discussion of Southey's *Lives of the Uneducated Poets* (1830–31) Kurt Heinzelman argues that Southey proposes a version of literary history that embraces working-class poets in order to "ameliorate" the possibility of class struggle (Kurt Heinzelman, "The Uneducated Imagination: Romantic Representations of Labor," in *At the Limits of Romanticism: Essays in Cultural, Feminist, and Materialist*

Criticism, Mary Favret and Nicola Watson, eds. [Bloomington: Indiana University Press, 1994] 100). However, in Southey's later vision, the worker poet is, if anything, a junior partner: "Southey wants to maintain the uneducated writer, the laborer-poet, as a self-educable amateur who is not entrepreneurial in his aspirations and whose gentrification, even if sustained by patronage, nevertheless symbolizes at the social level his autogenesis as an aesthetic producer" (p. 119). Chatterton, whose fame as a poet predates Southey's interest in him, is of course no exact figure for the worker-poet who requires Southey's complicated and qualified advocacy. It is clear at least that "class" does not play the role in Southey's 1800 formulations that it does in his 1830 discussion, as the latter is illuminated by Heinzelman.

7 "MINISTRY MORE PALPABLE": WILLIAM WORDSWORTH'S ROMANTIC PROFESSIONALISM

1 William Wordsworth, *The Prelude: 1799, 1805, 1850*, ed. Jonathan Wordsworth, M. H. Abrams, and Stephen Gill (New York: Norton, 1979), IX 222–226. Further citations will be given in the text.

2 Mary Moorman, *William Wordsworth: A Biography. The Early Years, 1770–1803* (Oxford: Clarendon Press, 1957), p. 213.

3 *Ibid.*, p. 170. See also *The Prelude* IX. 35–39.

4 To William Mathews, 23 May [1794], *Early Years*, p. 120.

5 It is a further irony that at least one factor in the Wordsworths' failure to master German was that they could not afford to circulate in Germany's literary society. See Moorman, *Wordsworth*, pp. 413–414.

6 Given Wordsworth's life-long intention to "do something" literary, his perpetual mingling of writing with earning, and his characteristic defensiveness about his varied plans in the face of familial resistance and possible rejection by critics and the marketplace, it is hard to state with certainty when Wordsworth committed himself to poetry. However, the German translation scheme is the last non-literary plan that Wordsworth ever proposes; coupled with the beginning of *The Prelude* and his subsequent, renewed attention to *Lyrical Ballads*, 1799 can certainly be proposed as the specific date.

7 For the details of Wordsworth's economic arrangements, see Wallace Douglas, "Wordsworth as Business Man," *PMLA* 62 (1948), 625–641.

8 For Wordsworth's monetary concerns and their bearing on his professional self-construction, see Charles J. Rzepka, "A Gift that Complicates Employ: Poetry and Poverty in 'Resolution and Independence,'" *SiR*, 28 (Summer 1989), 241–246.

9 Samuel Taylor Coleridge, Contributions to "Joan of Arc," May–August 1795, in *Coleridge Poems*, p. 215.

10 Ann W. Astell, *Joan of Arc and Sacrificial Authorship* (Notre Dame: Notre Dame University Press, 2003), pp. 34–35.

11 Lynda Pratt, "Coleridge, Wordsworth, and *Joan of Arc*," *Notes and Queries* 41 (239), No. 3, 1994.

12 To William Mathews, 7 November 1794, *Early Years*, p. 135.

13 Larson, *Rise*, p. 157. According to Larson, the struggle extends across the nineteenth century; "science" only becomes a basis for legitimation after World War One (p. 137).

14 For Wordsworth's activities after returning from Germany, see Moorman, *Wordsworth*, pp. 440–441.

15 Douglas, "Businessman," 631.

16 "Advertisement, Preface, and Appendix to *Lyrical Ballads*," *The Prose Works of William Wordsworth*, Vol. I, ed. W. J. B. Owen and Jane Worthington Smyser (Oxford. Clarendon Press, 1974), p. 126. Further references will be provided in the text.

17 David Simpson, *Wordsworth' s Historical Imagination: The Poetry of Displacement* (New York: Methuen, 1987), p. 12.

18 *Ibid.*, p. 5.

19 Siskin, *Historicity*, p. 46.

20 For David Sebberson, the Preface ultimately expresses the crisis attendant upon the cultural change from "practical reason," associated with Aristotelian well-being, to "technical reason," associated with Hobbesian "survival" and "manipulation." "Practical Reasoning, Rhetoric, and Wordsworth's 'Preface'," *Spirits of Fire: English Romantic Writers and Contemporary Historical Methods*, G. A. Rosso and Daniel P. Watkins eds. (Rutherford: Associated University Press, 1990), p. 95. Sebberson's account of technical reason in the Preface is consistent with my own reading of Wordsworth's new professionalism, but I maintain that it cannot be distinguished so easily from an expansive ethical prudence.

21 Kurt Heinzelman emphasizes the reciprocal labor required by the reader in Wordsworth's account, in *The Economics of the Imagination* (Amherst: University of Massachussets Press, 1980), p. 208. It is nonetheless important to note that the service ethic of the Preface preserves the special role of the poet, albeit within a set of common laws, and further to note that Wordsworth is "forging a new sense of contract" in the face of various levels of resistance. These latter tensions are noted by Klancher: "[Wordsworth] yearns to return to the space of 'reception' (symbolic exchange) from the historical ground of 'consumption' (commodity exchange)'', (p. 143).

22 On the central year 1802, see, in addition to Harrison and Rzpeka, Irene Tayler, "By Peculiar Grace: Wordsworth in 1802," in *The Evidence of the Imagination: Studies of Interactions Between Life and Art in English Romantic Literature* ed. Donald H. Reiman (New York: New York University Press, 1978), pp. 125–131. Tayler is also concerned

with Wordsworth's "renewed dedication to 'true' poetry" in this year (p. 140).

23 M. Jeanne Peterson, *The Medical Profession in Mid-Victorian London* (Berkeley: University of California Press, 1978), p. 287.

24 Thomas Pfau, "'Elementary Feelings' and 'Distorted Language': The Pragmatics of Culture in Wordsworth's Preface to *Lyrical Ballads*," *New Literary History* 1993 (24), 146.

25 To Charles James Fox, 14 January 1801, *Early Years*, pp. 314–315.

26 *Ibid.*, p. 313.

27 For a discussion of "Michael" which carefully illuminates the connection of this poem's treatment of property and "inheritance" to Burkean, politically conservative, "traditional" values, see James K. Chandler, *Wordsworth's Second Nature: A Study of the Poetry and Politics* (Chicago: University of Chicago Press, 1984), pp. 256–268.

Bibliography

Abbott, Andrew, *The System of Professions: An Essay on the Division of Expert Labor*, Chicago: University of Chicago Press, 1988.

Agutter, The Rev. William, "A Sermon Occasioned by the Death of the Celebrated Mr. J. Henderson, BA of Pembroke College, Oxford: Preached at St. George's, Kingswood, Nov. 23, and at Temple Church, Bristol, Nov. 30, 1788," Bristol: Bulgin and Rosser, 1788.

Amhurst, Nicholas, *The Convocation, or, Protestant Popery (1715)*, in *English Poetry Database* <http://ets.umdl.umich.edu>.

Anonymous, "Original Letters from Mr. Henderson to Dr. Priestley," *Gentleman's Magazine*, April, 1789.

"Review," *Claims of Literature, Anti-Jacobin Review and Magazine*, January–June 1802.

"Review," *Observations on the Political Conduct of the Protestant Dissenters; including a retrospective View of their History from the Time of Queen Elizabeth. In Five Letters to a Friend*, by the Rev. David Rivers, *Anti-Jacobin Review*, Dec. 1798.

"Review, Poems Written Chiefly in Retirement – Effusions of Relative and Social Feeling, &c. &c. – With a Prefatory Memoir of the Life of the Author, &c., by John Thelwall," *Edinburgh Review*, April 1803.

Armitage, David, "A Patriot for Whom? The Afterlives of Bolingbroke's Patriot King," *Journal of British Studies* 36, October 1997, 397–418.

Astell, Ann W., *Joan of Arc and Sacrificial Authorship*, Notre Dame: Notre Dame University Press, 2003.

Averill, James H., *Wordsworth and the Poetry of Human Suffering*, Ithaca: Cornell University Press, 1980.

Bacon, Francis, "Experiment Solitary Touching the Secret Processes of Nature," in *Sylva Sylvarum: or, A Natural History (1627)*, in *The Works of Francis Bacon (Volume IV)*, ed. James Spedding, Robert Leslie Ellis, and Douglas Denon Heath, Boston: Brown and Taggard, 1872.

Barfoot, Michael, "Brunonianism Under the Bed: An Alternative to University Medicine in Edinburgh in the 1780s," in W. F. Bynum and Roy Porter, eds., *Brunonianism in Britain and Europe*, London: Wellcome Institute, 1988.

Beattie, James, *An Essay on the Nature and Immutability of Truth, in Opposition to Sophistry and Scepticism (new edition, 1776)*, in *Essays*, New York: Garland Publishing, 1971.

James Beattie's London Diary, 1773, ed. Ralph S. Walker, Aberdeen University Studies 122, Aberdeen: The University Press, 1946.

Beck, Ulrich, *Risk Society: Toward a New Modernity*, trans. Mark Ritter, London: Sage Publications, 1992.

Benis, Toby R., *Romanticism on the Road: The Marginal Gains of Wordsworth's Homeless*, Houndmills: Macmillan, 2000.

Beshero-Bondar, Elisa E., "British Conquistadors and Aztec Priests: The Horror of Southey's Madoc," *Philological Quarterly*, Winter 2003 (82:1), 87–113.

Bewell, Alan, *Wordsworth and the Enlightenment: Nature, Man, and Society in the Experimental Poetry*, New Haven: Yale University Press, 1989.

Bialostosky, Don H., *Wordsworth, Dialogics, and the Practice of Criticism*, Cambridge: Cambridge University Press, 1992.

Bliss, Isabel St. John, "Young's *Night Thoughts* in Relation to Contemporary Christian Apologetics," *PMLA* XLIX, 1934, 37–70.

Bluestocking Feminism: Writings of the Bluestocking Circle, 1738–1785. Volume I: Elizabeth Montagu, ed. Elizabeth Eger, London: Pickering and Chatto, 1999.

Boehm, Alan, "Was Joseph Cottle a Liberal Bookseller?" *ELN* 32:3 (March 1995), 32–39.

Boswell, James, *Life of Johnson* (1791), ed. R. W. Chapman, Oxford: Oxford University Press, 1989.

Brantley, Richard E., *Wordsworth's "Natural Methodism"*, New Haven: Yale University Press, 1975.

Locke, Wesley, and the Method of English Romanticism, Gainesville: University of Florida Press, 1984.

Brewer, John. *A Sentimental Murder: Love and Madness in the Eighteenth Century*, New York: Farrar, Straus and Giroux, 2004.

Brown, Marshall, *Preromanticism*, Stanford: Stanford University Press, 1991.

Brunstrom, Conrad, "James Beattie and the Great Outdoors: Common Sense Philosophy and the Pious Imagination," *Romanticism* 3 (1), 1997, 20–34.

William Cowper: Religion, Satire, Society, Lewisburg: Bucknell University Press, 2004.

Burrage, Michael, "Beyond a Sub-set: The Professional Aspirations of Manual Workers in France, the United States, and Britain," in *Professions in Theory and History*, ed. Michael Burrage and Rolf Torstendahl, London: Sage, 1990.

Butler, Marilyn, *Romantics, Rebels and Reactionaries: English Literature and its Background, 1760–1830*, Oxford: Oxford University Press, 1981.

Literature as Heritage: Or, Reading Other Ways, Cambridge: Cambridge University Press, 1987.

Carnall, Geoffrey, *Robert Southey and His Age: The Growth of a Conservative Mind*, Oxford: Clarendon Press, 1960.

Carretta, Vincent, *George III and the Satirists from Hogarth to Byron*, Athens: University of Georgia Press, 1990.

Castoriadis, Cornelius, *The Imaginary Institution of Society*, trans. Kathleen Blamey, Cambridge: MIT Press, 1987.

[C.C.], "Anecdotes of Mr. Henderson," *Gentleman's Magazine*, April, 1789.

Chandler, David, "The Early Development of the 'Lake School' Idea," *Notes and Queries* 52 (25), no. 1 (March 2005), 35–37.

"Robert Southey and *The Prelude's* 'Arab Dream,'" *The Review of English Studies* (n.s.) 54: 214 (April 2003), 203–219.

"Wordsworthian Southey: The Fashioning of a Reputation," *Wordsworth Circle* Winter 2003 (34:1), 14–19.

Chandler, James, *England in 1819: The Politics of Literary Culture and the Case of Romantic Historicism*, Chicago: University of Chicago Press, 1998.

Wordsworth's Second Nature: A Study of the Poetry and Politics, Chicago: University of Chicago Press, 1984.

Chartier, Roger, *The Order of Books: Readers, Authors, and Libraries in Europe between the Fourteenth and Eighteenth Centuries*, trans. Lydia G. Cochrane, Stanford: Stanford University Press, 1994.

Christensen, Jerome, *Lord Byron's Strength: Romantic Writing and Commercial Society*, Baltimore: The Johns Hopkins University Press, 1993.

Practicing Enlightenment: Hume and the Formation of a Literary Career, Madison: University of Wisconsin Press, 1987.

Clark, J. C. D., *English Society, 1660–1832: Religion, Ideology, and Politics During the Ancien Regime*, Cambridge: Cambridge University Press, 2000.

Clark, Stuart, "The Scientific Status of Demonology," in *Occult and Scientific Mentalities in the Renaissance*, ed. Brian Vickers, Cambridge: Cambridge University Press, 1984.

Clifford, Alan C., *Atonement and Justification: English Evangelical Theology 1640–1790: An Evaluation*, Oxford: Clarendon Press, 1990.

Coleridge, Samuel Taylor, *Collected Letters of Samuel Taylor Coleridge, Volume I: 1785–1800*, ed. Earl Leslie Griggs, Oxford: Clarendon Press, 1956.

Collected Letters of Samuel Taylor Coleridge, Volume II: 1801–1806, ed. Earl Leslie Griggs, Oxford: Clarendon Press, 1956.

The Notebooks of Samuel Taylor Coleridge, Volume I:1794–1804: Notes, ed. Kathleen Coburn, New York: Bollingen, 1957.

The Collected Works of Samuel Taylor Coleridge: Lectures 1795 on Politics and Religion ed. Lewis Patton and Peter Mann, Princeton: Princeton University Press, 1971.

The Collected Works of Samuel Taylor Coleridge: The Watchman, ed. Lewis Patton, London: Routledge and Kegan Paul, 1970.

The Collected Works of Samuel Taylor Coleridge: Biographia Literaria, ed. James Engell and W. Jackson Bate, Princeton: Princeton University Press, 1983.

The Collected Works of Samuel Taylor Coleridge: Poetical Works I: Poems (Reading Text): Part 1, ed. J. C. C. Mays, Princeton: Princeton University Press, 2001.

The Collected Works of Samuel Taylor Coleridge: Poetical Works II: Poems (Variorum Text): Part 1, ed. J. C. C. Mays, Princeton: Princeton University Press, 2001.

Collings, David, *Wordsworthian Errancies: The Poetics of Cultural Dismemberment*, Baltimore: Johns Hopkins University Press, 1994.

Collins, A. S., *Authorship in the Days of Johnson: Being a Study of the Relation Between Author, Patron, Publisher, and Public, 1726–1780*, London: Robert Holden, 1927.

The Profession of Letters: A Study of the Relation of Author to Patron, Publisher, and Public, 1780–1832, New York: E. P. Dutton and Co., 1929.

Cook, Peter A., "Chronology of the Lake School Argument: Some Revisions," *Review of English Studies* (n.s.) 28, 110 (May, 1977), 175–181.

Corfield, Penelope, *Power and the Professions in Britain, 1700–1850*, New York: Routledge, 1995.

Cottle, Joseph, "Monody on the Death of John Henderson, A. B. of Pembroke College, Oxford," in *Poems: Second Edition. With Additions*, Bristol: Bulgin and Rosser, 1796.

Poems, Containing John the Baptist; Malvern Hills; An Expostulary Epistle to Lord Byron; Dartmoor, and Other Poems, New York: Garland Publishing, 1978.

Cowper, William, *Cowper: Poetical Works*, ed. H. S. Milford, with corrections and additions by Norma Russell, London: Oxford University Press, 1971.

Adelphi, in *The Letters and Prose Writings of William Cowper: Volume I, Adelphi and Letters 1750–1781*, eds. James King and Charles Ryskamp, Oxford: The Clarendon Press, 1979.

The Letters and Prose Writings of William Cowper, Volume II: Letters 1782–1786 eds. James King and Charles Ryskamp, Oxford: The Clarendon Press, 1981.

Croft, Herbert, *Love and Madness: In a Series of Letters, One of Which Contains the Original Account of Chatterton. A New Edition, Corrected*, London: G. Kearsley, 1786.

"A Letter from Denmark, to Mr. NICHOLS, Printer of the *Gentleman's Magazine*, by the Rev. Sir HERBERT CROFT, Bart. respecting an unprovoked Attack made upon him during his Absence from England," *Gentleman's Magazine*, February 1800.

"Young," in *Lives of the English Poets by Samuel Johnson, LL.D.*, ed. George Birckbeck Hill, D.C.L., Oxford: Clarendon Press, 1905, p. 391.

Cross, Nigel, *The Common Writer: Life in Nineteenth-Century Grub Street*, Cambridge: Cambridge University Press, 1985.

Croxall, Samuel, *The Vision (1715)*, in *English Poetry Database* <http://ets.umdl.umich.edu>.

Davidoff, Leonore, and Catherine Hall, *Family Fortunes: Men and Women of the English Middle Class, 1780–1850*, Chicago: University of Chicago Press, 1987.

Davidson, Graham, *Coleridge's Career*, New York: St. Martin's Press, 1990.

Disraeli, Isaac, *An Essay on the Character and Manners of the Literary Genius*, London: T. Cadell, 1795; repr. Garland Publishing 1970.

Doody, Margaret Anne, *The Daring Muse: Augustan Poetry Reconsidered*, Cambridge: Cambridge University Press, 1985.

Douglas, Wallace W. "Wordsworth as Business Man," *PMLA* 62 (1948), 625–641.

Dykstal, Timothy, *The Luxury of Skepticism: Politics, Philosophy, and Dialogue in the English Public Sphere, 1660–1740*, Charlottesville: University of Virginia Press, 2001.

Eilenberg, Susan, *Strange Power of Speech: Wordsworth, Coleridge, and Literary Possession*, New York: Oxford University Press, 1992.

Elfenbein, Andrew, *Byron and the Victorians*, Cambridge: Cambridge University Press, 1995.
    Romantic Genius: The Prehistory of a Homosexual Role, New York: Columbia University Press, 1999.

Elliot, Philip, *Sociology of the Professions*, New York: Herder and Herder, 1972.

Ellison, Julie, "News, Blues, and Cowper's Busy World," *MLQ* 62:3 (September 2001), 219–237.

Engell, James, *The Creative Imagination: Enlightenment to Romanticism*, Cambridge: Harvard University Press, 1981.

Epstein, William H., "Patronizing the Biographical Subject: Johnson's Savage and Pastoral Power," in Paul J. Korshin, ed. *Johnson After Two Hundred Years*, Philadelphia: University of Pennsylvania Press, 1986.

Erikson, Erik, "The Problem of Ego Identity" (1959), in *Pivotal Papers in Identification*, ed. George H. Pollock, Madison: International Universities Press, 1993.

Erskine-Hill, Howard, *The Poetry of Opposition and Revolution: Dryden to Wordsworth*, Oxford: Clarendon Press, 1996.

Fairer, David, *English Poetry of the Eighteenth Century, 1700–1789*, London: Longman, 2002.

Falkenstein, Lorne, "Hume and Reid on the Perception of Hardness," *Hume Studies* 28:1, April 2002, 27–48.

Felluga, Dino Franco, *The Perversity of Poetry: Romantic Ideology and the Popular Male Poet of Genius*, Albany: SUNY University Press, 2005.

Ferguson, Frances, "Coleridge and the Deluded Reader: 'The Rime of the Ancient Mariner,'" in Samuel Taylor Coleridge, *The Rime of the Ancient Mariner* ed. Paul H. Fry, Boston: Bedford, 1999.

Finucane, R. C., *Appearances of the Dead: A Cultural History of Ghosts*, Buffalo: Prometheus Books, 1984.

Fissell, Mary E., *Patients, Power, and the Poor in Eighteenth-Century Bristol*, Cambridge: Cambridge University Press, 1991.

Folkenflik, Robert, "Patronage and the Poet-Hero," *Huntington Library Quarterly* 48 (1985), 363–379.

Forbes, Margaret, *Beattie and his Friends*, Westminster: Archibald Constable and Co., Ltd., 1904.

Forbes, Sir William, *An Account of the Life and Writings of James Beattie, LL.D. . . . Including Many of His Original Letters, in Three Volumes*, 2nd Edition, Edinburgh: Arch. Constable and Co, 1807.

Ford, Jennifer, *Coleridge on Dreaming: Romanticism, Dreams, and the Medical Imagination*, Cambridge: Cambridge University Press, 1998.

Fosso, Kurt, *Buried Communities: Wordsworth and the Bonds of Mourning*, Albany: SUNY Press, 2004.

Foster, Harold, *Edward Young: The Poet of the Night Thoughts, 1683–1785*, Alburgh: The Erskine Press, 1986.

Franklin, Caroline, "The Welsh American Dream: Iolo Morganwg, Robert Southey and the Madoc Legend," in *English Romanticism and the Celtic World*, eds. Gerard Carruthers and Alan Rawes, Cambridge: Cambridge University Press, 2003.

Freidson, Eliot, *Professional Powers: A Study of the Institutionalization of Formal Knowledge*, Chicago: University of Chicago Press, 1986.

Freud, Sigmund, *The Interpretation of Dreams* (1900), ed. and trans. James Strachey, New York: Avon Books, 1965.

Fulford, Tim, *Landscape, Liberty, and Authority: Poetry, Criticism and Politics from Thomson to Wordsworth*, Cambridge: Cambridge University Press, 1996.

Galperin, William H., *Revision and Authority in Wordsworth: The Interpretation of a Career*, Philadelphia: University of Pennsylvania Press, 1989.

Gash, Norman, "The Crisis of the Anglican Establishment in the Early Nineteenth Century," in *Pillars of Government*, London: Edward Arnold, 1986.

Gerrard, Christine, *The Patriot Opposition to Walpole: Politics, Poetry, and Myth, 1725–1742*, Oxford: Clarendon Press, 1994.
  The Muses' Projector: Aaron Hill and his Circle, 1685–1750, Oxford: Oxford University Press, 2003.
Giddens, Anthony, *Modernity and Self-Identity: Self and Society in the Late Modern Age*, Stanford: Stanford University Press, 1991.
  The Consequences of Modernity, Stanford: Stanford University Press, 1990.
  The Constitution of Society: Outline of a Theory of Structuration, Berkeley: University of California Press, 1984.
Gladfelder, Hal, "The Hard Work of Doing Nothing: Richard Savage's Parallel Lives," *MLQ* 64:4, December 2003, 445–472.
Goffman, Irving, *Stigma: Notes on the Management of Spoiled Identity* (1963), New York: Simon and Schuster, 1986.
Goldstein, Jan, "Foucault among the Sociologists: 'The Disciplines' and the History of the Professions," *History and Theory* Volume 23, Number 2 (May, 1984), 170–192.
Goodlad, Lauren M. E., *Victorian Literature and the Victorian State: Character and Governance in a Liberal Society*, Baltimore: Johns Hopkins University Press, 2003.
Goodwin, Albert, *The Friends of Liberty: The English Democratic Movement in the Age of the French Revolution*, Cambridge: Harvard University Press, 1979.
Gray, Thomas, *Correspondence of Thomas Gray, in Three Volumes. Volume II, 1756–1765*, ed. Paget Toynbee and Leonard Whilby, Oxford: Clarendon Press, 1935.
Gregory, John, "Observations on the Duties and Offices of a Physician and on the Method of Prosecuting Enquiries in Philosophy" (1770), in *John Gregory's Writings on Medical Ethics and Philosophy of Medicine*, ed. Laurence B. McCullough, Dordrecht: Kluwer Academic Publishers, 1998.
Griffin, Dustin, *Literary Patronage in England, 1650–1800*, Cambridge: Cambridge University Press, 1996.
  Patriotism and Poetry in Eighteenth-Century Britain, Cambridge: Cambridge University Press, 2002.
Griffin, Robert J., *Wordsworth's Pope*, New York: Cambridge University Press, 1996.
Guillory, John, *Cultural Capital: the Problem of Literary Canon Formation*, Chicago: University of Chicago Press, 1993.
Habermas, Jurgen, *The Structural Transformation of the Public Sphere: An Inquiry into a Category of Bourgeois Society*, trans. Thomas Burger and Frederick Lawrence, Cambridge: MIT Press, 1990.
Haller, William, *The Early Life of Robert Southey, 1774–1803* (1917), reprint, New York: Octagon Books, 1966.
Hamilton, Paul, *Coleridge's Poetics*, Stanford: Stanford University Press, 1983.

Hanley, Keith, *Wordsworth: A Poet's History*, London: Palgrave, 2001.

Harrison, Gary, *Wordsworth's Vagrant Muse: Poetry, Poverty, and Power*, Detroit: Wayne State University Press, 1994.

Hartman, Geoffrey, *Wordsworth's Poetry, 1787–1814*, Cambridge: Harvard University Press, 1987.

Hawes, Clement, *Mania and Literary Style: The Rhetoric of Enthusiasm from the Ranters to Christopher Smart*, Cambridge: Cambridge University Press, 1996.

Hawkins, Michael, "Ambiguity and contradiction in 'the rise of professionalism': the English clergy, 1570–1730," in A. L. Beier, David Cannadine, and James M. Rosenheim, eds., *The First Modern Society: Essays in English History in Honour of Lawrence Stone*, Cambridge: Cambridge University Press, 1989.

Hazlitt, William, "On the Living Poets," in *The Selected Writings of William Hazlitt, Volume II: The Round Table, Lectures on the English Poets*, ed. Duncan Wu, London: Pickering and Chatto, 1998.

Heidegger, Martin, *Being and Time: A Translation of Sein und Zeit*, trans. Joan Stambaugh, Albany: SUNY Press, 1996.

Heinzelman, Kurt, "The Uneducated Imagination: Romantic Representations of Labor," in *At the Limits of Romanticism: Essays in Cultural, Feminist, and Materialist Criticism*, eds. Mary Favret and Nicola Watson, Bloomington: Indiana University Press, 1994.

The Economics of the Imagination, Amherst: University of Massachussets Press, 1980.

Heller, Deborah, "Bluestocking Salons and the Public Sphere," *Eighteenth-Century Life*, 99 (May, 1998), 59–82.

Henderson, John, "Postscript: Dissertation on Everlasting Punishment," in William Matthews, *The Miscellaneous Companions, Volume III, Containing Dissertations on Particular Subjects and Occasions; and Dialogues in the World of Spirits*, Bath: R. Crutwell, 1786.

Hess, Scott, *Authoring the Self: Self-Representation, Authorship, and the Print Market in British Poetry from Pope through Wordsworth*, New York: Routledge, 2005.

Hewitt, Regina, *The Possibilities of Society: Wordsworth, Coleridge, and the Sociological Viewpoint of English Romanticism*, Albany: SUNY University Press, 1997.

Hickey, Alison, "Coleridge, Southey 'and Co.': Collaboration and Authority," *Studies in Romanticism*, 37 (Fall, 1998), 305–349.

Hofkosh, Sonia, *Sexual Politics and the Romantic Author*, Cambridge: Cambridge University Press, 1998.

Hole, Robert, *Pulpits, Politics, and Public Order in England, 1760–1832*, Cambridge: Cambridge University Press, 1989.

Holloway, S. W. F., "The Apothecaries' Act, 1815: A Reinterpretation. Part I: The Origins of the Act," *Medical History* 10 (2), April, 1966, 107–129.

Holmes, Geoffrey. *Augustan England: Professions, State and Society, 1680–1730*, London: George Allen and Unwin, 1983.

Holmes, Richard, *Dr. Johnson and Mr. Savage*, London: Hodder and Stoughton, 1993.

Hughes, Everett C., "Institutional Office and the Person," in *The Sociological Eye: Selected Papers*, Chicago: Aldine, 1971.

Hume, David, "Of the Independency of Parliament," in *Essays Moral, Political, and Literary*, volume I, ed. T. H. Green and T. H. Grose, London: Longmans, Green, and Co., 1907.

"Of the Middling Station of Life," in *Essays Moral, Political, and Literary*, volume II, ed. T. H. Green and T. H. Grose, London: Longmans, Green, and Co., 1898.

A Treatise of Human Nature, ed. David Fate Norton and Mary J. Norton, Oxford: Oxford University Press, 2000.

An Inquiry Concerning Human Understanding, ed. Tom L. Beauchamp, Oxford: Oxford University Press, 1999.

Ireland, W. H., "Invocation to Genius," in *Neglected Genius: a Poem Illustrating the Untimely and Unfortunate Fates of Many British Poets From the Period of Henry VIII to the Time of the Unfortunate Chatterton*, London: George Cowie and Co., 1812.

Irlam, Shaun, *Elations: The Poetics of Enthusiasm in Eighteenth-Century Britain*, Stanford: Stanford University Press, 1999.

Jackson, Noel B., "Critical Conditions: Coleridge, 'Common Sense,' and the Literature of Self-Experiment," *ELH* 70 (2003), 117–149.

Jacobus, Mary, *Tradition and Experiment in Wordsworth's Lyrical Ballads (1798)*, Oxford: Clarendon Press, 1976.

Jager, Colin, "Natural Designs: Romanticism, Secularization, Theory," *European Romantic Review*, 12 (1), Winter, 2001, 53–87.

James, William, *The Varieties of Religious Experience: A Study of Human Nature*, New York: Mentor Books, 1958.

Janowitz, Anne, *Lyric and Labour in the Romantic Tradition*, Cambridge: Cambridge University Press, 1998.

Jarvis, Robin, *Romantic Writing and Pedestrian Travel*, Houndmills: Macmillan, 1997.

Johnson, Samuel, *Life of Savage*, ed. Clarence Tracy, Oxford: Clarendon Press, 1971.

Johnston, Kenneth R., *The Hidden Wordsworth: Poet, Lover, Rebel, Spy*, New York: Norton, 1998.

Wordsworth and the Recluse, Yale: Yale University Press, 1984.

Jones, Robert W., "'We Proclaim Our Darling Son': The Politics of Chatterton's Memory During the War for America," *Review of English Studies* n.s. 53:211 (August, 2002), 373–395.

Kant, Immanuel, *Critique of the Power of Judgment*, ed. Paul Guyer, trans. Paul Guyer and Eric Matthews, Cambridge: Cambridge University Press, 2000.

Prolegomena to Any Future Metaphysics, intro. Lewis Beck White, Indianapolis: Bobbs-Merrill, 1950.

Kaul, Suvir, *Poems of Nation, Anthems of Empire: English Verse in the Long Eighteenth Century*, Charlottesville: University Press of Virginia, 2000.

Thomas Gray and Literary Authority: A Study in Ideology and Poetics, Stanford: Stanford University Press, 1992.

Keen, Paul, "The Most Useful of Citizens: Towards a Romantic Literary Professionalism," *Studies in Romanticism*, 41 (Winter, 2002), 627–654.

The Crisis of Literature in the 1790s: Print Culture and the Public Sphere, Cambridge: Cambridge University Press, 1999.

Kernan, Alvin, *Printing Technology, Letters, and Samuel Johnson*, Princeton: Princeton University Press, 1987.

King, Everard H., *James Beattie's* The Minstrel *and the Origins of Romantic Autobiography*, Lewiston: The Edwin Mellen Press, 1992.

Klancher, Jon P., *The Making of English Reading Audiences, 1790–1832*, Madison: University of Wisconsin Press, 1987.

Korshin, Paul J., "Types of Eighteenth-Century Literary Patronage," *Eighteenth-Century Studies*, Volume 7, Number 4 (Summer, 1974), 453–473.

Kramnick, Isaac, *The Rage of Edmund Burke: Portrait of an Ambivalent Conservative*, New York: Basic Books, 1977.

Bolingbroke and his Circle: The Politics of Nostalgia in the Age of Walpole, Cambridge: Harvard University Press, 1968.

Krug, Rebecca, *Reading Families: Women's Literate Practice in Late Medieval England*, Ithaca: Cornell University Press, 2002.

Kucich, Greg, *Keats, Shelley, and Romantic Spenserianism*, University Park: The Pennsylvania State University Press, 1991.

La Vopa, Anthony J., *Grace, Talent, and Merit: Poor Students, Clerical Careers, and Professional Ideology in Eighteenth-Century Germany*, Cambridge: Cambridge University Press, 1988.

Lackington, James, *Memoirs of James Lackington, Who from the humble station of a Journeyman Shoemaker, by great industry, amassed a large fortune, and now lives in a splendid stile, in London*, Newburgh, New York, 1796.

Lamb, Charles, *The Letters of Charles and Mary Lamb, Volume I: Letters of Charles Lamb, 1796–1801*, ed. Edwin W. Marrs, Jr., Cambridge: Cambridge University Press, 1975.

Langan, Celeste, *Romantic Vagrancy: Wordsworth and the Simulation of Freedom*, Cambridge: Cambridge University Press, 1995.

Langford, Paul, *A Polite and Commercial People: England, 1727–1783*, Oxford: Clarendon Press, 1989.

Larson, Magali Sarfatti, "In the Matter of Experts and Professionals, or How Impossible it is to Leave Nothing Unsaid," in Rolf

Torstendahl and Michael Burrage eds., *The Formation of the Professions: Knowledge, State, and Strategy*, London: Sage, 1990.

"The Production of Expertise and the Constitution of Professional Power," in *The Authority of Experts and the Constitution of Expert Power*, ed. Thomas L. Haskell, Bloomington: Indiana University Press, 1984.

The Rise of Professionalism: A Sociological Analysis, Berkeley: University of California Press, 1977.

Lee, Debbie, *Slavery and the Romantic Imagination*, Philadelphia: University of Pennsylvania Press, 2002.

Lefebvre, Henri, *The Production of Space*, trans. Donald Nicholson-Smith, Oxford: Blackwell, 1991.

Levere, Trevor H., *Poetry Realized in Nature: Samuel Taylor Coleridge and Early Nineteenth-Century Science*, Cambridge: Cambridge University Press, 1981.

Levinson, Marjorie, *Wordsworth's Great Period Poems: Four Essays*, Cambridge: Cambridge University Press, 1986.

Liu, Alan, *Wordsworth: The Sense of History*, Stanford: Stanford University Press, 1989.

Loudon, Irvine, *Medical Care and the General Practitioner, 1750–1850*, Oxford: Clarendon Press, 1986.

Lovegrove, Deryck W., *Established Church, Sectarian People: Itinerancy and the Transformation of English Dissent, 1780–1832*, Cambridge: Cambridge University Press, 1988.

Magnuson, Paul, "Coleridge's Discursive 'Monody on the Death of Chatterton'," *Romanticism on the Net* 17 (February, 2000).

Coleridge's Nightmare Poetry, Charlottesville: University Press of Virginia, 1974.

Marcuse, Herbert, "*The Affirmative Character of Culture*," in *Negations: Essays in Critical Theory*, trans. Jeremy Shapiro, London: Allen Lane, 1968.

Martin, Roger H., "Evangelical Dissenters and Wesleyan-Style Itinerant Ministries at the End of the Eighteenth Century," *Methodist History* 16(3), April, 1978, 169–184.

Matheson, Ann, "The Influence of Cowper's *The Task* on Coleridge's Conversation Poems," in *New Approaches to Coleridge: Biographical and Critical Essays*, ed. Donald Sultana, London: Vision Press, 1981.

Matlak, Richard. *The Poetry of Relationship: The Wordsworths and Coleridge, 1797–1800*, New York: St. Martin's Press, 1997.

McCullough, Laurence B., "Introduction," in *John Gregory's Writings on Medical Ethics and Philosophy of Medicine*.

McDannell, Colleen and Bernhard Lang, *Heaven: A History*, New Haven: Yale University Press, 1988.

McGann, Jerome, *The Romantic Ideology: A Critical Investigation*, Chicago: University of Chicago Press, 1983.

McIntosh, Carey, *The Evolution of English Prose, 1700–1800: Style, Politeness, and Print Culture*, Cambridge: Cambridge University Press, 1998.

McKeon, Michael, *The Origins of the English Novel, 1600–1740*, Baltimore: Johns Hopkins University Press, 1987.

Mee, Jon, *Romanticism, Enthusiasm, and Regulation: Poetics and the Policing of Culture in the Romantic Period*, Oxford: Oxford University Press, 2003.

Milnes, Tim, *Knowledge and Indifference in English Romantic Prose*, Cambridge: Cambridge University Press, 2003.

Moorman, Mary, *William Wordsworth: A Biography. The Early Years, 1770–1803*, Oxford: The Clarendon Press, 1957.

Mossner, Ernest Campbell, *The Life of David Hume, second edition*, Oxford: Oxford University Press, 1980.

Negt, Oskar and Alexander Kluge, *Public Sphere and Experience: Toward an Analysis of the Bourgeois and Proletarian Public Sphere*, foreword by Miriam Hansen, trans. Peter Labanyi, Jamie Owen Daniel, and Assenka Oksiloff, Minneapolis: University of Minnesota Press, 1993.

Newey, Vincent, *Cowper's Poetry: A Critical Study and Reassesment*, Totowa: Barnes and Noble, 1982.

Nicolson, Marjorie Hope, *Mountain Gloom and Mountain Glory: The Development of the Aesthetics of the Infinite (1959)*, Seattle: University of Washington Press, 1997.

O'Day, Rosemary, *The Professions in Early Modern England, 1450–1800: Servants of the Commonweal*, Harlow: Longman, 2000.

Page, Judith W., *Wordsworth and the Cultivation of Women*, Berkeley: University of California Press, 1994.

Percy, Thomas, *Reliques of Ancient English Poetry, Consisting of Old Heroic Ballads, Songs, and Other Pieces of Our Earlier Poets; Together With Some Few of Later Date*, ed. Charles Cowden Clarke, in three volumes, Edinburgh: Nimmo, n.d.

Perkin, Harold, *The Origins of Modern English Society: Second Edition*, London: Routledge, 2002.

Peterson, M. Jeanne, *The Medical Profession in Mid-Victorian London*, Berkeley: University of California Press, 1978.

Pettit, Alexander, *Illusory Consensus: Bolingbroke and the Polemical Response to Walpole, 1730–1737*, Newark: University of Delaware Press, 1997.

Pettit, Henry, "A Bibliography of Young's *Night-Thoughts*," *University of Colorado Studies: Series in Language and Literature No. 5*, Boulder: University of Colorado Press, 1954.

Pfau, Thomas, *Wordsworth's Profession: Form, Class, and the Logic of Early Romantic Cultural Production*, Stanford: Stanford University Press, 1997.

"'Elementary Feelings' and 'Distorted Language': The Pragmatics of Culture in Wordsworth's Preface to *Lyrical Ballads*," (24.1) *New Literary History* Winter 1993, 125–146.

Pocock, J. C. D., "*The Mobility of Property and the Rise of Eighteenth-Century Sociology*," in *Virtue, Commerce, and History: Essays on Political Thought and History, Chiefly in the Eighteenth Century*, Cambridge: Cambridge University Press, 1985.

Porter, Roy, *Disease, Medicine and Society in England, 1550–1860*, second edition, Cambridge: Cambridge University Press, 1995.

Pratt, Lynda, "Revising the National Epic: Coleridge, Southey, and *Madoc*," *Romanticism* 2:2 (1996), 149–163.

"Coleridge, Wordsworth, and Joan of Arc," *Notes and Queries* 41 (239), No. 3, 1994, 335–336.

Prest, Wilfred. *Albion Ascendant: English History 1660–1815*, Oxford: Oxford University Press, 1998.

Priestley, Joseph, "The Use of Christianity, especially in Difficult Times; A SERMON delivered at the Gravel Pit Meeting House in Hackney, March 30 1794. Being the Author's Farewell Discourse to his Congregation," in *Two Sermons*, Philadelphia, 1794.

Priestman, Martin, *Cowper's Task: Structure and Influence*, Cambridge: Cambridge University Press, 1983.

Pyle, Forest, *The Ideology of Imagination: Subject and Society in the Discourse of Romanticism*, Stanford: Stanford University Press, 1995.

Radcliffe, David Hill, "Completing James Beattie's *The Minstrel*," *Studies in Philology* 100:4 (Fall, 2003), 534–563.

Ramsey, Jonathan, "Seeing and Perceiving in Wordsworth's *An Evening Walk*," MLQ September 1976 (37, 3), 376–389.

Reader, W. J., *Professional Men: The Rise of the Professional Classes in Nineteenth-Century England*, London: Weidenfeld and Nicolson, 1966.

Reid, Thomas, *An Inquiry into the Human Mind on the Principles of Common Sense: A Critical Edition*, ed. Derek R. Brookes, University Park: Pennsylvania State University Press, 1997.

Richetti, John J., *Philosophical Writing: Locke, Berkeley, Hume*, Cambridge: Harvard University Press, 1983.

Rieder, John, *Wordsworth's Counterrevolutionary Turn: Community, Virtue, and Vision in the 1790s*, Newark: University of Delaware Press, 1997.

Roberts, David, *Paternalism in Early Victorian England*, New Brunswick: Rutgers University Press, 1979.

Robinson, Roger, "The Origins and Composition of James Beattie's *Minstrel*, Romanticism 4:2 (1998), 224–240.

Roe, Nicholas, "Pantisocracy and the Myth of the Poet," in *Romanticism and Millenarianism*, ed. Tim Fulford, New York: Palgrave, 2002.

Wordsworth and Coleridge: The Radical Years, Oxford: Clarendon Press, 1988.

Rose, Mark, *Authors and Owners: The Invention of Copyright,* Cambridge: Harvard University Press, 1993.

Ross, Catherine E., "'Twin Labourers and Heirs of the Same Hopes': The Professional Rivalry of Humphry Davy and William Wordsworth," in *Romantic Science: The Literary Forms of Natural History,* ed. Noah Heringman, Albany: SUNY University Press, 2003.

Rule, John, "The Property of Skill in the Period of Manufacture," in *The Historical Meanings of Work,* ed. Patrick Joyce, Cambridge: Cambridge University Press, 1987.

Russell, Gillian and Clara Tuite, eds., *Romantic Sociability: Social Networks and Literary Culture in Britain,* 1770–1840, Cambridge: Cambridge University Press, 2002.

Ryskamp, Charles, *William Cowper of the Inner Temple,* Esq.: *A Study of his Life and Works to the Year 1768,* Cambridge: Cambridge University Press, 1959.

Rzepka, Charles J., "A Gift that Complicates Employ: Poetry and Poverty in 'Resolution and Independence,'" *Studies in Romanticism* 28 (Summer 1989), 225–242.

Sacks, Peter M., *The English Elegy: Studies in the Genre from Spenser to Yeats,* Baltimore: The Johns Hopkins University Press, 1985.

Saunders, J. W., *The Profession of English Letters,* London: Routledge and Kegan Paul, 1964.

Savage, Richard, *The Poetical Works of Richard Savage,* ed. Clarence Tracy, Cambridge: Cambridge University Press, 1962.

An Author To Be Lett (1729), intro. James Sutherland, The Augustan Reprint Society Publication Number 84, Los Angeles: William Andrews Clark Memorial Library, 1960.

Schoenfield, Mark, *The Professional Wordsworth: Law, Labor, and the Poet's Contract,* Athens: University of Georgia Press, 1996.

Sebberson, David, "Practical Reasoning, Rhetoric, and Wordsworth's 'Preface,'" *Spirits of Fire: English Romantic Writers and Contemporary Historical Methods,* G. A. Rosso and Daniel P. Watkins, eds., Rutherford: Associated University Press, 1990.

Shaw, W. David, *Elegy and Paradox: Testing the Conventions,* Baltimore: The Johns Hopkins University Press, 1994.

Sher, Richard B., *Church and University in the Scottish Enlightenment: The Moderate Literati of Edinburgh,* Princeton: Princeton University Press, 1985.

Shumway, David R. and Ellen Messer-Davidow, "Disciplinarity: An Introduction," *Poetics Today* volume 12, number 12 (Summer, 1991), 201–225.

Simpson, David, *Romanticism, Nationalism, and the Revolt Against Theory,* Chicago: University of Chicago Press, 1993.

Wordsworth's Historical Imagination: The Poetry of Displacement, New York: Methuen, 1987.

Siskin, Clifford, *The Work of Writing: Literature and Social Change in Britain, 1700–1830*, Baltimore: The Johns Hopkins University Press, 1998.

The Historicity of Romantic Discourse, New York: Oxford University Press, 1988.

Sitter, John E., *Literary Loneliness in Mid-Eighteenth-Century England*, Cornell: Cornell University Press, 1982.

"Theodicy at Mid-Century: Young, Akenside, and Hume," *Eighteenth-Century Studies* 12:1 (Fall, 1978), 90–106.

Smith, Christopher, "Robert Southey and the Emergence of Lyrical Ballads," *Romanticism on the Net* 9 (February 1998).

Somerville, James, *The Enigmatic Parting Shot: What was Hume's 'Compleat Answer to Dr Reid and to that Bigotted Silly Fellow, Beattie'?*, Brookfield: Aldershot, 1995.

Southey, Cuthbert, *The Life and Correspondence of the Late Robert Southey, in Six Volumes. Edited by his Son, the Revd. Charles Cuthbert Southey*, London: Longman, 1849.

Southey, Robert, *Letters Written During a Short Residence in Spain and Portugal*, 2nd ed., Bristol: Biggs and Cottle, 1799.

"Mr. Southey's Reply to Sir Herbert Croft," *Gentleman's Magazine* (March, 1800).

[Southey, Robert], *"Review," A Chronological History of the People Called Methodists, of the Connexion of the Late Rev. John Wesley; from their Rise in the Year 1729, to their last Conference in 1802, by William Myles. The Annual Review and History of Literature, for 1803 (Volume II)*, London: Longman and Rees, 1804.

"On the Means of Improving the People" [1818], in *Essays, Moral and Political, Volume I*, London: John Murray, 1832.

The Doctor, Second Edition, Volume I, London: Longman, 1835.

The Works of William Cowper, Comprising His Poems, Correspondence, and Translations. With a Life of the Author By the Editor, Robert Southey, L. L. D. In Eight Volumes, Volume I, London: H. G. Bohn, 1854.

The Letters of Robert Southey to John May, ed. Charles Ramos Austin: Jenkins Publishing Company, The Pemberton Press, 1976.

New Letters of Robert Southey Volume I: 1792–1810, ed. Kenneth Curry, New York: Columbia University Press, 1979.

Robert Southey: Poetical Works 1793–1810, Volume 2: *Madoc*, ed. Lynda Pratt, with the assistance of Carol Bolton and Paul Jarman, London: Pickering and Chatto, 2004.

Robert Southey: Poetical Works 1793–1810. Volume 5: Selected Shorter Poems c. 1793–1810, ed. Lynda Pratt, London: Pickering and Chatto, 2004.

St. Clair, William, *The Reading Nation in the Romantic Period*, Cambridge: Cambridge University Press, 2004.

St. John, Henry, Viscount Bolingbroke, *Political Writings*, ed. David Armitage, New York: Cambridge University Press, 1997.

Stafford, Fiona J., *The Sublime Savage: A Study of James Macpherson and the Poems of Ossian*, Edinburgh: Edinburgh University Press, 1988.

Stansfield, Dorothy A., *Thomas Beddoes M.D., 1760–1808: Chemist, Physician, Democrat*, Dordrecht: D. Reidel Publishing, 1984.

Steward, Dugald, "Account of the Life and Writings of Thomas Reid ... ," in Thomas Reid, *Philosophical Works* I, ed. and notes Sir William Hamilton, intro. Harry Bracken, Hildesheim: Georg Olms, 1967.

Strychacz, Thomas, *Modernism, Mass Culture, and Professionalism*, Cambridge: Cambridge University Press, 1993.

Sturrock, John, "Theory vs. Autobiography," in *The Culture of Autobiography: Constructions of Self-Representation*, ed. Robert Folkenflik, Stanford: Stanford University Press, 1993.

Swartz, Richard G., " 'Their terrors came upon me tenfold': Literacy and Ghosts in John Clare's *Autobiography*," in *Lessons of Romanticism: A Critical Companion*, ed. Thomas Pfau and Robert F Gleckner, Durham: Duke University Press, 1998.

Tayler, Irene, "By Peculiar Grace: Wordsworth in 1802," in *The Evidence of the Imagination: Studies of Interactions Between Life and Art in English Romantic Literature*, ed. Donald H. Reiman, New York: New York University Press, 1978.

Taylor, Anya. "Ghosts, Spirits, and Force: Samuel Taylor Coleridge," in *The Occult in Language and Literature: New York Literary Forum 4*, ed. Hermine Riffaterre, New York, 1980.

Thomas, Keith G., *Wordsworth and Philosophy: Empiricism and Transcendentalism in the Poetry*, Ann Arbor: UMI Research Press, 1989.

Thomson, James, The Seasons *and* The Castle of Indolence, ed. James Sambrook, Oxford: Clarendon Press, 1972.

Tracy, Clarence, *The Artificial Bastard: a Biography of Richard Savage*, Cambridge: Harvard University Press, 1953.

Tyson, Gerald P., *Joseph Johnson, A Liberal Bookseller*, Iowa City: University of Iowa Press, 1979.

Ulmer, William, "Necessary Evils: Unitarian Theodicy In 'The Rime Of The Ancient Mariner.' " *Studies in Romanticism* 43 (Fall, 2004), 327–356.

Vickers, Neil, *Coleridge and the Doctors, 1795–1806*, Oxford: Clarendon Press, 2004.

"Coleridge, Thomas Beddoes, and Brunonian Medicine," *European Romantic Review*, Winter, 1997 (8:1), 47–94.

Virgil, *The Second Book of the Georgics*, in *The Works of John Dryden, Volume Five: The Poems: The Works of Virgil in English (1697)*, eds. William Frost and Vinton A. Dearing, Berkeley: University of California Press, 1987.

Wallace, Anne D., *Walking, Literature, and English Culture: The Origins and Uses of Peripatetic in the Nineteenth Century*, Oxford: Clarendon Press, 1993.

Wallen, Martin, *City of Health, Fields of Disease: Revolutions in the Poetry, Medicine, and Philosophy of Romanticism*, Burlington: Ashgate, 2004.

Ward, W. R., *Religion and Society in England, 1790–1850*, London: B.T. Batsford Ltd., 1972.

Watts, Michael R., *The Dissenters: From the Reformation to the French Revolution*, Oxford: Oxford University Press, 1978.

Weinsheimer, Joel C., *Eighteenth-Century Hermeneutics: Philosophy of Interpretation in England from Locke to Burke*, New Haven: Yale University Press, 1993.

Wesley, John, "A Letter to a Clergyman" (1748), in Rupert E. Davies, ed., *The Works of John Wesley, Volume Nine: The Methodist Societies: History, Nature, and Design*, Nashville: Abingdon Press, 1989.

A Farther Appeal to Men of Reason and Religion, Part III (1745), in Gerald R. Cragg, ed., *The Works of John Wesley, Volume II: The Appeals to Men of Reason and Religion, and Certain Related Open Letters*, Oxford: Clarendon Press, 1975.

Wheeler, Michael, *Death and the Future Life in Victorian Literature and Theology*, Cambridge: Cambridge University Press, 1990.

Whelan, Timothy, "Joseph Cottle the Baptist," *The Charles Lamb Bulletin* July 2000 (n.s. 111), 96–108.

White, Daniel E., " 'Properer for a Sermon': Particularities of Dissent and Coleridge's Conversational Mode," *Studies in Romanticism* Summer 2003 (40: 2), 175–198.

Williams, David, *Incidents in My Own Life Which Have Been Thought of Some Importance (1802)*, ed. Peter France, Sussex: University of Sussex Library, 1980.

in Williams et al. *Claims of Literature: The Origins, Motives, Objects, and Transactions, of the Society for the Establishment of a Literary Fund*, London: William Miller, Bookseller to the Society, 1802.

Williams, John, *Wordsworth: Romantic Poetry and Revolutionary Politics*, Manchester: Manchester University Press, 1989.

Williams, Raymond, *Culture and Society: 1780–1950*, New York: Columbia University Press, 1983.

Woodman, Ross, "The Idiot Boy as Healer," in James Holt McGavran, Jr., ed., *Romanticism and Children's Literature in Nineteenth-Century England*, Athens: The University of Georgia Press, 1991.

Woodmansee, Martha, *The Author, Art, and the Market: Rereading the History of Aesthetics*, New York: Columbia University Press, 1994.

Wordsworth, Dorothy and William Wordsworth, *The Letters of William and Dorothy Wordsworth: The Early Years, 1787–1805* ed. Ernest de Selincourt, rev. Chester L. Shaver (Oxford: Clarendon Press, 1967).

Wordsworth, William, "Advertisement, Preface, and Appendix to *Lyrical Ballads*," The Prose Works of William Wordsworth, Vol. I, ed. W.J.B. Owen and Jane Worthington Smyser, Oxford: Clarendon Press, 1974.

The Salisbury Plain Poems, ed. Stephen Gill, Ithaca: Cornell University Press, 1975.

The Excursion, in John O. Hayden. ed., *William Wordsworth: The Poems, Volume II,* New York: Penguin, 1977.

The Prelude, 1798–1799 ed. Stephen Parrish, Ithaca: Cornell University Press, 1977.

The Prelude: 1799, 1805, 1850, ed. Jonathan Wordsworth, M. H. Abrams, and Stephen Gill, New York: Norton, 1979.

Descriptive Sketches, ed. Eric Birdsall, with the assistance of P. M. Zall, Ithaca: Cornell University Press, 1984.

Peter Bell ed. John E. Jordan (Ithaca: Cornell University Press, 1985).

"Note to the Ancient Mariner," from the 1800 edition of *Lyrical Ballads, in Wordsworth and Coleridge: Lyrical Ballads,* second edition, ed. R. L. Brett and R. A. Jones, London: Routledge, 1991.

Lyrical Ballads, and Other Poems, 1797–1800, ed. James Butler and Karen Green, Ithaca: Cornell University Press, 1992.

Wu, Duncan, "Looking for Johnny: Wordsworth's 'The Idiot Boy,'" *Charles Lamb Bulletin* 88 (October, 1994), 166–176.

Yearsley, Ann, "On Mrs. Montagu," in *Eighteenth-Century Poetry: An Annotated Anthology,* Second Edition, ed. David Fairer and Christine Gerrard, Malden: Blackwell, 2004.

Yolton, John W., *Perceptual Acquaintance from Descartes to Reid,* Minneapolis: University of Minnesota Press, 1984.

Young, Edward, *Edward Young: The Complete Works, Poetry and Prose* Volume II, ed. James Nichol (1854), Germany: Georg Olms, 1968.

Night Thoughts, ed. Stephen Cornford, Cambridge: Cambridge University Press, 1989.

Zimmerman, Sarah, *Romanticism, Lyricism, and History,* Albany: SUNY University Press, 1999.

Zionkowski, Linda, *Men's Work: Gender, Class, and the Professionalization of Poetry, 1660–1784,* New York: Palgrave, 2001.

Index

Abbott, Andrew 30, 31, 126, 232, 259
Aberdeen 100, 140, 257
Act of 1729 9
Addison, Joseph 52, 84
aesthetic autonomy 1–2
affiliation 196, 200–2, 207, 209
  and see Beattie, James; Croft,
    Herbert; Johnson, Samuel; and
    Southey, Robert
afterlife 21, 37–8, 40–2, 47, 72, 116, 182
  and see risk; Wordsworth, William
Agutter, William 149
  Henderson's funeral sermon 38–9, 40
Akenside, Mark 147
  as MD 8
  "Hymn to the Naiads" 147
ambition 107
  and see Beattie, James
Amhurst, Nicholas 67–8
  "The Convocation" 67–8
Anti-Jacobin Review 129, 209
Arbuthnot, Robert 112
"aristocratic ideology" 64, 69, 70–2, 83
  and see McKeon, Michael
Armitage, David 247
Astell, Ann W. 218, 219
audience 2–3, 55, 134
  and see Beattie, James; Hume, David;
    Reid, Thomas; and Wordsworth,
    William
authorship 125, 133, 176–7, 193,
    212–13
  and the professions, 5
  and see Croft, Herbert; Savage,
    Richard; and Southey, Robert
autobiography 146
  and see Beattie, James

Bacon, Francis 39–40, 131, 244
Balaam's ass 173
Battle of Trafalgar 185

Beattie, James 13, 21, 22–3, 59, 65, 125,
    128, 140, 146, 161, 169, 172, 185
  and the Church 121–2
  and George III 86–8
  as academic 8, 120–1
  identified with Wordsworth 90
  search for patronage 86
Works:
  Essay on Truth 86, 88, 91, 107, 108,
    112, 114, 121
  The Minstrel 86, 88, 90, 91, 104–6,
    107–18, 139, 142, 143, 153, 154,
    155, 219; affiliation in, 106–7;
    ambition in 104–5; as autobiography
    105–6; audience in 100–1, 103–5;
    evaluation and experience in 90,
    101–2, 108–9; 110–11; landscape in
    109–10, 110–11, patriotism in 107–8,
    114; patronage in 103, 111–13,
    114–21, 122; professionalism in, 90–1,
    102, 114, 118–22; space in 92,
    99–100, 109–10, 117–18
Beck, Ulrich 241, 242
Beddoes, Thomas 32, 35, 36
Bedford, Charles Grosvenor 147
Bellamy, George Anne 177
Benis, Toby 257
Berkeley, George 91, 94, 96
Beshero-Bondar, Elisa 186, 264
Bewell, Alan 175, 263
Bialostosky Don H. 235
Blake, William 122
Bliss, Isabel St. John 49
Boehmen, Jakob 40
Bolingbroke, Henry St. John, Viscount
    70–2, 73, 75, 80, 88, 230
  "The Idea of the Patriot King" 70–1
  "The Spirit of Patriotism" 71
Boswell, James 75, 76, 85
Brantley, Richard 258
Brewer, John 265

CAMBRIDGE STUDIES IN ROMANTICISM

General Editors
Marilyn Butler, *University of Oxford*
James Chandler, *University of Chicago*